The critics on Ge...

'The prose ... is never less than...
poignant moments ... Beattie, ...
and Ingle, drifts into the dark, terrifying wake of a world
champion, picking up the lives that have been left, fighting
for breath, there. It's simply fantastic'
Mick Middles, *Manchester Evening News*

'His previous book, *On the Ropes*, was hailed as a boxing classic,
and its sequel is equally good ... Great stuff' *Rated*

'Beattie can write about the low life of boxing like no one else
... [He] has got the smell of the gym in his lungs. He breathes
resin, sweat and soiled towels. He even goes three rounds
himself with Mick Mills. He writes for adults, and quite beau-
tifully' Julian Critchley, *Daily Telegraph*

'Beattie's control of his first novel is remarkable ... Writing
part in despair, part in miserable elegy, he has created a tre-
mendously involving, affecting novel whose simplicity is the
key to its punch' Carolra Matthews, *Scotland on Sunday*

'This brilliant and complex book is an unforgettable
pages' Phil Hamer, the *Irish Mirror* □

£3.58

'Easily one of the most brilliant works of fiction to come
out of North...
Grania McFad...

'A gifted journalist with ... for making people talk'
Sunday Times

Geoffrey Beattie is the author of several books of fiction and non-fiction. He is Professor of Psychology at Manchester University and has been a resident psychologist on the three series of *Big Brother*.

THE SHADOWS OF BOXING
PRINCE NASEEM
AND THOSE HE LEFT BEHIND

GEOFFREY BEATTIE

5

ORION

An Orion paperback

First published in Great Britain in 2002
by Orion
This paperback edition published in 2003
by Orion Books Ltd,
Orion House, 5 Upper St Martin's Lane,
London WC2H 9EA

A CIP catalogue record for this book is available
from the British Library.

ISBN 0 75284 979 4

Typeset by Selwood Systems, Midsomer Norton

Printed and bound in Great Britain by
Clays Ltd, St Ives plc

CONTENTS

ACKNOWLEDGEMENTS

I would like to thank Brendan Ingle, Johnny Nelson, Mick Mills, Prince Naseem Hamed and his brother Riath who, as always, gave their time so generously to a man who is still trying to make sense of what they do and why they do it. Writing is a lonely and insecure business, but not as lonely and insecure as boxing, and I would like to thank Robert Kirby, from Peters, Fraser and Dunlop, who was my agent and Ian Preece who is my editor at Orion, who were both very encouraging and enthusiastic throughout. Laura Meehan copy-edited the manuscript and as far as I can tell she did a very good job. *New Statesman* kindly gave permission for me to use four pieces, which I originally wrote for that magazine, pieces on 'Mad' Frankie Fraser, scoring Viagra, working for a few bob and a Kit-Kat and the piece on Val, the woman who made shorts for boxers in Salford. I would like to thank Peter Wilby personally for his enthusiasm for this kind of writing. Finally, I would like to thank Heather Shovelton who was extremely supportive both personally and professionally during the writing of this book.

THE CONTENDER

'There was this man and he was the strongest
   Of the strong.
He gritted his teeth like a cliff.
Though his body was sweeling away like a torrent on a cliff
   Smoking towards dark gorges
There he nailed himself with nails of nothing.'
TED HUGHES

ONE

His seat was empty. That's what I thought. I could even see the little blue plastic chair, with the complimentary programme sitting on it, in exactly the right position for a superstar like that – just along from the two pretty card-girls, one black with long, floppy, straightened hair and bright-red lipstick, the other white with milky-white skin and a slightly shy, nervous look. The two girls were sitting with their hands across their laps, almost demurely, both wearing long, clingy black dresses that hugged their bodies, sitting like débutantes waiting to be asked to dance on their first big social occasion, looking straight ahead most of the time, smiling in conversation, talking to each other with slow, polite turns in each other's direction, but without really making eye contact with each other or with anybody else. The chair was just waiting for him. But he wasn't there.

He would turn up – I knew that – to watch his old friend Johnny Nelson. Johnny Fantastic they tried calling him for a while, or perhaps that was just a TV company that gave him that name to make him sound like something from a Marvel comic, a jaw-busting superhero. Johnny was the WBO World Cruiser-weight Champion and was defending his world title in Sheffield. He was fighting for the championship of the world, not in Madison Square Garden or Las Vegas but in Steel City in the Ponds Forge leisure centre. World Championship boxing was now taking place in new and strange locations. In 1993, I had watched Johnny defend the WBF version of the world title against Tom Collins at the Mansfield Leisure Centre, and I had sat with Johnny after the weigh-in in the Buttercup Café in the Water Meadows swimming complex, where large inflatable pink elephants hung from the ceiling and dummy windsurfers, with unrecognisable facial expressions, clung to the walls. We were eating lasagne and chips, which were on the house for a bunch of celebrities like us. Frank, a dedicated fight fan who had gone on the sick from work to be present at the weigh-in, had told me that, in some ways, Mansfield was even better than Las Vegas for championship boxing, but he didn't elaborate.

We were all sitting there tucking into our free grub in anticipation of the big fight that night when Johnny got up to fetch some cutlery and gave a great hacking cough into his own drink. 'We always do that in my house to stop people touching our drinks when we're away,' he said to all those sitting at the long cafeteria table. I, and I think I alone, watched the thick globule of creamy spit float on the surface of the pint of orange juice before slowly sinking to the bottom of the glass, and I thought to myself this was an effective strategy, but a bit down-market given that this was the World Champion. In the days of Muhammad Ali surely someone else would have fetched the cutlery; there would have been no call for all that phlegm to be deposited in a glass.

Tonight, we have moved up-market from the leisure centre in Mansfield in a number of ways, but there was still no sign of Sheffield's real number one superstar. He would be there despite everything that had happened between him and Brendan, despite all their arguments about money. But what's money when it comes down to it, compared to everything that they'd been through together? Perhaps he was just late. That must be it; he was just late. I remember when he used to be late for training, late for everything. 'That Naz fella,' Brendan would say, 'he'll be late for his own funeral. You're the psychiatrist, isn't that right? Or the psychologist. You explain it to me.'

My fifteen-year-old son, Sam, was sitting beside me so closely on the narrow plastic chairs that I could actually feel his nervousness; his body seemed to be giving off heat. It was a warm evening outside. We had hurried along to the fight after training together in the gym opposite, and we had queued behind the Sports Minister, Richard Caborn, for our complimentary tickets. But Sam was so nervous that he hadn't cooled down. He had asked to borrow some of my own clothes to wear that night – a black top and some black trousers, which I had picked up cheap in Kendall's sale, designer labels but last year's fashions. He had said that he had nothing suitable, but he obviously felt that I knew how to blend in on nights like this, even in last year's clobber. I felt a little touched by his request, and then spoiled it somewhat by going on about the price. The top, I am not ashamed to say, had been reduced from fifty quid to twelve pounds fifty – it's well worth mentioning. I think it's a matter of pride to boast about these things; it shows that you haven't been ripped off like the muppets out there who pay above the odds for everything. I've had cut-price designer suits offered to me for fifty quid in club toilets by doormen – I know what I'm talking about.

I had asked Sam to join me just that afternoon. It was a last-minute thing. Brendan had rung me up in the morning. 'It'll be a great fight for you to watch,' he had promised. 'A great fight.' Brendan had a way of making you feel that you, and you alone, were the only one being invited in quite this intimate manner. That was his gift, but in reality I knew that I would be just one of a number of journalists and writers who would get the call at the last minute. 'It'll be a cracker. Bring one of your lads, if you like. There will be some great action for a lad like that to watch.'

My son had never been to a fight before. In fact, he had never been to anything like this with me. Perhaps that's why he was so nervous; he was going to get a glimpse of his father's other life. The other life only hinted at by my return to the family home in the early hours. I had spent years going to clubs. I have always liked staying up late. My mother always said that she could never get me to go to bed, even when I was young, or get me up in the morning. She would be at the bottom of the stairs, calling and calling, getting angry with herself because I would not budge. 'That boy would sit up all bloody night and then sleep all bloody day, if you bloody well let him.' Sometimes I think that I just found a lifestyle that allowed this staying up 'all bloody night' with the minimum of guilt.

Clubs until half past two in the morning and a piece in Thursday's *Guardian* on the 'Grassroots' page. That was a wonderful justification. 'I'm working,' I would say at two o'clock in the morning, 'I'm working, just like the guy who owns the club, or the doormen, or the girl who dances on-stage with the green rubber snake with the wonky eyes held between her hot, sticky thighs. We've all got our work to do, you know. We've all got to bring home the bacon.'

My column was a chance for the great liberal middle class in full employment to read about what the other half were up to in Thatcher's blighted Britain. The other half who were out of work or struggling to get by. The other half who knew how to enjoy themselves, as Rod, one of the club owners, liked to say. 'The *Guardian* readers want to see what they're missing, although they would never admit that to themselves.'

Sometimes, I would see Sam at his bedroom window watching me come home and leave the red BMW, bought from an after-hours associate, in the drive because the swing-over metal garage door made too much noise at that time of night. I would see Sam's light going off just after I slammed the front door shut. I may be an academic psychologist, but I spent a large number of years writing about life on the streets and in clubs and even in the boxing ring for a variety of newspapers and books. I thought that ultimately the life lived out there was something to do with psychology. Perhaps it was even the core of psychology, at least that's what I told my academic colleagues. It was human behaviour outside the laboratory. In fact, it was human behaviour well outside the laboratory. That was my justification, and it seemed to work. But I did try to keep this other life away from my family as much as I could, the *Guardian* notwithstanding.

However, one night a doorman from one of the clubs turned up at my home while I was out, and I came back to find him playing with two of my small children. I had never given him my address. I never talked about where I lived to him or to anybody else. I never talked about my marital status. I never talked about my personal life. But then again, none of them did. I saw one club owner almost every night for twelve years or more in the same club, and I never once found out where he lived. He didn't tell me, and I didn't ask. It just wasn't relevant. And why should I have talked about my own life? I always think that you need a degree of anonymity in this going-out business. But this particular doorman obviously thought otherwise. He was crouching on the floor of my living room with two of my sons. He looked up at me as I came in as if to say, 'Don't ever think you can keep secrets from me.' He was laughing in a really irritating way, more of a chuckle really, a false, deliberate laugh, a laugh that certainly didn't distract him from monitoring my every response. He was a great people-watcher. 'Well, well, well,' he said. I can remember his smile even today. That's the funny thing: that irritating look of his. He had a moustache then, which seemed to accentuate the smile rather than conceal it. It acted like a marker for his lips and its movements. Big Lenny, they called him. Big Lenny, the big mouth.

My mother always said that he was a typical bully on the basis of what I told her about him, but I don't really know what she meant by that. She thought that nearly everybody I talked about from the nightclubs was a bully of one sort or another. 'They can't all be bullies,' I said, using my famous university logic, 'because if everybody was a bully, then there would be nobody left to be the victims, they'd have no frigging victims.' But she just smiled at that. 'What about you?' she replied. 'You're always there for that.'

She never gave me credit for the way I changed. She always remembered me as a shy boy, a bit odd, as she liked to put it in social gatherings when I was a child. But there I was, in the know, in the clubs with a small glass of champagne in my hand. 'Marvellous,' I would say in that style they all use, although in my case I might have been saying it a little ironically. 'Fucking marvellous.'

My son Sam has also always remembered this small, trivial incident of Lenny turning up for some reason. But he says that it is *my* expression that he remembers most. Nothing that he can put into words, just something funny about how I looked. It was bits of different things; that's how he has always put it when pressed, just an expression made out of bits of different things. Sam says that he had never seen me looking like that before, and especially not brought on by such a harmless occurrence with such a friendly and engaging man. Sam was about six at the time, and this is one of his earliest childhood memories, like a flashbulb memory, bright and clear with all the details of the occasion encoded for all time in his memory. The stranger that just turned up one night at our house in Crosspool, the red truck that the stranger was pushing round the room, the way that the stranger made him laugh, me looking surprised or something, me not talking, the stranger laughing some more on his way out. All of this in a contracted sequence of images that do not quite flow from one to another. But bright and clear and memorable images nonetheless, despite having no coherent narrative to bind them together. It has always seemed slightly ironic that this other life, only hinted at by my absences, will be the cause of one of the clearest early moments in his own autobiographical memory.

'My absences', I love that expression. So vague, and so laden with thick emotional connotations of abandonment and guilt, and hints of drink and drugs and sex and sleaze. What was I up to in those clubs for so many years? There are two kinds of answer to this question, I guess. First, there is the serious answer that says I was repeating the pioneering work of Friedrich Engels in a different century. I started writing about the North soon after Thatcher came to power. Things were changing in my own life and around me. These changes needed to be documented. I was a young university lecturer and had recently moved to Sheffield. I wrote my first-ever non-academic piece because my wife fell below a train at Sheffield station and lost her arm. I wrote this first piece out of anger and frustration about what it was like for her to get a prosthesis, a false arm, a bionic arm that was made of dull plastic and did nothing. Her father made her a wooden slab with nails hammered through to cut meat on. This was the most useful device she acquired. When Paul Barker stepped down many years later as Editor of *New Society*, he wrote to me saying that this piece had always stuck in his mind for some reason. It was a powerful piece, he said, that had moved him. I moved on from there.

The very fabric of life in the North was in a state of flux as the traditional industries went, and unemployment rose, and I was there in the middle of it. Whole communities were destroyed and new cultures started to emerge – new romantics, new entrepreneurs, new drugs. I lived in Netherfield Road in Crookes, Sheffield in those early years; I called it Brick Street in one of my first articles about a street that didn't have to rise quite so early any more because nobody was working. I don't know why I changed the name. Netherfield Road sounded slightly posh. It didn't sound quite right for the street. It might have confused the *Guardian* readers. Then again, I didn't want to hurt anybody's feelings, even my neighbours', who might have seen the article by chance.

John Course, the Northern Editor of the *Guardian*, who commissioned my pieces, often used to ask me how I found the people I wrote about. 'Near by' was the answer. I lived next door to the first unemployed steelworker that I wrote about. It was all very handy. If the truth be known, all of the pieces that I wrote were opportunistic in this way – just whatever came up. There was no grand plan, no abstract scheme. I was summoned as often as I did the summoning. There were, of course, many other stories that I could have told, but didn't. My writing was just one set in a way – one version of life in the North under the Conservatives. When Engels wrote the preface to the original German edition of *The Condition of the Working Class in England* in 1845, he wrote, 'Working Men! To you I dedicate a work, in which I have tried to lay before my ... countrymen a faithful picture of your condition, of your sufferings and struggles, of your hopes and prospects. I have lived long enough amidst you to know something about your circumstances.' I would have loved to have been able to preface my work with these exact words. But life was constantly changing for the working class in the North of England during the successive Conservative governments from 1979 to 1997. There was no fixed picture of the condition of the working class to be lain before anyone. There was just a series of fleeting images of lives captured from different angles, a succession of vignettes and descriptions of people living sometimes in quite desperate circumstances. Then there was the multitude of self-constructions, self-justifications and emergent self-identities, which went along with all this, as we all changed. For ever. This, I suppose, was what my work was all about, and this was how it differed from Engels. My work was Engels for a post-modern world, that's how I thought about it sometimes. Perhaps there was no absolute truth, but it was serious nonetheless. It needed to be done. It was important work. That's what I could have told my son.

But then there is another sort of answer to the same basic question – what was I doing out there in clubs night after night? Not so much redoing Engels in a different historical and cultural epoch, but something different altogether. I was just out. It was as simple as that. Just out in a place that suited me. Out in a club within a club, just socialising really. Just hanging about with men in the know who knew what ordinary punters could be like at their worst, and really wanted nothing to do with them. Just out feeling a little bit special. We'd stay behind when the club closed. The bar would stay open, but no money was allowed to change hands. We were just getting by, in an exclusive kind of way, spending time, hanging out with other VIPs. A bit like a gang really, and it reminded me of the street in Belfast that I grew up in, with its own rules, regulations, obligations, duties and responsibilities, none written down but all to be understood implicitly and immediately. There was some sort of code of conduct. It was there in the club that I met many of the boxers that I came to write about. Herol Graham, Johnny Nelson, Naseem Hamed. When I subsequently became acquainted with them, they didn't recognise me as an academic psychologist, or as a journalist, or even primarily as a fight fan, but as a guy who hung out in the same places as they did, after hours like them, and was friends with many of the people that they knew and respected.

A little gang of sorts is how I would describe it, getting through the night separated from the ordinary punters out for their big night out, them wrecked again, bladdered, without a clue how to behave in a top nightclub, unlike us who knew exactly what to do to get by.

'What do you know?' Lenny liked to ask whenever he saw me and the rest of the lads out in the club where he worked. 'What do you know?' It was like 'tell me something I don't know'. 'Tell me what's happening around you. Tell me something I can use.' Lenny, like all the doormen, lived a very sociable life, talking to punters night after night on the door or as he did his rounds. He always needed new material to fill the long hours, you could see that. His stories about himself in the ring were all exhausted. He was never that good a boxer, he said so himself. We, the punters, but not the ordinary punters – the mug punters – all had an obligation to provide some new material. 'I don't know much,' I'd say towards the beginning of our long relationship as if that sort of response might do. It didn't. 'Well, you're no fucking use then, are you?' And he'd frown at the other doormen and walk off to engage somebody else who might have something to say to him.

After a while, I got to understand the rules of my interactions with him, my personal obligations, and I would collect bits of information for him, things from my own life or things that he might find useful, short facts about psychology because, of course, it hadn't taken Lenny long to realise that, unlike many of the people he knew, I had a day job, and an interesting day job at that. 'Do you know, Lenny?' I would say, and I would relate some story about the workings of the human mind. He had a great memory for stories about classic obedience experiments – 'You mean we're all like the fucking Nazis, that's what I expected anyway' – or illusions or aversive conditioning, anything that he could pass on and trade. I heard many of the stories back after they had done the rounds. They had become more interesting in the meantime, the way that stories do. One night, I told Lenny that I had discovered that if you spray a live ant with pheromones associated with ant death the other ants will carry it outside the nest and bury it in the nearest refuse heap. I had read this somewhere in one of those big American textbooks designed to capture the imaginations of eighteen-year-olds. It seemed a little far-fetched to me, but interesting nonetheless. Big Lenny was mesmerised by this fact. 'And the ants will keep burying their friend until the chemical wears off,' I explained. I made a face at him as if to say, 'I'm not big in psychology for nothing, you know.'

'I'd like to see that,' he replied. 'It would be a great little experiment for us in the wine bar. Can you get hold of some of that gear for me, some of that spray, and we'll give it a go?'

I confessed to him that this was not really my specific area, and that his request was quite impossible, and that I only really had an abstract knowledge of the spray and of the experiment. 'I'll fucking abstract you' was his response, and then he went all quiet on me in that threatening way of his. 'I'm still trying to find out what your fucking specific area is, do you know that?' But he wanted the spray, and he wanted a lot of it. 'Get me the one hundred mil one,' he said as if it were perfume. 'Enough for quite a few sessions.' Whenever I saw him after that he would shout over at me, 'Have you got that fucking spray for me, yet? Where's my fucking death spray? You've been promising me it for weeks.'

The other doormen wanted to know what kind of death spray this was.

'Is it like CS gas?' one asked.

'It's for ants,' I said. 'He wants death spray for fucking ants.'

11

They assumed that it was insecticide for his garden.

'You'd better get some of it for him anyway,' said wee Steve, 'because he's like a fucking elephant – he never forgets.'

So eventually I have to confess – and I have never told anyone this before – I brought him a little empty bottle of aftershave and filled it with some plain water, just to shut him up. I assumed that he would just walk around showing off this little bottle of liquid for a while and that eventually he would lose interest in it, and it would just be lost, along with the coshes that had belonged to the Polish security guards and the airguns from Spain. But, of course, this never happened.

'Now then,' he said, 'now then,' sounding like Jimmy Saville, that other well-known wit. I should have known that he had plans for me and my death spray. The following night I watched, with more than a little bit of an anxious feeling inside, as he gathered a small crowd of VIPs, hangers-on and tired doormen around him at about three o'clock in the morning for a special demonstration of this spray at work.

'But you haven't got any ants, Lenny,' I pointed out helpfully.

'Who hasn't?' he replied, and he reached into the top pocket of his jacket and pulled out a matchbox, which he opened on the chrome table. There were three ants in it, all very much alive and, if my memory serves me correctly, all trying to crawl up the side of the box and away into the candlelit aura of the top-notch nightclub.

'What's in the box?' asked Linda, a woman with long, flowing blonde hair and dark roots covering what I guessed must have been her natural grey. Her hair, I always thought, was like something of a geological rock formation with layer upon layer of sediment covering formative stages in her life. She was smoking a long cigarette, which had bright-red lipstick along a surprisingly large section of its length. They called her 'deep throat' for this very reason.

'Ants,' said Lenny, 'as you can see. Live ants. Here for a little psychological experiment that I've devised with the help of the Doctor over there.'

'This isn't going to be cruel, is it, Lenny?' she said. 'Because I'm a vegetarian, as you well know.'

'There's no cruelty involved at all, luv,' said Lenny. 'This is just nature. In this bottle', he pulled the little blue bottle of Cool

Water out of his right pocket, 'is something very special indeed.'

Linda stared blankly at it. The cigarette disappeared into her mouth again. I watched her lips inch along it for a fuller drag, as if she might swallow it whole.

'It's not that special, Lenny. It was a few years ago, but we sell it to everybody these days.'

'But it's not Cool Water in this bottle, Linda. It's something else.'

Becksy, another doorman, started nodding as if he had got the point, which he probably hadn't because he never got the point. 'It's snide gear, Linda. Lenny's got a new supplier. You're the expert, luv. See if you can tell the difference between what Lenny has got in that bottle and the real thing that you make the punters pay through the nose for.'

Linda had worked on the perfume counter of a large department store in Sheffield for years. I would see her every Saturday afternoon with that practised mask of a smile of hers, her whole face covered in an additional mask, thick and cosmetic, hiding at least some of those late nights and bad experiences that she was always going on about. Before Lenny got a chance to say anything, she had picked up the 'aftershave' and sprayed the inside of her wrist with it. She held her cigarette in the other hand, well away from her face, in case it should interfere with her olfactory sense. Lenny glanced at me and sighed. Linda was caught in something of a double bind; this was Lenny's gear, after all.

'I've smelt stronger to be honest,' she said. 'It's a little bit weaker than the real thing. But then again, Lenny, I am an expert on this. When you've worked behind a perfume counter for ten years . . .'

'Twenty years more like,' interrupted Lenny.

'. . . then you can discriminate things that the average person can't.'

'Linda,' interrupted Lenny, 'this isn't weak Cool Water. This is a strong death spray for ants.'

There was a momentary hush as the small group of VIPs, hangers-on and doormen all looked at each other to see if this was one of Lenny's little nobbles. Then they all laughed as Linda started spitting and choking all over the red, patterned carpet. She dropped her cigarette.

'Some of that went right up my nose, Lenny,' she said. 'It's fucking disgusting. If it kills ants, what does it do to humans?'

You could see by her expression that she was imagining vividly what it might do to humans. She ran down the steps to the ladies' toilet. You could hear her stomach heaving all the way down. It didn't sound very ladylike.

'That's the last we'll see of her for the next hour or so while she does her make-up again,' said Lenny. 'This stuff doesn't kill ants. Isn't that right, Doc?' He glanced over at me. 'You tell them . . .'

Nervously, I explained all about the ant's great sense of smell and the way it reacts to the scent of death, with nervousness drying my tongue, as I had no idea how ants would react to another ant sprayed with water with just the merest hint of eau-de-Cologne.

'Are you ready then, folks?' asked Lenny. 'Who's going to spray this little fucker here for me?'

He looked at me as if to indicate that this was my responsibility, and then carefully extracted one of the ants from the box, the liveliest of the three, indeed the one that looked farthest from the point of death. Having just emptied the ashtray onto the floor, he placed the ant carefully inside it, and sat it in the middle of the chrome table.

'Right, Doc, give it a spray.'

I aimed the very watery eau-de-Cologne at the ant and sprayed it once. It seemed momentarily stunned, presumably surprised to be covered in sweet-smelling water at that time in the morning.

'Right, folks,' said Lenny. 'It's now covered in death spray, but look how it's wriggling away trying to get out of here. Now wait until you see what these other two little fuckers are going to do to it. They're going to pick it up and carry it out of Sheffield's ultimate nightspot and bury it in the nearest refuse heap. Now just watch this.'

He gingerly picked up first one ant and then the other and placed them on either side of the wet ant. They seemed to pause for an instant, and then all three of them headed for the edges of the table, in three quite separate directions.

I don't know if ants can run, but these three appeared to be running very fast indeed. Lenny watched them as they ran all the way down the legs of the table and out of view. Nobody dared say anything. Becksy was pretending not to look at me, but he was; he was doing these little nods in my direction. I took my cue.

'We forgot one thing, Lenny,' I said.

'What?' he said, irritated. Indeed, more than irritated, he was slipping and sliding into anger, like a man out of control on an icy pavement.

'There's no refuse dump near by,' I said, 'nowhere to bury the ant – perhaps they sensed that.'

'Oh, like a sixth sense?' said Becksy, who had an uncanny ability to look, as well as sound, absolutely idiotic at times.

'Yeah,' I said.

'Like ESP?' said Becksy.

'Oh,' said Lenny. 'So you would need the death spray *and* a refuse dump for it to work.'

I could see him thinking it was the kind of thing that would be hard to make up on the spot if you were frightened, which he guessed through his own sixth sense that I was.

'I'll give it a go when I get home,' he said. I could feel my fear fading, a calm spreading over me. 'It gives me something to look forward to,' said Lenny, 'when I'm having a quiet drink at home later tonight.'

It was already 4 a.m.; Lenny's late-night drinks could be very late indeed.

'If I can find any more of those little fuckers in my garden, that is. I think that I might have caught them all for this experiment.'

Linda came back out of the toilet. She had a fresh coat of make-up on, expertly applied, indeed professionally applied. Everybody was looking relieved.

'Have I missed anything?' she asked.

This was the kind of moment that this existence after hours in the club was made up of. I have a series of them in my head, all vivid and real. Powerful images. You would see Herol Graham out there and Johnny Nelson, and later a boyish Naz, far too young really for a club like this. All keeping themselves amused, hearing the same stories from Rod, Lenny and Mick Mills. Herol and Johnny together, working their way through the crowd to the far bar. Herol in his brown suit with loud, large checks. He got it in London, I remember he told me that, 'somewhere near

Bond Street'. Naz laughing too loudly at the other bar, with a face that suggested he was up to something, and a small gang of lads around him, egging him on, in whatever it was.

When my son asked me what I used to get up to, out in nightclubs every night, I sometimes didn't know what to tell him. I didn't know whether to claim that I was the new Friedrich Engels or the man who just ducked and dived with ants in an ashtray, and chatted away to Herol Graham about a suit with loud, brown checks. I didn't know which version to go for because I suppose that in reality I didn't know which version I actually believed myself.

Sam liked to ask me nevertheless. I think that he liked making me feel guilty.

'It's a long story,' I would say. 'It's a long story and you might not understand. You're too young.'

TWO

I had told Sam that afternoon that we would probably be ringside at the Johnny Nelson fight. I thought that he would be delighted to sit with the VIPs, but he asked whether any blood would land on us. He seemed nervous about this. 'It's Johnny Nelson,' I said. 'There won't be too much blood about. Not if old Johnny Fantastic can help it. A bit of sweat maybe, but no blood and guts.' And then I regretted saying it. I sounded like all the rest of Johnny's legion of knockers. Johnny, it was always said, had taken Brendan's defensive boxing to heart. But I had been to watch Johnny's attempt to take the world title from Carlos de Leon in Sheffield City Hall in January 1990, and all I remember about the fight was the caution, that terrible creeping caution of Johnny's, and the distinct lack of blood, resulting in a twelve-round draw and boos from the audience. The Sheffield public took a long time to forgive Johnny Nelson. I looked around at the audience in Pond's Forge leisure centre. It was far from full and this was world championship boxing in the heart of Yorkshire.

The official programme, 'The Magic Is Back', said it all:

With interest in Britain at an all-time low, the Yorkshireman journeyed abroad for work. Johnny plied his trade in France, South Africa, Australia, Belgium, New Zealand, Thailand and Brazil, often taking fights at heavyweight, and winning. For four years Johnny lived in virtual exile as he beat Jimmy Thunder and got robbed against Adilson Rodriguez twice.

That's why Brendan had rung me, of course. Johnny needed some positive publicity. Brendan would never be that blunt, of course. 'Oh, the action and the craíc will be great,' Brendan said. 'Bring your tape recorder; you might get a wee story out of it. And I've more to talk to you about.' It was July 2001 and there had been race riots in Bradford and other British cities. Brendan explained that he was doing his bit to stop Sheffield erupting in the same way. 'I'm taking some of my boxers up to Attercliffe with me, including Killer Khan, and inviting some of these young Pakistani lads with real attitude problems to put the gloves on and have a go. They all want to be Naz; he's their hero, their Islamic warrior. Let them get rid of their frustration in the ring, that's what I say. You can come with us next time.' I sometimes felt that Brendan could talk me into anything.

My son and I had walked in midway through some bout, and we sat on the second row back from the ring, beside a large white-haired man, who I assumed quite rightly was a ref because of the way he was watching the action in front of him so intently, as if he might miss something. I also assumed quite rightly that he was American. He looked well fed and prosperous. He was rocking slightly from side to side, his eyes narrowed a little, refusing to blink, refusing to miss a thing.

'Hey, buddy,' he turned my way, 'do you know what time the main bout is on?'

I shook my head. 'Sorry,' I said. 'No idea.'

'Oh,' he replied, and turned again towards the ring, the whole head movement executed in one smooth action, without pause, as if he could tell that I wouldn't know much.

The VIP enclosure felt very exposed. You could sense other members of the audience looking at you from elsewhere in the room, trying to work out who you were and whether you were worth knowing or not. There was a strong smell of lemony aftershave, quite pricey. I can tell these things. It was a sharp sort of smell that reminded me of raw, shaved skin, reddening and blotchy in the light. The man in the row in front was talking loudly about his German shepherd dog to a woman with heavy, gold jewellery and thick, brown crocodile-like skin. 'As good as gold,' he was saying, 'until that morning. I don't know what happened. I wasn't there. I just don't understand it. As good as gold.'

I looked around to get my bearings. The boxers were standing behind a low barrier at the back of the room, as if they didn't quite belong. It wasn't quite like amateur boxing, which always shocks me a little, where the thin, gaunt boys at the back are brought out in pairs and led to the blood-splattered ring, which usually resembles a sparse Jackson Pollock with thin, faded pink, almost grey lines, and spots and splodges in the same dull colour, watched by corpulent red-faced businessmen now on their cigars and brandy. But nevertheless it looked like a discernibly different social group at the back there, separated from the rest of us.

When I say 'the back', I say it with caution because there was no front of the room. The ring is, after all, square and there are entrances on a number of sides. But I say 'the back' because the lights from Sky Television were set up on that side. The boxers were behind the lights, which were directed away from them. They were standing in the shadows, so to speak. I looked around to see how many I would recognise after this period of time. I had written a book about Brendan's gym around five years previously. It had evolved out of my nights spent in the clubs. Many of the doormen were ex-boxers, the owner was a fight fan, and on many nights the boxers themselves would come into the club for a bit of social intercourse, as the owner liked to put it. But I had moved on to other things, academic matters, which demanded all of my time. I was now Professor of Psychology and Head of Department at the University of Manchester. I was fully engaged in my academic work. But I had seen Naz a number of times in the intervening period, and Brendan would ring me up regularly to ask me when I was going to come back down to the gym to talk to him and the lads again. I always think that he liked unburdening himself to me, although that may just be vanity on my part. On a Sunday afternoon, he would ring me at home and talk for an hour, sometimes without any discernible pause in his speech. 'Alma [his wife] says to me, "Brendan, do you know what your trouble is . . .?"' I would listen and encourage with my little 'hmms' and 'yeahs', like some cheap therapist, until he had finished.

I had often considered going back to see them all again to finish the story, which was really incomplete. I had, after all, watched the beginnings of this great tale. I had watched the dreams being nurtured like a tender plant in the back streets. I had watched Naz taking the world title and I had seen a dream being realised in a northern town in decline. And then I had disappeared. 'You've gone on the fucking missing persons list,' Big Lenny said when he finally caught up with me. I had got close to some of these key players but perhaps closer still to some of the bit players, although perhaps you can get a little too close sometimes. My life had started to resemble theirs in some odd and unexpected ways. It's not all about money in the world of boxing, as I discovered. There's money and there's reputation and there are all the obligations you build up along the way. You can become obligated in ways that you hadn't even imagined before. For example, I wrote an application for a job as a probation officer for a bouncer and ex-boxer that I knew. (I should point out that he didn't get the job, although apparently he was told that it was one of the most well-written applications that they had ever seen in the probation service.) But one of the real reasons I wanted to see them again was because a lot had happened to Brendan and Naz since I first became involved, and part of me wanted to know if I saw any of it coming: the disputes, the arguments, the falling out, the resentments, the hurt, all of the kind of stuff that had poisoned a great and successful relationship. I am a psychologist after all. Could I have predicted well in advance what was going to happen?

My friend, Mick Mills, a bouncer and ex-boxer, said that he could, and that there was never any doubt in his mind that it would all end in tears. 'When there's money like that on the table there's bound to be a fucking row over it. Who isn't going to go to war for that kind of money?' But that's because he always takes the pessimistic view on things like that. I like to be more open-minded, more objective, more balanced, more fucking naïve, as Mick and my mother both like to say.

The end of Naz and Brendan's relationship came long after my first book was finished, but before the fight against Kevin Kelley in 1997. In his insightful book *The Paddy and the Prince*, Nick Pitt says that the end can be traced to a single moment in the back of a stretch limo travelling from Los Angeles International Airport to the Sheraton Hotel in Los Angeles with Frank Warren, Brendan, Naz, Ryan Rhodes and Joe Calzaghe, the WBO Super-Middleweight Champion, all crammed into the car and all heading for the World Boxing Organisation annual convention. According to Pitt, the whole thing finished after an argument brought on by Naz teasing Brendan once too often. Naz is reported to have taunted Brendan with, 'What did you win, Brendan? Nothing. You never even won an area title.' Brendan apparently reacted to this, and then Naz administered the *coup de grâce* with, 'You know your trouble, Brendan? You never stood up to anybody. You never stood up to anybody in your life. You always let people bully you. Like the time with Mickey Duff when he slagged you off and you just stood for it.'

These words are quoted verbatim in the book, but I guess all that we really have is the gist, as remembered by Brendan. But I can imagine it. This kind of teasing is what boxers in the Wincobank gym – and Naz in particular – engaged in all the time. I can hear the words coming out in that cocky tone of his. Frank Warren apparently told them that they were worse than an old, married couple. I can even hear him saying that but, according to Pitt, the damage had been done. Pitt says:

> Brendan became obsessed by what Naseem had said, as if Naseem had stained his whole life ... They were poisonous thoughts that Brendan allowed to fester in his head for the three days of the convention. While Naseem, Frank Warren and the others flew on to New York to publicise the Kevin Kelley fight, Brendan flew home alone. He had eleven hours to sit and think with no one to deflect or diffuse his ruminations. By the time he arrived at Heathrow, Brendan wished he'd grabbed Naseem in the limousine and tried to hit him.

The reason, according to Pitt, for Brendan's reaction is spelt out in the pages that follow. Pitt says that the comments stung so much because there was an essential truth in them, 'But the person he had failed to stand up to was not Mickey Duff, or indeed any of the others who had given him trouble over the years. It was Naseem. Brendan had allowed himself to be bullied by the bully he had, in part, created.' When Naz got back from America, again according to Pitt, Brendan pulled him to one side and told him that he didn't want to work with him any more. Sal, Naz's father, came down to Brendan's house to see him and, in Pitt's book, Brendan listed his grievances to Sal, including his cut of the money, down from 25 per cent to 16 per cent and then by Brendan's calculations to nearer 4 per cent.

It's a neat story. It's based on the power of the word, on the remark that cuts deeper than any punch thrown in that splattered ring. Its premise is basic psychology. The money side of things is just slipped in almost as an afterthought. The story is based on a certain psychological vulnerability in Brendan. The remark from Naz made Brendan finally realise his own weakness and recognise what he had helped to make. I can even imagine Brendan passing on the story; it fits in well with some of his deeper views on the boxers he had helped create. I remember him once telling me that Alma had commented that he was really in the business of creating monsters. I heard this comment in the early 1990s. He said it in a matter-of-fact sort of way. Then, it was directed against Herol Graham, with whom Brendan had also had a father–son relationship, although, of course, things were to change there too. Later, I heard the same comment repeated, only this time it was directed at Naz. I don't think that he remembered saying it to me the first time round.

Nick Pitt's story seems entirely plausible in a way. Perhaps we have to trace everything back to a point in time, to say that that was the moment; that was the moment when Brendan realised it couldn't go on, that there was some sort of epiphany in the back of that stretch limo. But when you have talked to Brendan over the years the way I have, you sense that this realisation that things with Naz would not really work out in the end was not all that sudden. Perhaps a bit of Mick Mills has rubbed off on me. That moment in the limo on the way to the Sheraton wasn't the *cause* of the breakdown; it only acquired its special significance retrospectively.

I have always thought that one particular short passage from Joyce Carol Oates about the psychology of boxing in her excellent book *On Boxing* is particularly poignant.

A boxing trainer's most difficult task is said to be to persuade a young boxer to get up and continue fighting after he has been knocked down. And if the boxer has been knocked down by a blow he hadn't seen coming – which is usually the case – how can he hope to protect himself from being knocked down again? And again? The invisible blow is after all invisible.

This seemed to be both a good way of thinking about behaviour in the ring and a good metaphor for thinking about the life of boxers outside it. To finish the story about Naz and Brendan and the pursuit of boxing greatness involved thinking back to all that I had observed and heard in the gym in Wincobank in order to ascertain whether what had happened when Brendan and Naz had squared up was indeed the 'invisible blow', with all its devastating consequences, or whether it had been signalled like one of Tom Collins' haymakers against Johnny Nelson that night in the leisure centre in Mansfield, with much less serious consequences. It may be part of all of our basic psychology to believe that we live in a world that is predictable, in which things happen for a reason and where causes and consequences can be isolated and identified, like that comment in the stretch limo on an American highway. But I wanted to see if this were true here.

That is why I was at the fight with my son, to continue the story about those guys behind the barrier back there, including Brendan, who was making himself busy as usual, and the others who weren't here or weren't here yet like 'the Naz fella', as Brendan always called him.

But perhaps there was another reason why I had gone back. A more personal reason. Perhaps I had to prove to myself that all the time spent away from my young family in those clubs and bars was not time wasted. That it was not just time spent with people who were not really worth knowing in the first place: 'the cheats and the bullies', as my mother always called them. 'You shouldn't have been giving them the time of day.' But I always reasoned that if a boxing legend had been moulded in that environment, a true boxing legend that would transcend time, space, religion and creed, and if I had seen it all first-hand, and if this legend had not been destroyed or overtaken by events, then it all really was worthwhile in the first place. It was worth being there and seeing it all directly and knowing that ants with death spray in bottles of Cool Water really did have their own part to play in the social construction of that small *demi-monde*. And that it all added up to something, even for those around the legend, including me, way out there on the periphery. This could easily have been the reason for me returning to this world, if I am being totally honest with myself.

There is something quite strange about this process of looking back, which is both exciting and forbidding at the same time. In the light of what occurred between them, I like to read statements

23

from old interviews with Naz and with Brendan when they were still striving for a world title to take back to Sheffield. We all enjoy that bitter-sweet process. I have in front of me some quotes from Brendan from before Naz's fight with Laureano Ramirez in 1995. I remember that fight well for a number of reasons. I remember Ramirez turned away after complaining that he had swallowed his tooth. I remember thinking at the time that this was a very unfortunate thing to have happened to a boxer, getting your teeth knocked out like that in public, like something that happens on a street corner. I also remember Naz wearing a gum-shield that night that was white in the centre and black elsewhere, so that it made him look like Bugs Bunny. The fight also sticks in my mind because it was the first contest in which Naz publicly thanked Allah for his victory. He did it in a way that made Allah sound like an experienced corner man, 'Allah said to me, "That was your round."' He then went on to remind everybody that 'It hurts being this good', which he was prone to saying at the time. I have notebooks in that scribble of mine filled with these words, over and over again. I read the sentences from their interviews with that awful feeling that you have when you look back knowing how things turned out. Brendan discussing how he and Naz were planning to spend all the money they were going to make. Naz with his 'forty million quid', which Brendan had been promising him for years, always that same figure. I don't know where he got that number from. And Brendan with his ten million, that one quarter cut. Brendan always seemed to have this need to signal their basic financial agreement, his twenty-five per cent cut, just in case anybody tried to forget it. It was as if the insecurity was always there. Perhaps that's the way in boxing; make few assumptions and that way you won't be disappointed.

And I read some of Brendan's other words again. 'There are a lot of people around who would like to spoil the relationship I've got with Naz. But I think that a lot of people are going to be disappointed in this particular case. This time I've got a boxer and me and him are going all the way.' I smile a mournful sort of smile to myself and wonder why dreams always have to end up like this.

I think of the sheer intimacy of the relationship between the two of them, the intimacy of two lives so bound up together. I remember Naz and Brendan standing in Brendan's parlour in front of a pair of scales. Brendan, a grey-haired man in his fifties, with pale, translucent skin, a little loose around his frame, and a small, slight Arab boy with darker, taut skin, standing at ninety degrees to one another. On one side of the room was a large bookcase. There were a lot of books on Irish history at the time, I remember that. Black covers with the green of the shamrock. It was serious reading. It could have been the parlour of a minor academic or a priest. On the other wall was a large framed photograph of Herol Graham, the Graham of years ago, the Graham of eternal optimism and promise. Not the Herol that I was used to seeing about at that time. I remember that the grey-haired man got onto the scales first.

'Twelve stone dead. Now it's your turn, and don't forget I've been warning ye.' His Irish brogue was as thick as buttermilk, but inviting at the same time.

The small Arab boy stepped forward in a mock swagger. He always had that cockiness about him. I can never remember him without it.

'It'll be all right, Brendan, don't worry.' His was a cocky Sheffield accent. 'I'm young, fit. I *am* the business.'

Brendan averted his gaze from the scales just for a moment. He felt that he needed to explain.

'The problem with Naz is that he knows he's good. At that age it's bound to go to your head. He loves himself and why not?'

I must have nodded. 'And why not indeed?'

I remember Naz being prepared for greatness, having to make sacrifices, and Brendan going through the whole thing with him. In *On the Ropes* I wrote about Naz climbing onto the scales in Brendan's front room with a look on his face that wasn't quite so cocky.

'These scales never lie, Naz, remember that,' said Brendan. 'Eight stone nine. What did I tell ye? What did I say? You were boasting about all the crap you'd eaten yesterday. Fish fingers and chips. Well this is what you get. You're three pounds over the weight. I've said to you time and time again – you're eating all wrong, and you're sleeping wrong. You're up far too late, playing snooker.'

And that almost whining tone of his. 'But, Brendan, I'm beating everybody. I'm knocking them all out. You know how good I am.'

'You may be the greatest thing since fried bread, but this is your comeuppance. Three pounds over weight two days before a big fight can be hard for any fighter to shift, let alone a bantamweight. You've got less than two days. This will be a test of what you're made of outside the ring.'

I always remember those words, 'what you're made of outside the ring'. Never just half the battle.

And I remember Brendan talking one month later. 'I always knew that young Naz would fail to make the weight some day,' said Brendan. 'That lad could eat for England. I didn't allow him to eat anything for the remainder of the Monday or on the Tuesday morning. At lunch-time on the Tuesday I weighed myself again – I was twelve stone again. I explained to Naz that by the time we got down to London, with the stress and strain of me driving all that way, I'd have lost two pounds. It wouldn't be so easy for him. We were staying in a flat above the Thomas à Becket gym. I brought my scales with me. When we got to London my weight was down to eleven stone twelve pounds, exactly as I'd predicted. Naz had lost a pound on the drive down, but he still had two extra pounds to shift. Naz's room was cold. I took the blow-heater out of my room to give to him. I also switched on the sunbed in the corner of his room. It's my job to see he's as comfortable as possible before a big fight. I explained to him that he'd lose nearly one pound sleeping. We were both starving. I hadn't had anything to eat or drink all that day either. It's no good me trying to motivate or inspire somebody else if they're trying to make the weight, and I'm eating.

'It was a rough night, the bed was damp, and somebody down below was playing some old Beatles records. By the next morning, I was down to nearly eleven stone eleven pounds; I'd lost almost another pound. Now I was counting in ounces. I went to the toilet and I was now only six ounces over the weight I'd set myself – I had to lose three pounds just like Naz. Naz was less than a pound over the weight. So I went to the toilet again. Naz accused me of having something to drink. He said that I must have sneaked a drink. I kept going to the toilet and my weight kept dropping. Naz couldn't believe that I was going all these times without having something to drink. But the proof was on the scales. He could see the ounces coming off. He knew I wasn't cheating, and that he and I were going through this thing together. But every time that I went to the toilet I had to reassure him by stepping on the scales again to show that the weight was coming off, and that I wasn't sneaking a drink. We were watching each other like frigging hawks. I took him for a walk and by the time we got to the weigh-in he was half a pound under the weight. He hadn't had anything to eat or drink since the Monday, that's thirty-six hours without anything. I took him to a restaurant after the weigh-in, but he couldn't finish his soup or his spaghetti. His stomach had shrunk. But he felt good. I told him that that day he'd grown in my estimation.

'Naz has this little routine when he gets into the ring – he jumps over the ropes, just like Chris Eubank, but then he does a flip holding onto the ropes and then three flips across the ring. He's a bit of a showman. But I told him that night that I just wanted one flip from him, then he was going straight to work. I told him that he was going to mentally and physically destroy his opponent. Incidentally, his opponent was unbeaten before that night. Naz had him down three times in the first round. He knocked him out in the second. I told him afterwards that there is nothing to stop him becoming world champion. "Who's going to stop you now?" says I. "Nobody," says he. "Right," says I.'

I remember all that and I always thought how sad it was that they had parted on such bad terms. I had been telling my son repeatedly that there was more to the fight game than he might think. I tried to explain what Brendan had done for Naz, and what goes into making a world champion. But some young people aren't that interested in ancient history, which this was to him. I was there when the great journey started with Brendan and Naz. I saw what went into it.

'It's the Irish blarney,' they always said, in a demeaning sort of way. 'He used the blarney on them all.'

'Herol Graham, Johnny Nelson, Naseem Hamed? The blarney did all that?' I would ask incredulously. 'That's some blarney.'

I remember the boys turning up to the gym in those days, the waifs and strays, looking to learn. Matthew was just another one of them; he was twelve, with a round, open face. Brendan was perched on some wooden steps by the side of the ring. Brendan called Matthew over. 'How long have you been coming to the gym?'

'Three years,' said Matthew.

'Tell him what it was like before you came to the gym.'

'It were terrible. I had no friends and I was being bullied all the time at school.'

'Tell him what it's like now,' said Brendan.

'It's great. I've got lots of friends and I'm not bullied now.'

Brendan squeezed his arm tighter and looked at me. 'This lad here can't fight. He'll never be able to fight. I'll teach him to dodge a bit in the ring. I'll teach him to fuck his opponent around, to make the other fella look bad. I'll build up his confidence. I taught him that if anybody comes up to him in the street and starts to bully him, that he should just shout "fuck off" and run away. I'm teaching him personal and social skills for life. My job is to get these lads through life as safely as possible – both inside and outside the ring. It can be rough around here. I was the one to bring the first blacks in this area to my gym. So the National Front put posters all over my house and scrawled their name on the walls of the garages outside the gym. You can still see their graffiti to this day. But they've gone, and I've survived, and that's what it's all about. I knew this guy who was big in the National Front, and he ended up marrying a black girl. So it was all a load of bloody bollocks anyway.'

The rumour at the time was that Brendan painted 'NF' on the garage walls himself.

In the ring above us there were five boxers. Two were black. One was a powerfully built novice boxer, the other was Johnny Nelson. Two were small, white boys, probably no more than ten, the fifth was a serious-looking Asian youth, dressed in a black polo shirt and black tracksuit bottoms, who stalked his opponent, before unleashing incredibly ineffectual-looking punches. They took turns at sparring with each other, with one always left out. Johnny Nelson with the muscled black novice, then Johnny with one of the boys.

'Only body-shots up there. I won't stand for any boxer in this type of sparring giving his opponent one accidentally on purpose to the head,' said Brendan. 'TIME!' shouted Brendan and all five boxers walked slowly around the ring in an anti-clockwise direction. 'In my gym the professionals train with the novices.

They can all learn something from each other. Bomber Graham used to stand in the middle of this ring and the lads would try to land a punch on him. They never could. CHANGE OVER!' The boxers touched gloves gently, as if they were in some barn dance and then started again with a different partner.

A sixteen-year-old stood by the ring bandaging his hands. Brendan called him over. It was Ryan Rhodes.

'How old were you, Ryan, when you came to the gym for the first time?'

'Six.'

'What did I say to you?'

'Do you know any swear words?'

'So I got him to tell me every swear he knew – "fuck", "bastard", "wanker" – the lot. So I says to him, "From now on you don't swear when you're in this gym and you do as you're told." It took him by surprise, you see. Then I says to him, "What do they say about the Irish where you come from?" and he says, "They're all tick bastards." But this "tick bastard" says that this lad will be winning a gold at the Olympics in three years. When the English shout, "Fuck off, you tick Irish Mick" at me, I just remind them that they were riding around on dirt tracks before the Irish came over.'

Brendan pulled out a book that he had been carrying around in the pocket of his anorak to show me. It had pages of political cartoons from the nineteenth century on the Irish problem. 'This shows you what the English thought of the Irish. The Irishman was always portrayed as a wee monkey. Here's the Irish Guy Fawkes, a wee ugly monkey in a hat, sitting on top of a keg of gunpowder before setting light to it. The tick wee monkey bastard. But the Irish are too cunning for the English. I've had the British Super-Middleweight Champion. When I was starting him off, I called him Slugger O'Toole. The Irish are great boxing fans, so I reckoned that they'd turn out in force to see an Irish boxer with the name of O'Toole. Slugger would come into the arena dressed in green, and it wasn't until he'd taken his dressing gown off that they would see that he was black. So they'd all be shouting, "He's not Irish," and I'd say, "What's the matter with you? Can't you have a black Irishman?" And then when they asked me his real name, I'd reply quite truthfully, as it turns out, "Fidel Castro Smith." They'd not believe me anyway.'

Brendan pulled Ryan closer to him.

'Who's the only person who is ever going to lick you?'

'Me, myself.'

'Who's responsible for you?'

'Me, myself.'

'Correct.'

This was a routine that they had rehearsed many times. Ryan knew when to come in, and he knew all the unvarying responses. It was like the litany from a church service.

'Some people think that it's easy to be a boxing trainer and manager. You just cream off your twenty-five per cent, and the lads do all the work. But that's not how it is. I take these lads in when they're kids and I have to work on them. I have to build up their confidence. I have to teach them about life, and replace all the crap they've learned. They come here and their head is full of it.'

He called over a somewhat shy-looking boy with a thin moustache and dull, greyish shorts. His girlfriend had been sitting in the corner of the gym biting her nails all afternoon. 'What school did you come from, Matt?'

'Arbourthorne.'

'What kind of school is it?'

'Special needs.'

'What were you there for?'

'Because I was a thick bastard.'

'What are you now?'

'A clever bastard.'

The responses were instantaneous, starting almost before the question finished. He pulled Matt closer until their faces were almost touching.

'Who didn't you like when you first came here?'

'Pakis.'

'Pakis and blacks?'

'No, just Pakis. I always thought that the blacks were all right.'

'Who don't you like now?'

'Nobody.'

'When that lad came here, he had nothing going for him,' said Brendan. 'Now, he's a part of the team in here. There are a lot of Pakistanis in the team. He trains with champions. He'll be sparring with Johnny Nelson in a couple of minutes. I can identify with these lads. When I was a boy I had what you would call now 'learning difficulties'. Over in Ireland I was just a "tick bastard". I struggled with my spelling, my reading and everything else. I struggled with Latin and Gaelic. I can still say in Gaelic, "What is your name?" "My name is Brendan Ingle." "Where do you live?" "Dublin City." "Do you have any money?" "No, I haven't." I can recite all these verses in Latin, but I've no idea what any of them mean. These verses were beaten into me. One of the nuns was a right bastard with her leather strap. I was beaten because I was "tick". But this taught me a valuable lesson – you can't change people's attitude by mentally or physically abusing them. The only way that you change people is by engaging in dialogue with them. Only dialogue.'

He shouted over to Matt, 'Who is the only person who can beat you?'

'Myself,' replied Matt across the crowded gym.

'My lads come to me with all their problems. I always say to them that if you haven't killed anybody, then you haven't got a real problem. I can sort everything else out.'

He turned to the boxers in the ring. 'Now lads, before you get down out of the ring, I want to see you jump over the ropes one by one.' Johnny Nelson did it with some flair. The rest struggled to get over. 'I let them jump off the second rope, if they can't manage it,' said Brendan. 'I do it to build their confidence in all aspects of life. Boxing isn't just about punching and how to slip a punch. It's about building confidence and learning to survive.'

He shouted up to Matt, now sparring with Johnny Nelson, 'Matt, what do you say if some dirty pervert comes up to you in the street?'

'I shout "fuck off".'

'What do you do then?'

'I run like fuck.'

'I'm teaching them how to survive inside and outside the ring,' said Brendan, 'which isn't that bad for a "tick Mick".'

And it was in this milieu that he taught Naz everything he knew, and a lot more besides.

THREE

I have a much more recent image of Brendan sitting in his front room one wet Sunday afternoon about six months ago. It's a sad, emotive image. Brendan had managed to get hold of a video of a television interview, not yet broadcast, with Riath, Naz's brother and business manager, discussing his brother's rise to stardom. He wanted me to watch it with him. Brendan sat in the corner with the remote in his hand. I observed his face carefully. He assumed that I would be watching the screen and so was moment- arily caught off guard. I watched the micro-expressions of pain and anger, fully formed expressions of emotion, register fleetingly each time Riath spoke. It was as if Brendan were a boxer who was not entirely in control of his own body and who was taking hard punches to the ribs.

'By the time Naz turned professional, he was ready-made,' said Riath. 'Brendan has no right to say he's made Naz ... He may have enhanced and nurtured his talent, but no one apart from the Creator can say, "I made this person" ... When Brendan once said to me that he had done the hard job, and that I was feeding off his rewards, I saw him for what he was ... Brendan didn't let Naz grow up.'

There really was a sadness in how Brendan watched the tape, a sadness that formed slowly and engulfed his whole face. The room was quite dark; he must have thought that I couldn't see his face.

Brendan played the tape again, and this time he watched me for my reaction. I shook my head, which was the one sign he wanted, and then I watched him carefully as he grimaced self- consciously to conceal his emotions. He was silent for a while, and then, without any warning, he started to talk about the gates of his house. I kind of knew what was coming next. Brendan has always lived in the same modest house opposite the gym in Wincobank. The house was never finished and was always being worked on by Brendan and gangs of lads, and sometimes the odd girl, who were on YTS schemes. Brendan's 'gang of waifs and strays', as he always put it. Anyway, Brendan would have them do a bit of work, and then introduce them to the gym to teach them how to get by in the world.

He had told me before about kids like these, saying, 'I had fourteen boys and girls with me on this council scheme and they were all nutters. I had this girl and all she ever said was "Go and get fucked, you Irish bastard." I was teaching them a bit of gardening, and a little bit of this and that, and sometimes I'd take them down to the gym to teach them some more survival skills. I'd let them put the gloves on, and I'd teach them how to get by. Kids would come in sexually abused by their parents. Kids would come in sexually abused by their neighbours, and I'd think to myself, "I'm supposed to be teaching bleedin' gardening skills, me." One time this lad comes over to me and says, "I was painting under there and this fella comes and grabs me by the testicles." I told him that in future if anyone tried to sexually interfere with him just tell him to "bollocks" and run off. I've been teaching survival skills for years.'

You would often see them all working on the house that was never finished. But a few years ago, wrought-iron gates appeared outside Brendan's house, with spikes and gold curls. He had apparently decided on these gates after Naz had won the world title. It isn't hard to pick out Brendan's house now in that street in Wincobank. The gates were always a sensitive issue; some have talked about *la folie des grandeurs* on Brendan's part. I never mentioned them. I pretended that the gates had always been there, or that they were so insignificant that you wouldn't really notice them. Brendan told me several times that Naz had criticised these gates to his face. Naz had said they were too big. He had said that they were out of place outside his house, that they were ridiculous and then, according to Brendan, he had bought the same gates for his mansion on the other side of the city.

'He says that they're too good for me, but they're not too good for him,' Brendan had told me. 'That's the kind of person he's become.' These gates had acquired some terrible symbolic significance in the feud between the two of them. It was all about what each of them could aspire to, what each of them had earned, what each of them had achieved. These were gates fit for a king, or perhaps a 'king-maker', but not for both. I listened to the tirade against Naz on the subject of the gates and I nodded again and said all that I could say. 'They're lovely gates, Brendan. Really lovely. You've worked for them. You deserve them.'

I understood why Brendan felt so hurt. That afternoon, after he had calmed down about the video, and after his anger over the elaborate black and gold wrought-iron gates had blown itself out, he couldn't have been clearer. He said quietly that Tara, his daughter, had told him that he had given Naz more time and more attention than any of his own children when they were growing up and this comment, which he knew to be true, had hurt Brendan deeply. 'I shake hands with my kids rather than put my arms around them,' he said. 'That's just the way it is.'

There was a terrible sense of loss emanating from Brendan; you could see it in his face. All those years spent with Naz, and now he felt that he was being slowly and deliberately written out of the history of the legend. 'Just remember all I taught him,' he said. 'That knowledge doesn't come from nowhere.' Brendan needed his role to be publicly reaffirmed by Naz himself. He needed to know that all those years devoted to Naz had not been in vain. That afternoon, I understood something of Brendan's mental state because I felt something a little similar. I too felt that I had to justify to my children what I had been up to during those years. Not just passing the time in a northern city wrecked by what seemed like deliberate government policy. Not just ducking and diving with loose fast-talk. But out there documenting the process through which a legend was being slowly and painstakingly formed, witnessing something significant and important and true. Perhaps that was why I had arranged to go back to see all the boys again, to finish the story, to find out what had become of them, to re-evaluate what we had all been through, to re-examine the legend that was Naz, to re-examine myself.

FOUR

Mick Mills was standing in his usual spot in the narrow part of the club, with the smoke and the perfume and the expectancy hanging in the air. He is small and squat for a doorman, but not to be messed with. You can tell that just by looking at him. His fist, capable of breaking jaws, was holding a small lager. The boys who know the score around here always drink halves of lager. He was sipping from the glass. He reached out a large, horny hand and I squeezed it as I walked past. 'Long time no see, stranger,' he said. He looked genuinely pleased to see me. 'Where have you been hiding?' he asked me. He was standing with a punter with narrow-framed glasses and a yellow shirt that hung out over his trousers. A blonde girl in a small PVC top and tight, matching trousers squeezed past the two of them. The man with the glasses protruded his lips and went 'Oooooo' right into the side of her face. She appeared to take this as a compliment. She smiled at Mick, but not at the man with the glasses. Mick winked at me, as if to say, 'Did you clock that?'

'He knows them all,' said the man with the glasses. 'Every decent-looking bird in this town walks through the doors of this club sooner or later and Mick clocks them all.' I leaned back against the metal bars of the bar. It was an old, familiar haunt and an old, familiar feeling. I watched the girl as she weaved her way away from us; she was a little unsteady in her high shoes. Mick smiled over again and wrinkled his nose. It was just men doing what they do.

'What are you doing back here?' he said. 'I'd heard that you'd moved up in the world. I'd heard that you'd moved over to Manchester.'

The man with the glasses laughed loudly without looking at

35

anyone, as if this might be one of Mick's jokes, as if moving across the Pennines to 'the Smoke' and moving up in the world were mutually contradictory statements.

'You know,' Mick said, 'I wouldn't live over in Manchester for all the money in the world. They use guns over there. They're dead keen on drive-by shootings. In Sheffield, at least you know that you're not going to be killed when you go out for a night.'

'What about that guy that time in the toilet?' said the man with the glasses, who still had not been introduced to me. 'He were killed that night.'

'That were different,' said Mick. 'He got a crack on the head all right, but it was the way he fell. It was the way he fell that did him. It wasn't really intentional, not the way it is in Manchester. There, they mean to kill you over there. Here, they only kill you by accident.'

Mick tilted his head to the side when he looked at me. It reminded me of my mother when she had said something that she thought was profound.

I smiled back at him. 'True,' I said.

I sipped my lager. 'It isn't so bad,' I said as reassuringly as I could. 'I haven't seen anything really, to be absolutely honest.'

'That's because you haven't been out,' said Mick. 'You've probably been hiding away from it all. If Gary and Steve and me took you out for a night, you'd see some action all right.'

For a while, I had trained with Mick, Gary, Steve and the rest of the lads on a Saturday morning in Brendan's gym. It was how I had started my first book on boxing. My publisher, unbelievably now when I look back, had suggested I might like to engage in a few professional fights to write a book about the experience of boxers, along the lines of George Plimpton's *Shadow Box*. Plimpton had gone three rounds with Archie Moore despite, I always thought, Plimpton's totally implausible build for a boxer. I thought that my publishers lived in another world, and I suggested to them that it might be useful to learn to spar a little first. So I did. For a year, I packed my gear and went down to Wincobank every Saturday morning. What was it like? It was much harder than I had ever imagined. I can certainly remember some of the sensations of the fight. Some of the strongest sensations were the sounds that came from me. The sounds and the pain.

'Ooooooommmmmppphh.' The noise had erupted from the pit of my stomach. From way down low. It didn't sound human. It was an involuntary response, way beyond my control. Way beyond anybody's control. That's what I tried to tell myself. It was out before I could do anything about it, and there was no way to apologise or make amends now. That noise sealed my fate. Gary, who was standing at the side of the ring, laughed. I wanted to. I wanted to smile and to clown about to show that I wasn't taking any of this seriously. But I couldn't. It was all serious, and this was obvious to even the casual spectator. I was grimly determined. Just try saying the word 'grim' and watch how it makes your lips purse in an ugly manner. My lips wanted to hang open, bleeding, sucking in the air through the gum-shield. It took all my effort to keep a face together. I was past caring whether it looked aggressive or like the face of somebody who should be respected. It was a grim mask.

To spare my embarrassment Gary kept glancing away, shouting to his mates still on the bag routines. But I could see him looking back towards me, looking out for little signs from my body. To see how I was taking it. To see what kind of a man I was. I covered up. I watched the eyes of my opponent. I was looking for signs from him. I didn't know of what.

But I was already starting to slide down the greasy, phylogenetic scale of respect. If I had started the morning at the gym on my first day of boxing at the level of hamster or dormouse, I was now fast approaching the level of amoeba. I had been warned, you see, not to make any noise when hit. 'We have lads who've come down to train once or twice and they've taken a good shot and then they're down on the canvas,' Gary had warned me before we started. 'The rule down here on a Saturday morning is if you're hurt, you box on. If you're hurt, you don't make any noise – you don't make a song and dance about it.' But it was too late. I had made a noise, and not just any noise. I had managed to produce a low moan that had played its own tune on the way out. I had never heard that noise before, although I had seen it written down several times in comics when the filthy Bosch had been butted in the stomach with the handle of a gun by some Tommy or other. I was the filthy, cowardly Bosch. Or an amoeba. I didn't much like the thought of being either.

I was now watching my sparring partner's face for a sign of

recognition of my infringement. I had broken the rule. I had violated the code of manly conduct in the ring. But there was no such sign, just that quiet look of satisfaction from Mick 'The Bomb' Mills of work well done. My 'song', which had started so softly and which had risen to a sort of crescendo, was music to his ears. There was a sign at the side of the ring that read 'Boxing can damage your health'. It was meant to be funny. I now knew that it wasn't. I was trying to remember where my spleen was and trying to imagine how it would feel if it had burst. Or was merely ajar. Leaking. Seeping.

I was more determined now. It might have been just the impetus I needed. Sweat dripped into my eyes. It stung. I tried wiping it away with the edge of my glove. It left my stomach exposed. My vest was soaked with sweat. My biceps ached. Never had I imagined that a man – even in his thirties and a novice at boxing – who had been performing bicep curls virtually continuously from the age of eleven upwards, would ever have to endure aching biceps. Not biceps, for God's sake – those curious muscles that run up the back of your arm, maybe – but not the bicep. But just try that movement – out and back, out and back, out and back with the left arm – a hundred times, now a thousand times. Continuous defensive movement. I ached. All of this effort expended on my jab was meant to be effective. It was meant to keep my opponent at arm's length but it was no defence at all. Mick walked right through them. His jabs, on the other hand, landed with great dull thuds on my upper arm and forearm with hypnotic regularity. My arms were stuck rigid in a defensive posture.

He bobbed and weaved as I tried to land one good punch on him. Just one, Lord, just one. I wanted him to respect me. I was desperate for some respect. But I knew that I was going to have to earn it. I wanted to start scrambling up the other side of that deep hole that I had managed to dig for myself through my whimpering. But I was telegraphing my shots, and he didn't even have to block them – he just had to bob and weave. He was about my height – five foot eight – but his forearms had similar dimensions to my thighs. My shots were landing harmlessly on those great slabs of meat. And, by the time they had landed, they had no power whatsoever. As Mick had said earlier, 'Boxing looks easy enough, especially on the telly. You may even be able to land a good punch on a bag. But connecting well with someone who's moving is a lot more difficult.' It's all in the timing. And my timing was off. It was as simple as that.

The problem was that I always thought that I could have done a lot better even with a moving target. I had always fancied myself in the ring, you see, although for the life of me I couldn't remember why. I had been brought up on boxing. My uncle had been an amateur boxer in his younger days, and on Saturdays when he and my father got back from the pub I would be invited to box him. Me and the dog both. Spot, our black and white fox-terrier, would only ever attempt to bite him on a Saturday night when he reeked of Guinness. Spot would be on his shoulder biting his neck and I would be clambering over the back of the settee boxing his ears. My uncle was by then about five stone overweight, but it didn't matter. My aunt was always very proud of the fact that I had managed to give my Uncle Terence a black eye – never mind the scars that Spot managed to inflict. My uncle would sit hunched up in his suit, sweating, with the Guinness coming back out through his pores. The dog would distract him and then 'wham' I got one in. My uncle would hurl the dog to the floor. 'You have to show them who's the boss,' my uncle would say.

My mother would agree. 'Your uncle is very good with animals. Your father's too soft. You have to be cruel to be kind.'

We always worked ourselves up into a great lather, all salty sweat and sickly foam from Spot's mouth. The dog would have to go and lie down afterwards to cool down, and then it would sneak round the back to drink the porter out of my uncle's glass. But that was all a lifetime ago and it was no preparation for this. A one on one. Man to man. No Spot to help me out.

Mick never stopped moving this way and that. Impossible to pin down. My punches left my body hard and determined, but they fizzled out somewhere in that gap between us. Mick's glory days in the ring might have been behind him by then – and I say 'might have been' because there were those who were still talking about a comeback for him – but even so he was still several classes above me. An untouchable. He was always a good crowd pleaser, and his punch had definitely not left him. 'The boxer with the hardest punch since Randolph Turpin,' Harry Gibbs, the referee, had said. They had warned me on the way to the gym that Mick could be a bit heavy-handed. I thought that it meant that he was not very tactful. Now I knew that it was meant in a more literal sense altogether. 'But', they told me, 'he won't hurt you. He knows that you're a nobody. He'll have nothing to prove.'

Sweat was closing my eyes. I was working in the ring. Voices from within. Nothing to prove indeed. A nobody. Acidic little drops in my eyes. Narrower and narrower. Imagining a commentator on this fight. 'So the countdown for the end of the first and the steam is already showing now.' The steam was showing, rising from the solid, thick torso in front of me. Steaming bull on a cold winter's morning. No, raging bull. Majestic. How would I look in the ring if the camera were on me? How was my footwork? Just try a little shuffle. I looked down and another heavy jab nearly broke my shoulder. Careful, steady now. Blocking. The raging of the beef brigade. Steaming bulls. Steaming. Steam. Two steam trains speeding towards a head-on collision. A clinch. Our heads collided. My arms compressed at the elbows. Locked in tight. My breathing slowed. Like an animal caught in a trap. I didn't want to breathe on him. I didn't want my breathing to tell him anything. I felt his forehead grinding against the side of my head. I could hear the wet hairs rubbing. Short, spiky, wet hairs grinding against my temples. I tried to pull back. Then again. Stuck fast. Just that noise in my ears, and my elbows feeling as if they were about to shatter. No referee in this sparring. Just one on one.

Suddenly, the trap flew open. He let me go. Bored. Everything on the proximal horizon was now a blur. He was the only focus, the sole figure towards which my attention was directed, and when he moved, which he did continuously, his whole body was a great white blur. Out of this haze, I felt only these slow, methodical blows. A man at work. Not sharp, stinging blows that might leave you annoyed or irritated, but great, solid, dull thumps. Every time they landed on my chest, I thought that they might stop my heart. I had never heard of a boxer's heart being stopped by a punch before, but in those moments I thought that it was a real possibility. My heart was racing and then 'boom', it slowed. The involuntary noises coming from my body as I was winded reassured me that I was still alive. A sudden surge of energy. The body in full flight. Adrenalin pumping. A strange feeling of optimism. Noises from within and without. Alive and working now. Harder! Faster! I was listening for the bell and hearing other voices. 'This is the most professional that I've seen Beattie.' 'Beattie was never intimidated; he got on with the job.' 'I'm proud of Geoffrey Beattie because he did the job fantastic.' Gary stood there saying nothing, too embarrassed to watch.

Out through the haze and way out somewhere in the corner of my eye, I could see that we were now being watched by another bouncer with a teeshirt that said 'Kiss my ass'. I had dreaded this moment. I thought that I might be able to survive in the ring with Mick, as long as there was no one there spectating, except for Gary who was only half watching anyway, but now there was a crowd of two to egg him on. My heart was sinking fast. My wave of optimism had broken on the shores of this grimy bloodstained ring. Paul, the bouncer in the 'Kiss my ass' teeshirt, with a black belt in ju-jitsu, who also happens to own a couple of fitness clubs, called across the room, 'You're not running are you, Mick?' It was an inoffensive question really. My eyes told Mick to ignore it. They pleaded with him to ignore it. But his feet started to grind to a halt. My knuckles were already bleeding after the bag work. Left jab, left jab, right jab, left uppercut, left hook – the opening routine in the bag work. Ten times. It was the upper-cuts that had done the damage. It was they that had brought the knuckles of my two smallest fingers on my left hand into contact with the bag. It was probably the first time that they had ever been brought into contact with anything in their entire life. After one routine, they were bleeding. After six or seven routines, all of my knuckles were bleeding. What damage was I going to inflict on him with those hands?

I had been talking to a climber the previous day who had just fallen off a rock face. He had told me that it was the longest second and a half he had ever experienced. As 'The Bomb' drew to a halt, I could understand exactly what this climber had meant. I remembered what Joe Louis had once said, 'You can run, but you can't hide.' But I couldn't even run, at least not backwards. Mick had let me go after him. I now had a little experience of moving forwards and defending myself, but none whatsoever of moving backwards and staying upright, especially not with those jabs coming at me.

The first blow came to my shoulder. It jerked my body around,

41

as if someone had rotated me in a dance. He squared up for a second punch. 'Don't forget, no head shots,' shouted Gary. I covered my stomach, and I started to make an involuntary but very quiet 'uuurrrrggghhhh' sound even before the shot had landed – in preparation, I think.

'Time!' shouted Gary, laughing. 'We never time rounds here. We play it by ear, so to speak.' I wasn't sure whether he intended the pun or not, but I was relieved anyway. 'He was just playing,' said Gary reassuringly.

We touched gloves and I climbed slowly out of the ring. My legs were trembling. Mick started to shadow-box the air where I had stood. The air probably put up more resistance. Steve climbed in beside him. Steve had also been a professional boxer, but he never had the same kind of talent as Mick. One of Brendan's old boys, a spoiler. He knew how to look after himself in the ring and that was about it. Now, he looked after himself on the door of a nightclub. He still had a full-time job as a sheet-metal worker. He was no challenge to Mick. 'Bastard,' said Steve under his breath, as one of Mick's bombs landed within the first few seconds.

I had a chance to look round the gym. Old, faded posters, heavy bags and sweat-stained floor. Everything hinted of work. There was a lot to be done. This was my first day of training. They were the bouncers at Sheffield's ultimate nightspot – all sunbed tans and snide watches. They had been asking me for months to join them in the gym, but I had always managed to get out of it without losing too much face. I had said then that I wanted to learn about boxing. They had told me that there was only one way, and that was by stepping into a ring. This ring was famous; Bomber Graham had bobbed and weaved in that small confined space. Kids would queue up to try to land a punch on him. Graham would stand with his hands behind his back, dodging every one. And then there were Johnny Nelson and Prince Naseem Hamed and here I was. The song and dance man with leaden feet. On Saturdays Brendan let Mick and the lads borrow the gym for a workout. 'We just play at boxing,' explained Gary. 'It helps us to get rid of all that pent-up aggression, which builds up after working on the doors of a nightclub all week.'

'It's also useful to build up team spirit,' explained Mick. 'We all come from different backgrounds – professional boxing, karate, ju-jitsu, and then there's Lloyd who's been a professional heavyweight boxer and is now a body-builder. He's currently "Mr Central Britain". Mick Quirke is also a body-builder and he owns his fitness club. Oh yeah, and then there's the DJ from the club where we work. That's him trying to skip over there. After the bag work today, he took off his gloves and his hands were all red. He thought that his hands had been cut to pieces. It was the dye from the gloves! But it's good for us all to get together and know what we're all capable of.'

'Or not capable of,' I thought, in my case.

Mick now climbed into the ring with Paul, the black belt in ju-jitsu. Paul had something to prove. Mick winded him in the first few seconds. Unlike myself, Paul made no sound. Gary watched this bout with me. 'Everybody here has a lot of respect for Mick. You only appreciate how good he is when you step into the ring with him. Although we only play at boxing down here on a Saturday, you've still got to think very carefully about what you're doing. It's a very good way of finding out what it's like to be hit. It's also a very good way of getting rid of any aggression. Working on the door of clubs, you rarely get called upon to do anything, and when you do it's usually out of the blue. A while ago, in Dinnington, some kid managed to get my coat over my head and put my head through a glass door. The kid was well respected in the area. Mick was working with me at the time, but he didn't help out. In fact, he was standing taking bets on who was going to win. But it was important for me to get the better of this kid, who had a big reputation in the area. Mick knew I had to come through it on my own. It was like an initiation ceremony. It must have been harder for Mick to stand there and watch than to join in. He could have punched holes in the kid. Mick is still very good. Although Lloyd is good and very, very big, he still doesn't have the same kind of talent that Mick has. These regular training sessions down here let you get all of that kind of stuff sorted out. You soon get to know what kind of talent everyone has, and who to respect.'

I kept thinking of deer rutting, and hierarchies in the animal kingdom, but what had any of this to do with mating, for goodness' sake? The DJ, who had trouble skipping and even more trouble with his upper-cuts, had his girlfriend and newborn baby along to watch, as if to emphasise the point.

'I'd never done any boxing in the past, so Mick has taught me everything,' continued Gary. 'I regret not taking up boxing earlier. The club where we work recently put up a glass case with photographs from all the door staff's fight days. They had boxing photos of Mick and Steve, boxing and wrestling photos of Big Jim Moran, and boxing and body-building photos of Lloyd. I had nothing to put in the cabinet. Mick says that, although I'm thirty, I should try a few fights in the ring. He says that I'd be okay. It would be something to look back on, something for the glass case.'

In the changing-room, with the paint hanging off in great flakes, sat another Gary, an up-and-coming heavyweight boxer who works as a bouncer in a club in Nottingham. He was wearing a black teeshirt with 'Rhythm Killers' on the back. 'When you face up to guys like Mick Mills on a Saturday, then you know you can handle whatever comes off the streets the rest of the week. Training always makes me feel very calm afterwards.'

I wished that I could have agreed with him. I had by now realised that there were people out there who could punch holes in me. I think that I was happier in my ignorance, but I kept my mouth shut. This was my initiation. I sat in the changing-room examining my body. My upper arms and forearms were black and blue. Bruises were appearing on my back as if the pain and injury had been conducted right through my torso. Mick laughed. I promised faithfully that I would become a regular on a Saturday. I told them that I wanted to understand boxing: what it felt like, where the boxers came from, why they did it. Mick told me that I had started well. 'You mean that I now know what it feels like?' I asked.

He wiped his face with the back of his glove, and looked at me with little expression in his eyes. There was no sparkle there, no real warmth, certainly no respect but perhaps just a little curiosity.

He had a good look at me before he replied. 'I wouldn't go that far but at least you know what a sickener it is to get one in the stomach. Boxers have to get used to sickeners. So at least you've made some kind of start.'

It all seemed like such a long time ago. The funny thing was that I had missed Mick and the lads. I suppose that academic life just doesn't allow the same feeling of camaraderie, of togetherness. In the meantime, I had tried to stop Mick from smoking by buying him a book about how to do it in ten easy stages, and I had written some adverts for Gary and a friend who were setting up a debt-recovery agency. 'You've tried the rest, now let Top Notch Security get your money back without a blood fest' was one of my earlier efforts. Unfortunately, they didn't find my humour that amusing. 'We're in a bit of a rush actually,' said Gary. But at least I had a computer and a printer, and I could spell. But now I was working in Manchester, I had started to fall out of touch with them, although I thought about them a lot and wondered how they were getting on now that their early thirties were giving way to their early forties. I had fond memories of that time, and one or two slightly less fond memories that make me feel a little embarrassed even today, like what happened one particular Monday night. It was a bad night for me, not because of what happened physically, but because of what it made me realise about myself.

I got home that particular night about ten past three and looked in the mirror. It was worse than I thought. My nose was about four or five times its normal size, a huge plateau of blue, swollen cartilage right in the middle of my face. In the toilets, Paul had stuck a plaster across my nose to stop it moving out of place. My nose was broken. I was wearing a new cashmere and wool jacket that now looked about twenty sizes too big. Some of the seams had been split. Paul had spent an hour with me, trying to remove as much blood as possible with chewing-gum remover. At least, I think that's what he called it. All I remember was my blood was splattered all over the ceiling of the club. It was there for a few weeks afterwards in the corners of the ceiling where the cleaners had missed, as a reminder, just in case I needed one.

It had happened in the club foyer just as I was leaving. I don't remember what was said. All I remember was feeling confident because of my boxing skills, because I was training with Mick and the lads at the door. I thought that now I could look after myself and, failing that, they'd look after me. We were like brothers, that's how it felt.

I can't remember who threw the first punch, but it couldn't have been me. How would that have looked? 'Doc goes out looking for trouble.' That would have been some headline in the local paper. I think that it was his friend. The punch seemed to come from the side. I never saw it coming. I was facing the guy, whoever he was, but I've no idea what was being said in the confrontation, if indeed it was a confrontation. I remember a hard, solid blow from the side and then the guy in front of me getting a straight right in. It felt hard, like one of Mick's, really. That sort of level. It was only later that I learned this guy was also a boxer. But he was a professional boxer, that was the difference. Mick and the boys knew him.

'He's an all right lad,' Mick said afterwards. 'I don't know what went off there or what you said to him.'

There were a few punches thrown in the fight. I think that I threw some – I was too embarrassed to ask afterwards – and then the doormen jumped on all of us. I thought that I would get special treatment because I was training with the lads who worked the door, but I didn't. I am pretty sure that whilst I was being held back by Mick or Gary or whoever the other guy still managed to get a few more punches in, which didn't seem quite right somehow.

All I remember was my head jolting back and the blood spurting out and afterwards looking up at the ceiling – perhaps because my head was still being banged back but I'm not sure about that – and thinking that there was an awful lot of blood up there and that it had all come from me. After everything calmed down, I was told by Mick that this guy, whoever he was, was waiting outside to 'finish it off'.

'Finish what off?' I asked Mick.

'Whatever it is,' said Mick. Mick was trying to be helpful. 'Don't go out there, he'll give you a hammering.' And he was very apologetic. 'We would have helped you out more but we got into a spot of trouble ourselves last week in a fight. The police are investigating it. We're on our best behaviour tonight.'

Paul, who was the toilet attendant, tried to clean me up. I could tell by his facial expression that I was a real mess.

'What was all that about?' asked Paul who was standing in front of the wall-to-wall mirrors with row upon row of aftershave sitting in front of them.

'I've no idea,' I said.

He told me not to look at myself. 'You stand with your back to the mirror,' he suggested helpfully.

Mick came into the toilets. He was smoking a cigarette. I had bought him a book on how to stop smoking. He had told me that it was working and that the craving had gone. He tried to hide the cigarette from me.

'What was all that about?' Paul asked Mick.

Mick shook his head mournfully. 'I've no fucking idea. I didn't really see it. I was in the foyer but it was all over in a flash.'

'Was it over some bird?' Paul asked me.

'I was talking to some girl,' I said. 'But I don't know who she was.'

'Was she that good-looking blonde bird with the big tits?' Paul asked helpfully.

'Possibly,' I said. 'It's all a bit of a blur now.'

'Well, you know what they say about good-looking, big-titted blondes in nightclubs?' said Paul.

'No,' I replied.

Paul looked over at Mick, as if to say 'for goodness' sake'. 'You should avoid them, Geoffrey. You should avoid them until after hours when all the aggressive cunts have gone back home, where they belong. Everybody knows that.'

I thought I had better sit down. I sat in the cubicle with the door open. My nose was bleeding again and dripping onto the floor. There was some wet toilet paper down there so I aimed the drip onto it. I felt sick.

'I think something was said,' said Mick loudly from outside.

'Like what?' asked Paul.

'Ask him,' said Mick.

'I've no idea,' I said.

'What are you going to say when you get home?' asked Mick.

'I'll say I walked into a door.'

'Ditch the jacket then,' said Mick, taking my excuse seriously. 'Nobody will believe you if you keep that jacket on. That jacket's fucked anyway. Ditch the fucking coat. You've no chance of getting away with it wearing that fucking coat.' I removed my coat and Paul, despite having spent a good hour working on it, crumpled it into the litter-bin by the urinal.

'That's better,' said Paul. 'You don't look so bad now.'

'Are you going to give lectures in the university with that face tomorrow?' asked Mick. 'Let me give you a bit of advice. You'd better ring in sick, for fuck's sake.'

Mick studied his own face in the mirror. He fixed his hair carefully and delicately with his right hand, flattening a few hairs at the front, and then he checked his white shirt for spots of my blood. 'You see,' said Mick with a slight smile, trying to cheer me up, 'that's the problem with boxing; you think that you can handle any situation. It's not as simple as that.'

'It's a very dangerous sport is boxing,' said Paul.

I had second thoughts about the coat. I didn't fancy going home without a coat. I stood up, feeling slightly dizzy, walked over to the bin and carefully pulled it back out. I smoothed out the creases and very slowly put it back on. The coat smelt of peppermint now, for some reason. Mick and Paul just stared at me.

'Are you feeling all right now?' asked Paul.

'If you're not used to a good dig,' said Mick, 'it can be a bit of a shock to the system. If you hang on for about twenty minutes, I'll walk you to your car.'

I went back and sat on the bog again. The other doormen were coming in to take off their bow-ties before setting off home. I could see Paul in the mirror indicating where I was sitting. They didn't want to embarrass me further by asking how I was. I was sitting in silence as Paul cleared all of his aftershave into a large Tesco carrier bag with a hole in it.

Later, Mick walked me out to my car. 'Your man has gone home,' he said. 'When you see him again, just nod and say hello,' said Mick. 'That's just my advice. Don't bear any grudges. It doesn't do any good. Just nod and say hello, as if nothing has gone off between the two of you.'

'But I don't know what he looks like,' I said. 'He's just a blur.'

'You'll recognise him all right,' said Mick. 'You probably couldn't describe him, but you'll recognise him. Don't worry about that. I know the kid. He's all right. I'll put a word in for you. I'll tell him you're a doctor. It sounds better than telling him that you're a frigging psychologist.'

'And what about his friend?' I asked. 'What about him? Who was he, by the way? Do you know him as well?'

'What friend was that?' asked Mick.

'The friend that got the first punch in, the punch from the side. That's why I didn't see the other punches coming. That punch caught me by surprise.'

We stood in the underground car park. Mick was lighting up another cigarette and was looking at me a little puzzled. 'He had a friend in the club with him,' began Mick, 'but I think that he just backed off when the trouble kicked off.'

'What about that punch then?' I asked. 'The one from the side, the really hard one I didn't see coming?'

'I think that's called a left hook, Geoffrey. That was just a left hook. But I'll tell you something, it were a fucking beauty. It was a right fucking corker and you took it slap-bang on the side of the fucking head, and then that straight right-hander on the fucking nose. It's not a bit of wonder you feel sick. It were a fucking beauty.'

Then Mick slapped me on the shoulder, got into his car and drove off. I drove home slowly and carefully, climbed into bed and tried to sleep on my back all night. I had trouble breathing and the funny sounds coming from me woke my wife up. 'Could you be a bit quieter?' she said grumpily. 'Some of us have to get up in the morning.'

That was all I remember about that night. I never discussed this with Mick again, and I didn't want to now that I was back, not even with him standing just over there, not even as a joke. 'Remember the night I had my nose broken, Mick? It were a right laugh that, eh?' I couldn't ever bring myself to mention it. Not now. Not ever. But I dwelt on it. That was my problem. Mick and the boys would have just forgotten about it. 'These things happen,' they would say. 'You take one, you give one, that's what men do. You take the odd punch, you fight back, you don't back off, you just get stuck in.' I realised that this difference in the way we reacted to such a simple situation was quite significant.

I just stood there in silence, thinking back to that night. 'What's the matter?' Mick asked. 'You haven't got some bird up the duff, have you?' I think that he was trying to cheer me up.

'No, no, no,' I said. 'Nothing like that.'

It was quite strange to be back here where I had spent so many nights with Mick, Rod and Big Lenny. Another doorman with a shaved head and jug ears approached Mick. There had obviously been some sort of trouble earlier. You can always tell this by the way doormen talk. There's a sort of excitement about it, but it's talk that's done at very close quarters, to exclude outsiders. The

49

jug-eared bouncer's hands were gesturing wildly as he talked. I could just make out what he was saying. 'He did this,' he said, talking about some unfortunate punter. 'So eventually,' he stressed the word 'eventually', 'I had to respond.' His gestures, however, said something different. His left hand was held flat and represented the unfortunate punter. His right fist was Mr Jug Ears himself, and was part of him at the same time. It was iconically a whole person and, a little more transparently, a fist. 'He did this,' he said, and the flat hand wandered across to the middle of his chest, 'so eventually I had to ...' And I watched the fist of his right hand slam hard into the left hand, which fell to the point just below his belt. It went down like a sack of spuds.

I watched Mick's eyes. He always loved to hear about violence. The man with the glasses noticed this as well. 'It's a blast to you, Mick,' he said. 'A real blast.'

'Fighting and fucking,' said Mick. 'The two best things in life.' He corrected himself: 'The only two things in life.' He was almost smacking his lips as he said it. He just wanted to remind me of this other world. He wasn't that crude.

I wanted to make a note of this small slice of life because in the morning, with all the halves of lager, I would have forgotten it. So I stepped back into the shadows of the club and pulled a small notebook out of my trouser pocket. A thickset man with a completely shaved head, wearing a dark suit and black teeshirt, came up to me. 'What are you writing?' he enquired. It sounded chummy at first. He was smiling at me. I thought that he might have recognised me from the past.

'Notes,' I said. 'I'm just making notes.'

'What sort of fucking notes?' he asked. 'You're not the filth, are you?' His friend took up a position on my other side. The thickset man reached across me to light his friend's cigarette. There must have been something wrong with his lighter because there was a very strong smell of petrol in my face. It was a pleasant enough smell, but I thought that the lighter might flare up.

'You want to be careful with that lighter,' I said.

'What?' said the thickset man. 'Is he the filth?' he said to his friend. It was more menacing this time but I couldn't tell if he really meant it. He had stopped smiling. 'Because we couldn't have the filth standing here making notes right in front of us. We'd have to shoot him.'

I stood writing this down as well. 'I can't believe this character,' said the thickset man. It was time to extricate myself from this situation, so I beckoned Mick over.

'Don't be stupid,' said Mick to the pair of them. 'He's not a copper.'

'Oh, I was only checking, Mick,' said the thickset man, almost deferentially. 'You have to watch your back in here sometimes.'

I thanked Mick, the man who knew everybody, and offered to get him a small lager. A girl of about twenty, quite pretty with a mole above her mouth, approached with her boyfriend who could possibly have been Italian. 'Hi Mick,' she said in a high, girly voice. 'This is Carlo.'

Carlo shook Mick's hand.

'Mick looked after me about a year ago,' she said, 'when I had a bit too much to drink and this guy started bothering me. Mick took me home and put me to bed, didn't you, Mick?'

'Oh yes,' said Mick. 'A lot of birds need looking after.'

'He was a real gentleman,' said the girl with the mole.

'Let me shake your hand,' said Carlo, 'for looking after my woman.'

Mick looked a little embarrassed, but he stretched out his hand.

'All part of the job really,' he said modestly.

The girl started heading up towards the wine bar. 'I'm taking it nice and steady tonight,' she said. 'I might get tipsy but that's as far as I'm going tonight.'

Mick waited until the pair had left. 'I looked after her all right,' he said. 'I got her home, and I got her face down, and I gave it to her. She's never mentioned it again. I was horned up that night. I'd popped a tab of Viagra. The one hundred gram one. My dick was like that pole there.' He pointed at a long shiny pole with some greasy fingerprints on it. 'It was full on that night. It was like fucking toothache. The ache from down there is terrible when you've had one.'

He reached into his pocket and retrieved a packet of blue pills. 'Yours for only twenty-five quid a tab. The best hard-on you'll ever have. It's like having your cock pumped up with a bicycle-pump.' He passed me one of the pills. 'Are you fixed up for the night? Because if you're not, don't be taking one now for fuck's sake. But if you are fixed up, go ahead and pop one now.'

Another of Mick's friends joined us. It was Dave who always wore a slightly bewildered expression, slightly perplexed. He never looked happy. Mick obviously thought that it was time for a bit of a sales pitch. 'Tell him what Viagra is like, Dave,' said Mick. Dave just made a blowing sound like he had just tasted a very hot curry. He screwed his face up at the same time.

'What did I tell you?' said Mick. 'Words can't describe it. It's that good. When I first got them I was a bit reluctant to try them as well so I used my next-door neighbour as a guinea pig. He's unemployed so he popped a tab one afternoon. He sat there all afternoon in his dressing gown staring down at his dick. 'It's not working, Mick,' he kept saying. 'Nothing's happening.' But I thought to myself that they have to do something or there wouldn't be so much fuss about them. So one Sunday afternoon I took one whole tablet at three o'clock. By a quarter to four I had the biggest hard-on you've ever seen. It was like somebody else's dick down there. My bird thought I was a different bloke. Honest to God. I was waiting for her to call me by a different name when we were on the job.'

Dave just stood there nodding away. He was the rick in this sales pitch. I could feel the pressure to buy. But I thought I saw a way out. 'But I've been drinking lager,' I said. 'Presumably they don't work if you've been drinking.'

'Oh no,' said Mick. 'You'll not get brewer's droop with Viagra. It will be up there hammering away.' I noticed that his fist was making a piston-like movement. So was Dave's, but his piston gesture was less forceful, less convincing in a way.

'It is twenty-five quid, though,' I said. I was trying a different tack; I was starting to quibble about price.

'You mean to say that a man like you can't afford a few quid for the fuck of a lifetime?' said Mick. 'What do you think of that, Dave?' Dave just gave a short, disdainful laugh and looked at me pityingly. 'I mean,' continued Mick, 'what would you rather spend your money on than the fuck of a lifetime?'

'I haven't got twenty-five quid on me,' I said.

'You mean to say that you go out to a top-notch club and you haven't even got beer money?' retorted Mick.

'I'm sorry about that,' I said.

'Listen,' said Mick, 'to be honest, when I take a whole tab my face goes like a carrot. I walk around looking like a fucking beetroot. I sometimes think that my head is going to explode. You'd be better off with half a tab. Twelve pounds fifty for a half. That would do the trick, and you must have that kind of money on you for taxi fare. Or are you planning to walk home?'

Dave gave a kind of derisory laugh. 'Walk home,' Dave repeated. 'That's a good one. This guy knows how to have a good time all right. Go to a club, have a skinful of beer and then walk home.'

I joined in the laughter, but I don't know why.

'I've been getting into some right skirmishes,' said Mick, 'since I started taking Viagra. Last week I went home at half five in the morning with only one sock on. I couldn't find one of my socks in this bird's house. My girlfriend went berserk when I got home. She had waited up for me. I tried to get undressed in the dark but she put the light on. She said to me, "Where's your bloody sock?" I swore to her that I had been working the door all night with only one sock on, but she didn't believe me. She said, "I may be stupid to put up with you, but I'm not that bloody stupid."

Tom Jones was singing in the background, 'Sex bomb, sex bomb, you're my sex bomb.' There was just no getting away from it.

'I've got a lot of regular customers now,' said Mick. 'I've got one Chinese guy who comes down from Worksop to get some. He buys ten at a time. He's a big spender.' He looked straight at me, as if to say that here is somebody who is clearly not.

But none of his hints were working. Mick eventually gave up. He broke one of the blue tablets in front of me. 'Hold out your hand,' he said impatiently, and he dropped one neat half into the palm of my hand. 'Don't lose it,' he said. 'And don't take it until you are fixed up with a bird.' He left without payment. I went off and wandered round the club. It was nearly two in the morning. That time of the night when you can feel the desperation from the men still on their own. I saw Dave standing in a quiet corner looking wistfully across the dance floor at a dark-haired female. 'She used to be my girlfriend,' he said when I walked up to him. 'We lived together for nearly seven years.'

His ex-girlfriend was talking to a young, good-looking man with short, spiky hair. Dave looked crestfallen. His little routine with Mick seemed a very long time ago. He paid no attention to me. It was almost as if I wasn't there. He just stood there watching quietly. 'To be honest,' he said eventually, 'I don't really need Viagra. What I need is a good woman.'

I had a good laugh that night, and I fitted back in comfortably, if a little self-consciously. 'It's like you've never been away,' said Mick. I liked the idea of waking up in the morning and writing about the night before. I told Mick that I was planning a new book about life in the shadows of boxing. 'About me again? I'll be famous one day,' said Mick, 'if you keep writing about me.' I told him about my plans but I left out my own more personal motivations. I still wasn't talking about my children to him. I told him that my new book was going to be Friedrich Engels all over again. It was going to be 'a faithful picture of your condition, of your sufferings and struggles, of your hopes and prospects'. I told him that I was planning to 'live long enough amidst you to know something about your circumstances'. Not quite in these words, but he knew what I meant. 'Oh,' he said. 'That sounds good to me.' I told him that I would also try to get back into the shadows of boxing all on my own over in Manchester, in the clubs of Salford and Moss Side, to remind myself of what it was like to meet up with new boxers that I didn't know, to see the process afresh. I would make some field notes in these new encounters like the professional stranger that I knew I could become. I was full of great ideas but, of course, I did not grow up and change through the years with the guys from Salford, unlike with Mick and the lads from Sheffield, and I think it shows. Engels must have had the same basic problem, but the funny thing is that Engels never admitted it.

FIVE

I had been told to turn up at five o'clock in the morning to be first in the queue for work. I would be paid at the end of the day. It was an American concept. Work today, get paid today. It represented the casualisation of labour. But there had been a storm the night before in Salford and the wind and the rain had been lashing against my window. I had started to drift off to sleep but the rain had begun to sound like a fire crackling. I know that this is an unlikely image, but that's how it sounded. Like a fire just outside my window, threatening and irregular enough to keep me awake. I got up a bit later than I had intended, bleary-eyed. It was just after 5.00 a.m. I had to walk. There was no sign of any buses at that time of the morning so I didn't want to risk waiting at the bus-stop, and there were very few souls about in the freezing rain to ask.

I got there after six, but I wasn't the first. I looked around to get my bearings. One man in his late twenties sat huddled under his coat in an armchair. A girl of perhaps nineteen sat on a settee. She had tinsel in her hair. They were watching *Goldfinger* on a large screen and drinking coffee. James Bond was enunciating 'Pussy Galore' very carefully. 'Poooooosy,' said the man peeping out from beneath his coat, sensing my presence. I must have smiled because he said it again.

I went up to the reception desk and registered for work. A surprisingly cheerful young man explained to me that I would have to complete a safety questionnaire. 'It's all right,' he said. 'It's multiple choice.' He told me to fill it in at a large table. I assumed that it would be very easy. 'When are drugs permitted at a job-site?' it asked. 'Never' was the first answer. I was just about to tick 'a', chuckling quietly to myself at the idea that

55

some people might think that you are permitted to bring a large lump of hashish to a building site, when I noticed that the second answer was 'Only when prescribed by your doctor'. 'What is the most common site injury?' was the second question. 'What is the safest way to carry objects up a ladder?' 'How should you carry a power-tool?' I had no idea, so I guessed.

The young man behind the counter smiled at me benevolently when he gave me my score. 'You got sixty-five per cent, but don't worry. Oh, and you got today's date wrong.'

'I'm sorry,' I said, trying a wry smile. I always thought that it was part of my charm. 'I get dates mixed up sometimes. I've often got a lot on my mind,' I said. He looked at me as if he felt a bit sorry for me. I couldn't help noticing that my Irish accent had grown noticeably stronger. I don't know why. That soft Northern lilt comes and goes. It seems to have a mind of its own. But I didn't try to explain this to him. I wanted to stop while I was ahead.

He didn't tell me any of the correct answers. He just told me to take a seat, and help myself to coffee and a doughnut. I sat next to the girl with the tinsel, who didn't look at me. 'This film is crap,' said the man from below the coat. 'So is the latest James Bond film. They're all crap.'

I could hear American voices from behind the counter. Young men with co-ordinated shirts and ties. Immaculate at this time of the morning. I noticed that there was a sign above a full-length mirror on the far wall. I went over to read it. I stood there in front of this mirror, looking at myself, padded against the cold of a Salford morning, with a thermal vest below my sweatshirt and an old leather jacket. Not fashionably old, just unfashionably old: 1991 rather than 1950. Something to wear on a building site. My eyes were red from the sleeplessness caused by the crackling noise of the storm the night before. The lower lid of my left eye was twitching. I had never seen this happen before, and I found myself staring at the little spasms of the lower lid. 'Would you hire this person?' the sign above the mirror read.

I sat down and sipped my coffee. I read the other notices on the walls. 'No guns, knives or other weapons are allowed on the premises.' 'Anybody caught drinking before or during work will be terminated.'

They wandered in individually. Young men with shaved heads

and the remains of attitude. The young man behind the counter knew most of their names. Most of them were regulars. Two teenage girls came in together and immediately went outside for a smoke. A man sat down beside me and we started talking. He had a South African accent. He told me that he had to get out of his home country. Luckily, his wife was entitled to an Irish passport. 'There's a rape every twenty-six seconds at home,' he told me. His brother had been hijacked. 'He was stripped naked and kicked to pieces. That was when we decided to leave.' The man had been in the quality assurance field in South Africa. Last week he was cleaning aircraft seats with high-pressure hoses for four pounds fifteen an hour. But life was better here, he told me. His wife could walk the streets at night. 'There are some gang-related shootings in Salford, but it's nothing compared with back home. You're very lucky here,' he said. 'You should count your blessings.'

I laughed politely and went back to looking at the big screen, counting my blessings. Goldfinger was raiding Fort Knox, and Pussy was co-ordinating her team of foxy girls. The man under the coat had got a laugh once so he tried again, 'Poooosy Galore'. Nobody responded this time, so he pretended to go to sleep. I sat and waited. I noticed that a lot of those who had arrived after me had been sent out on jobs before me. *Goldfinger* was ending. Mr Bond, at least, was on the job. I assumed that I was being passed over because of my score on the safety quiz and the fact that I didn't seem to know what date it was. Or perhaps it was because I could claim none but the most basic of labouring skills.

The girl with the tinsel put on a new film. It was *Judge Dredd* with Sylvester Stallone. I found myself watching it. 'Would you care to explain that, Citizen,' said Judge Dredd who was judge, jury and executioner all rolled into one. I wanted to know why I was still there. I went to the toilet but there was no toilet roll. I came back to my seat, feeling slightly soiled. There were only two of us left now: me and some latecomer. I tried to start up a conversation but he wasn't interested. I asked what the work was like here. 'Shit,' he said. 'I'm only staying to half nine and if nothing comes up I'm going home,' he said. I thought about going back to bed. It was nearly nine o'clock. I had been there for almost three hours. Then I got the call. It was all first names.

'It's factory work, Geoff,' said the young man with the open smile. 'It's warm and dry and not that bad. It's putting zips on jackets. To be honest with you, the firm wanted women, but we don't have any. I've just sent a carload up, but one of the staff will give you a lift.'

I went out the back and jumped into a small car with an American who had thick, heavily lined skin. He was under pressure because they had sent up a group the day before but they had not made the target. It was a rush job before Christmas. Some jackets had the wrong zips and they had to be fixed. 'We're bailing out China,' he said in a way that only an American could. 'That's where the cock-up occurred. Are you ready for this job today?' he asked.

'I am,' I replied.

'Are you really ready for it?'

'Definitely,' I replied. I noticed that there was now no trace of my Irish lilt. I was becoming more posh by the minute. I wanted him to notice that there was something different about me. It was pathetic really, but I wanted to stand out like I did when I was a student on summer jobs on building sites. But I didn't. On the drive up, he didn't once ask me anything about myself. I was just another hard-up punter. We raced through town following another of the American employees in his car because he wasn't sure where the factory was. He was crunching the gears. 'I'm not used to this kind of little tin car,' he said.

I asked him about the agency. 'Well, in the States we get a load of homeless working for us,' he explained. 'They queue around the block for a job, but you lot in Salford are a lot better off. You all have houses.'

I nodded vigorously. 'Indeed we do,' I said. I was now emphasising my vowels like a classically trained actor.

I asked about the rate of pay, but he said that he couldn't remember it offhand. And then he returned to the stresses he was under, with the guys letting him down. 'I could train four monkeys to do this job,' he said. But I wasn't sure where that left me, the untested monkey, so I said nothing.

We arrived at the factory in a part of Manchester that I didn't know, but there was trouble already. The man who liked to say the word 'pooosy' didn't want the job when he saw what it involved, and he wanted a lift back. The two Americans were discussing whether he deserved the lift or not. I was led in past the regular workers who looked at me with cold condescension. I sensed my place. It was all in the way they looked. The guy who had been huddled under his coat was walking up and down, a little agitated. 'This is a crap job,' he said. 'I'd rather play with my dick than work here.' The two decided that he should be taken back, and he was led away.

I was shown the ropes by Phil, who had been there for a week. 'It's fiddly,' he said, 'and as boring as hell, and the pay is shit. But apart from that ...' Our boss, sensing the mood, decided to stay for an hour to motivate us. He talked about us bailing out China, and then talked about us bailing out the company.

'Do we get extra if we make the quota?' asked Phil.

'We'll see,' said the boss.

He positioned me right beside him and offered to race me in the assembly of the jackets, and for some reason or other I agreed. I could tell by the looks of the others that they thought that I was a bit soft in the head for going along with it, but I agreed to try to fasten fleeces to jackets, file down the zips, fold them and bag them quicker than him. The boss talked incessantly throughout. I beat him, and his retort was, 'Gee, if you and the rest of the guys keep that up all day, then we might be out of the woods.

'You see, guys,' he said, 'this can be fun.' He was quite serious. I could see Phil making wanking movements with his hand. The boss stuck it out for about forty minutes. He left us to it, after suggesting that Phil should be the new boss for the day. 'I'll do it for six pounds an hour,' said Phil.

'We'll see,' said the American. 'We'll see.'

Our gang stood in a huddle away from the rest of the factory. You could tell that nobody really trusted us. It was hot and, as I had dressed for a building site, I had to strip off to my thermal vest. It wasn't yet 10.00 a.m. and I was feeling done in already, red-eyed and yawning. I started chatting to one of the lads with a shaved head. Kev told me that he had stayed up all night decorating his girlfriend's flat because he thought that he might not get any work that day. He was worried about getting through the day.

The girl with the tinsel in her hair worked away on a bench in the far corner. She had a personal stereo and seemed to be in a world of her own. Occasionally she danced, sometimes she burst into song.

A few of the Salford lads formed a clique within our group. They told each other tales of gangland Salford as they fiddled with the zips. One of them, who had been a professional boxer, was talking about his form, 'five wins out of twelve; it's better than it sounds', and then he told us that he had told off one of the Salford godfathers for giving toffee to children. 'The kids might get confused and accept it from perverts,' he explained. 'Your man agreed with me and admitted that he was in the wrong. It's just as well for me, otherwise I'd be dead meat.'

Another told the story of how he took his daughter to visit his mother in hospital and passed armed officers guarding another Salford gangster who was recuperating in hospital. 'Daddy,' his daughter said, 'the gun you keep in the cupboard at home is bigger than his.' They all laughed, but they made sure I was listening. Big men reduced to this.

'If I'd invested my money when I was younger, I wouldn't have to do this crap,' said the man with the gun at home.

I noticed that three of them had mobile phones that didn't go off once that day.

After the introductions, nearly all the talk was about money. I kept myself to myself. 'Do you know how much you're getting today?' Phil asked me.

'Not really,' I said.

'You'll be lucky if you clear twenty quid. So slow down, for fuck's sake. You're not on piece rate,' he warned.

Every time U2 came on the radio, Kev with the shaved head shouted over, 'I bet you like U2. They're Irish as well.' And just in case I missed them, he'd shout a warning every time they came on.

Management in suits passed us, occasionally making friendly little quips our way, and Phil, Steve and Darren would smile back and whisper 'fuck off, cunt' under their breath in one single exhalation. We were told at lunch-time that if we all went to the chippy our half-hour for lunch would commence as soon as we put on our coats. Only two could go. I ordered a fish, but it wasn't much of a chippy because I was told there weren't any fish. 'You can have chips or chicken or a sandwich. That's all,' said the girl with the tinsel very loudly over the music from her personal stereo.

We had our lunch together in the canteen as the regular workers carried in food and drink for their Christmas party. Phil kept asking them if we would be invited. Some said they would ask the boss, but you knew that we weren't welcome. You could just tell. 'If I was a woman,' said Steve, 'I'd be a fucking millionaire. I'd lie on my back and make fucking millions.' According to one of the regular factory workers, who supervised us, one of our lot that week had been an escort. 'And a lesbian,' he added for good measure.

The day seemed like a month. I have never looked at my watch so many times or felt that an hour could last an eternity. I always thought that time flew. Not here it didn't. In the afternoon tea break we got the leftovers from the Christmas party and a can of lager each 'to take home with us'. We all drank them on the spot.

We knocked off at 5.00 p.m. The young lad in charge of us said that we had done loads of jackets that day. He also told us that the factory paid six pounds fifty-five an hour. We were on four pounds fifteen; the agency pocketed the rest. I felt that we were being watched as we left the factory, as if we couldn't be trusted not to attempt to relieve the boredom of the work with a few fleeces under our coats. Sometimes, I feel that you can understand the motivations that underlie petty thieving. A couple of the guys picked up a fleece each and stuffed them inside their coats. I declined. 'What's the matter, Paddy?' one asked. 'Are you good living or something? Or chicken?'

'Just chicken,' I said. 'That's me. Chicken Geoff.' And they all laughed at me.

Phil raced us back to the depot where we queued for our money. I got a cheque for twenty-three pounds ten pence. The rest got two quid less because they had money deducted for the lift to the factory. They forgot to deduct mine.

Our American boss was back at the depot, beaming away. We told him that the factory were pleased with our performance. Phil asked about our bonus for making the target. He told us to hang on and he went into the back room. He emerged 'with something for each and every one of us'. He gave us a Kit-Kat each and told us that because we had done a good job we would be picked first on Monday for the zip factory. 'You'll be first away,' he said. I heard Phil whispering, 'Fuck that for a laugh.' I pocketed the Kit-Kat and made my way out into the freezing cold Salford night almost exactly twelve hours after I had started the day. My left eye was still twitching. I don't know why.

SIX

The following day I slept in because I could afford to. I drove around Salford thinking about Mick and the boys from the club. I wondered to myself whether, coming from a working-class home in North Belfast, I would have had the guts to step into the ring to try to make a living, if 'I hadn't had those bloody brains that get you into so much trouble', as my mother liked to put it, or whether I would have ended up in that factory messing about with zips and nicking the odd fleece or two at the end of a long, monotonous day.

It was a hard, tough place around here, in this particular area of Ordsall. It reminded me of the 'turn of the road' in North Belfast where I grew up, and I knew that I should not be judgemental. There were young lads like I was as a boy, growing up in these houses with graffiti on the walls and broken glass outside. Red, metal shutters like cages covered the shop-fronts. They stayed on during the day. Most of the shops were closed down, even behind the iron cages. There were large chunks of uneven rock positioned on the pavement, presumably to stop ramraiders. I sat in my car looking out, almost hesitating. The graffiti was written in what looked like tar and was a yard high. 'Jimmy L is a grass', it read. I watched some kids on bikes watching me as I sat in my car, watching them. Strangers are both a threat and an opportunity in this small, confined, concrete space. Perhaps in equal measure. They looked at my car and then at me, as if they were trying to work out if either one or the other was worth rolling. I got out to have a walk around. The small supermarket near by had a very large security guard with a malevolent stare and a shaved head. I noticed a sad-faced woman in the supermarket with a black eye, and then I noticed a second. It seemed like more than a coincidence. I heard something that sounded like glass crackling beneath my feet. I looked down to see a couple of smashed LPs scattered on the pavement. I crouched down and pieced the bits of one of the records together slowly and carefully. One kid on a bike was staring at me with an expression that was a blend of curiosity and menace. It turned out to be a Cliff Richard LP, lifted, I imagine, in some burglary and dropped. First, because it was Cliff Richard and, second, because it was an obsolete form of playing music. There were yards of yellow tape, the kind used to cordon off dangerous buildings or to mark out a threatening hole in the road, blowing in the gritty wind. There was some guttering lying on the road. Passers-by just stepped over it, as if it weren't there. This is where Val decided to set up her business last January. Right here.

Val makes made-to-measure sportswear for boxers in Ordsall. She called her business 'Val to Victory'. She was going to call it 'Val 'n' U' 'because it sounds like "value",' she explained. Silk shorts, satin tops, shiny dressing gowns that shimmer and glisten in the artificial light. I worked my way through some of her samples at the front of the shop. Red flashes of lightning on a white silk background, red, white and blue chevrons on cream silk, shiny purple shorts with long gold tassels and the words 'bounty hunter' at the top. 'Why bounty hunter?' I asked Val.

'That's just what this heavyweight likes to call himself,' she said. 'It sounds threatening. A lot of the boxers like a really hard nickname and then the names of their kids further down on the same pair of shorts.'

Every pair of shorts is made by hand. Every strip of coloured, shiny material is sewn on slowly and meticulously. One pair of shorts can take a week for Val to make. Plain, made-to-measure shorts start at twenty-five quid, a plain poncho thirty-five, a gown sixty and a boxer's jacket seventy-five. 'Don't forget,' she said, 'a boxer's jacket has got very wide sleeves which means that there is a lot more fabric involved in it.' The boxers, however, know that they are starting to make it in the fight game when they come to her shop to choose something more elaborate, something designed for them personally. Val said that she likes to watch her clients box before she decides which costume to make for them. 'Their outfit', she said, 'should reflect how they box. It should tell you whether they are a hard boxer or a fancy boxer. It should tell you a lot about them and what they're really like.' She went to watch Ricky Hatton box, and she decided that he was a really big hitter so she wanted his shorts to indicate this. 'As soon as I saw him,' Val said, 'I knew that I wanted to do something with really long tassels. I knew that the tassels would reflect his punching power. The harder he punches, the more the tassels whip round his body. So I gave him twelve-inch tassels. You wouldn't want much longer than that. He loves them, but his grandad apparently hates them. Richard has had me do four pairs since then, all with the same long tassels.'

I asked whether the tassels ever distracted the boxer. 'Oh no,' she said. 'But they can be very distracting for his opponent. Once the tassels start flying they know that they're in trouble.' I asked her how she got into this business. She told me that her husband, who died recently 'of emphysema, heart failure, diabetes – you name it, he had it', was a keen fight fan. 'He liked going around boxing gyms during the day. He met one young boxer who had rung up a company that made outfits for boxers because he wanted some shorts and a poncho, but the company asked him to measure himself and he hadn't a clue how to do it so he asked me. He didn't know how to measure his inside leg, his waist or anything. So I measured him up and then made the outfit for him. That's how it all started.'

Now she has forty to fifty clients, and she even has had orders from abroad. 'Well, it was a guy working in a bar in Tenerife, actually,' she added. 'He was a relative of a boxer but he wanted his own individual shorts to give him a bit of credibility on the street so that everyone would think that he had been a somebody in the ring at one time or another.'

Prince Naseem Hamed's shorts have been a big talking-point in and out of the ring. 'Everybody wants something a little bit different now,' she said. 'That's where I come in.'

'I also have fans coming along as customers,' she told me, 'wanting the same outfit as their boxing hero.' She showed me a satin-backed, crêpe-towelling poncho for one of Michael Gomez's fans in blue and white. 'He's a keen Man City fan,' she explained, pointing at the coloured sections. 'All of his fans wear sombreros at his fights, and those with some cash to spend all get the same matching top.'

'Is Michael Gomez Mexican?' I asked naïvely.

'Oh no, he's just a local Manchester lad. But everybody needs a gimmick these days, as well as their boxing ability. Michael has got his well sorted now.'

A woman came into Val's shop with a green and white checked shirt with a hole in the front. This is Val's daily business – repairing clothes for the local people and washing bin bags of dirty laundry for a fiver a throw. 'Can you fix it so that you can't tell?' the woman asked anxiously. 'My son won't wear it otherwise.' Val inspected it carefully. 'They were giving something out next door,' the woman said. 'I thought that they were giving out something for nothing, but it just turned out that they were giving away leaflets with "Jesus loves you" on them. It's just as well somebody does around here.' Val looked at the shirt carefully, and then told her that she couldn't do anything with it except turn all the fabric inside out and that would take for ever. The woman looked crestfallen. The incident was a reminder, if one were needed, that this is a very poor area.

I looked around her work area, and noticed that there was a message pinned up that read 'Visualise and Actualise'. The one beside it read 'If it's to be, it's up to me'. Val observed my line of regard. 'These are inspirational messages from my business manager,' she said. 'He's been provided by Salford City Council to help me get my business off the ground. He's really excellent. I visualise at the start of every day and then I actualise.' But not with the checked shirt provided by the woman who clearly couldn't afford anything else.

Two young lads came into the shop rather sheepishly and asked Val if they could look at her boxing pictures. They were two of the lads who had been staring at me earlier from their bicycles. Around the walls of her shop are pictures of Michael Brodie, whose outfits are paid for by a local security firm, Ricky Hatton with his tassels flying, and Michael Gomez with his fans in their matching sombreros and their blue and white tops. The lucky ones from around here. Val talked to the boys quietly. She showed them the pictures. I listened in to what she was telling them. 'Wait until you can order some of these outfits,' she said. 'Then you'll know you're really on your way.' Her dream was to open the local Kwik Save as a boxing gym. 'The kids around here deserve more than they're getting,' she said. 'They need something to aspire to. My silk shorts remind them of what they could achieve one day.'

I didn't mean the story to stop here. This was only the start. Val told me that she had decided to make a go of turning the Kwik Save into a gym, and she said that I could follow her progress over the next year. So I went back regularly to talk to her about the intricacies of planning applications and listened to her reports of dealing with men from the council, and, over many months, I watched the kids watching me, watching them. But nothing came of it. I even bumped into one of the lads who had been putting zips on jackets with me. I saw him and his friend sauntering through the city centre and he walked straight past me, as if he didn't recognise me. Perhaps he didn't. I wasn't a face around here. Nobody knew me. It was just like 'There's that Chicken Geoff guy. A right fucking muppet. Let's ignore the fucking cunt or he might end up following us around town. He doesn't look as if he's got any friends. Give him a wide berth, for fuck's sake.'

SEVEN

Once again, I looked back at the faces of the boxers in the leisure centre. There were so many new faces. I suppose Brendan always has new boys coming through. It's hard to find an appropriate metaphor for this. A factory has all the wrong connotations, but it does suggest a relentless stream of products of varying quality, all to be graded, all with distinct commercial possibilities. A cutlery factory, perhaps, one of those that survived Sheffield's recent industrial past. I knew a little about this. When I wasn't researching life in nightclubs every night, I went to the cutlery factories to find out about what Mrs Thatcher's Conservative governments had done to the manufacturing base of this country of ours during a period that political economists call 'negative de-industrialisation', which saw the number of people employed in manufacturing decline from seven million to four and a half million during the first fourteen years of Conservative rule. At that time, Sheffield was full of ex-steelworkers with shopping bags. You would see them in the supermarkets in the afternoon. They didn't talk a lot, even to each other. It was embarrassing. Straight in and straight out. Back to the house. Back to Wimbledon, cricket, old films and housework. Many of them quite liked the housework. They didn't like to be seen doing it, mind, but it was still all right. It was still something. One former steelworker I knew had just got a job on a building site, so his brother, another unemployed steelworker, slipped in to do the housework one day each week. He slipped out as cautiously as he went in. Burglars would have envied his stealth.

But even so, some cutlery factories were surviving, and there the talk was different. The owner of one such factory talked to me about the British disease that had blighted British industry.

'In Britain errors are acceptable – you just build them into your calculations. This firm doesn't accept this and I don't accept it.' And he explained how his firm had not succumbed to this particular illness. Perhaps that was why boxing and steel were good metaphors for one another – the survival of the fittest, the rhetoric and the triumphalism of those who somehow made it, the huge pool of ex-workers who were no longer required and found whatever work they could in the grey streets of Sheffield.

It was a bit like a steel factory up there in Wincobank, and it was the way that Brendan graded his boxers like products in the steel industry that I found most interesting, and the way that he negotiated the commercial possibilities of each and every one of them. 'We might make a bob or two yet,' he would say. 'Trust me.'

I was down at the Savacentre in Wincobank one afternoon with Brendan in his car. He was going to pick up one of his boxers for a fight in Sunderland that night. I had gone along for the ride. The boxer's car had broken down and we were going to give him a lift. The fighter had rung Brendan the night before and told him that it was about time that he had another professional fight. Brendan rang him the next morning to say that he was in luck, and that he had fixed him up with a fight for that very night. The fighter thought that this was rather short notice, but Brendan was ready for him. 'What's the matter with you?' he said. 'You know that you have to be ready and willing in this game if you want to get ahead. You don't think that Muhammad Ali would have said, "I'm sorry, I don't want to fight. It's too short notice." You have to be willing.' This fighter, I could tell, needed some convincing. Brendan was talking him up in the car. 'Don't worry about the fight. He'll not get past your left hand, take it from me. Tonight you'll not be moaning; there'll be a big smile all over your face.' The barrage was more or less constant. The boxer, who was from Birmingham, put on a Lenny Henry accent. He was smiling and he had a friend with him.

'I know I will because I'm going to knock him out.'

This was not what Brendan wanted to hear. 'Knock him out! Knock him out!' shouted Brendan. 'Knock him out and we're out of business. I want you to beat him up, but nicely, over a few rounds. I want it to last a bit. He'll come in like this to you, and I want you to go bomp, bomp, bomp and then walk away. He won't get near you. Shuffle, walk away from him, fiddle him around. That way we might make a few bob.' This was how some of his fighters made money from the fight game: by shuffling, walking away, fiddling other boxers around, standing them on their head, bamboozling them. Brendan used the same words to describe what Naz did to his opponents. Brendan had a few hours to teach this young black boxer his script for the night.

It is easy to think in terms of stereotypes when it comes to the fight game, and my mind was working that way when I scanned the faces behind the barrier at the back of the room. There was 'the slugger', 'the gallant loser', 'the scrapper who wouldn't give up', 'the pretty boy who the audience might want to see beaten up', 'the overweight heavyweight with love handles who will go down in the second to help some toned, well-muscled young fighter build up a series of wins'. But Brendan was much more subtle than that. He would take them to Hull or Bethnal Green or Belfast or Glasgow. He knew what each of the different audiences wanted. He knew what each of those hands resting on that barrier at the back of the room could do, what they were capable of, how they would handle the fight, how they would handle their role. Their role, the role that would be given to them. They only had to look in the mirror. That's what I thought sometimes when I was feeling cynical about the fight game. When you saw them in the ring for the first few seconds, you can almost read their script for them, out loud. You could warn them if you wanted. But they knew the script as well as anybody. You could see it in their faces sometimes – the fear that gave the game away. They would know when they were out of their class, and they would know what was going to happen in the next few minutes. The crowd would be baying for blood – and sometimes 'baying' is not too strong a word here – and they knew whose blood was on the line. You would watch the boxers shuffling their feet. Psychologists claim that we leak our emotional state through the region of the body that we have the least internal feedback from, and therefore the least control over, namely the feet and the legs rather than, say, the face, which is more or less constantly monitored. I sometimes wonder if fear is the ultimate source of all those great boxing shuffles that we have seen or read about. The boxers stand there, waiting for the introductions to end, shuffling on feet that feel like lead. There is sweat on their faces. The commentator says, 'This young boxer has properly warmed up, you can see that, and he is ready to do the business.' But you know different.

Brendan's boys would always put on a good show. They weren't the kind of boys to dive to the canvas when a glove merely touched them, 'like they've been shot between the eyes by some fucking sniper' is how Big Lenny always put it. They would have to listen to Brendan for the next four hours on the way back from Sunderland or wherever if they did. They only hit the deck when they really needed to, even though that glove banging their chin right back might be the first fist that they have ever felt there, as Brendan never allowed head shots in training. He didn't allow head shots because he would say you never knew what damage they could do. 'When Michael Watson got that pounding from Chris Eubank, you don't know what punishment he had taken over the years, some of it training in the gym,' Brendan would say. But having watched his fighters over the years, I have always thought that he didn't allow head shots for another, quite different, reason. His was an egalitarian gym, where Naz, Bomber Graham and Johnny Nelson would spar with that little tubby Asian kid with the round face and the spiky hair from up the road. Head shots wouldn't allow that. They wouldn't allow twelve boxers from as far across the talent spectrum as you could possibly imagine all to spar together at the same time and, on the sound of a bell, to change partners, as if they were involved in some folk ritual. This was Brendan's way of fostering hopes and dreams. All the kids had sparred with Naz and, even when they looked in the mirror on the night of a fight, they might still have thought, 'I've got a chance here. Naz The King Of The World never liked that jab of mine. I've got a chance. You never know. If Naz didn't like it, what about this guy here?'

Brendan taught the art of boxing, the science of boxing as he called it, in this egalitarian gym. Sometimes the boxers would slip in a punch to the head, 'accidentally on purpose, like', Brendan would say, 'as if I wouldn't fucking notice'. But they knew that they were breaking the rules. 'Read the frigging sign,' Brendan would shout. 'What does it say? That's right, "Boxing can seriously damage your health". What's the only sport where you can legally kill your opponent? That's right, frigging boxing.

And you want to come in here and pound somebody's head. Now what did I tell you? No more shots to the bleedin' head or I'll take you out of there. I don't care who you are. Do you understand what I'm saying?'

There are, however, some obvious disadvantages of not allowing punches to the head. When Daniel Teasdale, one of Brendan's protégés, had his first amateur fight in Leeds when he was twelve years old, he only threw punches to the body of his opponent in the first round. John Ingle, Brendan's son, who was working the corner, had to instruct him explicitly to aim for the head. In the second round he did and won the fight.

The word 'factory' has all the wrong connotations, really, and yet the gym had produced so much new commercial product since I was last there. Brendan would ring me up and say that he'd got a great story for me. 'I've got a new kid, miles better than the Naz fella at the same age.'

'How is Naz?' I would enquire, making my enquiry as innocently and as delicately as possible.

'Well, let me tell you,' Brendan would begin, and I knew what was coming next. It was another story about St Peter betraying Jesus in the Garden of Gethsemane. It was a story of a betrayal of biblical proportions. It was a story of Naz's shortcomings as a boxer and as a man.

Once I travelled across the city to a hotel, built sometime in the 1970s, which had its own gym with a pool and a sauna. There was a young Irish lad there. He had had the treatment from Brendan. I could tell that. 'Tell him what you had going for you when you left Dublin,' said Brendan. I sat back in the sauna with the two of them and watched the young fighter's face. It was his manner of telling that was so familiar. It was like going through confirmation. The recitation of the catechism would never be the same again after that, nor the intimate disclosure about one's life after being with Brendan.

'I was in trouble at school,' he began, his head slightly bowed. 'I was in trouble at home. I was in trouble with my parents.' It was the Father, the Son and the Holy Spirit all over again, rhetorically at least. It was the classic three-part list. He looked down at the bench of the sauna. I always noticed that all of Brendan's boxers kept their underpants on in the sauna, Muslims and non-Muslims both. They were the only ones I knew who did this. I always wondered why that was. He was a good-looking lad, quite thickset with a solid, hairless chest and broad shoulders – a natural middleweight. There was a certain honesty about his expression. Brendan had already told him what he could achieve over and over again. I had seen it happen with Naz. This lad looked, in some ways, like even more promising material. He seemed more obedient, almost docile. 'Brendan has taught me discipline. Brendan has taught me belief in myself. Brendan has taught me that it's all down to me. And him,' he added after a pause, creating, I thought, the perfect structure in the confessional rhetoric.

That was three years ago. I don't know what became of him or Daniel Teasdale or some of the other lads who were supposed to be better than Naz at the same age. They didn't make the boxing headlines, that's for sure. They came and they went, the more favoured fighters against the steady stream of lads that would fill fight nights in Bethnal Green or Belfast and put up a good show. They got special treatment, though. Brendan sent Daniel Teasdale to gymnastics and tap-dancing classes to help improve his movement in the ring and gain a little bit of extra publicity when his time came. 'Naz could only do the flip into the ring. You'll be able to flip in and tap-dance across to your opponent in the centre of the ring,' said Brendan. Brendan had Daniel standing singing in the middle of the ring, like all the others. 'Red and yellow and pink and green/Orange and purple and blue/I can sing a rainbow/Sing a rainbow ...' 'I'm teaching personal and social skills,' Brendan said. 'And confidence ... you can't have too much confidence. Sing up, Daniel, I can hardly hear you.'

Again, I scanned the faces of the lads behind the barrier. I could see Ryan Rhodes who had changed, in terms of his facial appearance, since I last saw him. A few years ago, he was billed as the Spice Boy and tipped for greatness. But two defeats had left him rethinking his plans. Everything had been stripped to its foundations to be started again. I made a mental note to ask Brendan how he would set about doing that, repairing the damage to somebody who could almost taste the success that was virtually there in front of him. He had lived his teenage years just a couple of years behind Naz. They climbed into the Ferrari together. Ryan felt the weight of the Rolex watches that Naz had

73

been given as gifts. He listened to all the talk. He was nearly there himself. And there he was now, waiting for Johnny to climb into the ring. Sky Television would be long gone, and most of the VIPs too, before he made it to the ring that night.

'Where's Naz?' my son asked.

'He'll be here in a minute,' I replied.

My son, Sam, had almost stopped believing that I knew Naz, even though Naz was in my book *On the Ropes* and Brendan had arrived at my house at proof stage and gone through the manuscript carefully on my settee, insisting that I delete a few lines and more than a few of the f-words. 'I don't talk like that all the fucking time,' said Brendan, as he sat with a pencil in his hand shaking his head and scoring out some of the offending words. 'Alma would be really upset if she thought that this was how I got on when she wasn't around.' But Naz had not been with him that day and Sam had somehow convinced himself that I had never met the man himself. That was how big Naz had become in the meantime.

'I haven't seen any photographs of you actually with Naz,' my son liked to say. His images of Naz were of the cool dude in the black leather jacket arriving in New York in the Adidas ad, of Michael Jackson turning up to Naz's training sessions or images of the twenty-two-storey-high poster of the Prince on Sunset Boulevard in Hollywood. 'More than Gloria Swanson ever got,' a paper had said. 'Who's Gloria Swanson?' my son had asked. My son wanted proof that I knew him. I had none. 'You haven't seen any photos of me with anybody' was my lame response.

Sam and I had watched Naz's fight with Marco Antonio Barrera on television five months previously. Father and son together, the way it should be, the way that I had done with my father in front of the black and white television when we used to watch Muhammad Ali. The Barrera contest was the fight that they had all wanted: the fans, the pundits and those cynics who thought – even beforehand and against the evidence – that Naz's record of 35 wins out of 35 fights, with 31 knock-outs, was somehow not as impressive as it might at first seem. I suspect that one of the problems was that Naz always said that he would be the greatest fighter of them all, bar none. He was bound to attract some critics along the way. They waited for their moment to be proved right.

When he was still in his teens, Naz had always told me, and

anybody else who was prepared to listen, that he would not only be the world champion one day, but that he would also be the world champion at three or four different weights – the number varying depending upon exactly how cocky he felt that day. He was going to be the greatest boxer of them all. Later, when he had won the world title, he was asked by a leading magazine to nominate the three best boxers of the past thirty years. He put himself in first position, with Muhammad Ali in second, and Sugar Ray Leonard in third. He said, 'I'm going to retire undefeated, a living legend with all the belts. I know I've got something a lot of fighters haven't got: I've got God on my side. Both Ali and Leonard lost a few times, but I just can't see myself getting beaten.'

Before he took the world title, they used to call him 'Motormouth', and laugh a little behind his back. I remember those days well. The musty smell in the gym, like the smell of old sweat and stale spunk – some people tell me that it's the smell of testosterone but I'm not so sure. The dust in the air that makes you cough. The repetitive, regular sound of the leather bags being hit again and again. The sharp grunts of hard, uneven effort. The dust on the hard wooden floor resembling beads of sweat that had somehow become solid over the years. The floor marked out in a mysterious array of lines and circles, so that Brendan could teach the 'science of boxing' to his eager apprentices. The bell in the corner sounding every three minutes throughout the day, whether there was someone in the gym or not – time was measured not in hours and minutes in this hard, dusty place, but in rounds. The bell making its irritating buzzing sound. Brendan up in the corner, shouting out his instructions. Naz sitting on the side of the ring with yet another grey-haired man from the newspapers with a tape recorder in his hand. And some posse of visitors, who were in to look around the gym, smiling shyly towards the wonder kid. Naz would be on stage for them all.

'He's at it again,' they would say, 'old Motormouth in the corner. Just listen to him.' And Brendan would be weaving around, 'making himself busy', as he always liked to put it. 'Leave the lad alone. He's only young.' And you would see Naz winking over at him and Brendan winking back, as if the rest of us didn't notice. That great, silent signal of collusion between the two of them, the wink always including some and excluding others.

But the laughing had stopped a long time ago. The press and the fans had been listening for a while – sometimes I thought too much now – as if every word of Naz's was a sign, every statement a prophecy. Opinion was divided, the way it should be before a great fight. It was no sure thing. Many were saying that he had never been tested before in the way that Barrera was going to test him in Las Vegas. Barrera was the WBO Super-Bantamweight Champion (8 stone 10 pounds) who was stepping up to the nine-stone featherweight limit for this fight. It was said that he was much stronger for those extra few pounds. There were rumours, however, that Naz was struggling to make the weight. I could believe them. He had always had trouble making the weight ever since I knew him. Running, he liked to say, was for runners, not boxers.

But the Barrera fight was the big one, and his critics were saying that the talking had to stop. I had watched Naz on television in the week up to the fight, as he trained in the bright sunshine of Palm Springs, a million miles from Sheffield on a rainy night, where I was sitting. He looked a little older than the last time I saw him. I noticed the difference. He was twenty-six, still young but a little more mature in his looks. I thought back to the Naz whom I had watched develop and change.

I have many different images of Naz; I am bound to have. There is the runt, four foot nothing of him, hanging about with the boxers on fight night at the City Hall in Sheffield fifteen years ago. The little Arab boy whom they used to call 'the little Paki'. 'He's here again,' they would say, 'that little Paki lad. You just can't get fucking rid of him.' Brendan took Naz with him every-where to demonstrate to him the essential truths of boxing, to show him what happens to boxers both in the ring and out of it. There was always a bit of the Catholic priest in Brendan, that's what I always thought. He was always going on about the evils of sex and drink being responsible for the downfall of most boxers. 'People are dying of Aids, but it hasn't stopped the popu-lation having sex,' he liked to say. 'I've had boxers before with great talent but they never had the discipline. I've seen boxers throw their careers away.' He knew that I liked Mick Mills enor-mously, and he would often bring Mick into his stories at times like that. 'He would go outside with a girl on a wet night before a fight. You couldn't talk to Mick. He would be out there in the freezing cold with a girl when he should have been resting.'

Brendan took Naz to see the downside of boxing for himself. The boxer in hospital after a drug overdose, or after a street fight, or after depression had got the better of him and had driven him to attempt to end the whole thing. 'Just look,' Brendan would say. 'Look at that and fucking learn.' Naz had a number of advantages over Mick and the rest of them. He was a Muslim for a start, and he was a Muslim from a large and supportive family. He was 'clean-living', in Brendan's words, and that was a huge advantage in the fight game. Plus, of course, he had tremendous power in his punch, a punch that could be thrown as he swayed back in a manner that reminded you of his idol, Muhammad Ali. 'Awesome', Mick Mills said, 'for a little fucker like that.'

As he liked to tell anyone who was prepared to listen, Brendan had been training Naz since he was seven years old after he had seen him fighting three older white lads in a school playground. It was an important part of the story: that raw courage, the aggression there from the start, the chance encounter, fate, racism.

'Just remember,' Brendan would say over and over again, 'boxing is the only sport where you can legally kill your opponent.' He was always working on Naz's fear, on his dreams, shaping his body and his mind.

I have other images of Naz, as well. In the years when he was starting to make it and his face was starting to appear on the telly, I bumped into him one afternoon in Sheffield's Meadowhall shopping centre. The American shopping mall transferred to Sheffield's Don Valley to fill some of the space left by the closure of Britain's industrial past on the banks of the stagnant and polluted River Don with its dead branches, rubber tyres and empty chemical drums. Meadowhall, that temple to consumerism, with cameras to monitor the behaviour of the customers and to pick up and identify any customer not doing what they are there to do, which is to engage in the goal-directed behaviour of spending. Naz would probably have been picked up by one or more cameras that day. He was there with another lad, just mooching around, 'chillin'' he would have called it later, but it was just hanging around then. He and his friend looked as if they were a couple of kids taking the afternoon off school. They call it 'wagging it' in Sheffield. I know that because in the psychology department where I worked we once had an educational psychologist come in and give a talk about truancy in Sheffield. She was using qualitative research illustrated with many direct quotes. In one of her interviews one young lad said, 'We were wagging it in Burger King.' And she explained for those of us who did not know that 'wagging it' meant playing truant. My professor was sitting beside me and he turned to me and asked what 'Burger King' meant. He wasn't joking. The afternoon that I bumped into Naz, I was with a female friend who knew nothing about boxing, but she knew all about Naz. Or so she said. She read the tabloids and she was always dropping information about different celebrities into the conversation. 'Did you know that so-and-so is getting a divorce?' she would say, as if she were a personal and intimate friend of theirs. She knew a lot about Naz. She had just been telling me about his favourite car, his favourite colour, his favourite drink, and some endless list of facts about nothing. It was that famous cross-over effect of Naz's, appealing to a new audience who were more interested in the walk, the talk, the music and, of course, the success than the boxing itself. She thought that Naz was great. Then this small, insignificant lad in a grey hooded top came up in the middle of the shopping arcade and said, 'Hi, Geoffrey. How are you?'

'Who was that?' she asked, with a look of mild distaste, after he had left.

'Naseem Hamed,' I replied. 'Soon to be the boxing champion of the world.'

'Get lost,' she said. 'Whoever that was, it wasn't him. That was just some young lad wagging it from school, some young Asian lad. Naz is nothing like that. He's taller for a start, and he's a lot more muscly.'

She never did believe me. We had an argument later that night. 'You're a right fucking bullshitter,' she said. 'You pretend to know important people to make yourself look good. You don't know fucking anybody. You said that little Asian lad was the Prince. Well, I know that you were talking crap. My best mate went out with two Sheffield Wednesday players, you know. I can recognise a fucking real celeb when I see one, and he wasn't a celeb. No way, José.' And she stormed off.

But she didn't know Naz at all. Naz was the newest and brightest celeb around. At that time he was fast becoming the biggest thing in British boxing for years – better than Chris 'Simply the Best' Eubank, more destructive than Nigel 'The Dark Destroyer' Benn, more marketable than Frank 'HP Sauce' Bruno, men whose bruising careers we have already started to forget, who appeared in advertisements that we already have forgotten. He was also very young, very hip and achieving rock star status in the ring. He was attracting a much younger crowd to his fights. Then aged just twenty, he was due to fight for the WBO Featherweight Title.

But there was something else about the Prince. Interviewers were saying that he made Chris Eubank look like a shrinking violet. Experienced boxing commentators said that he had a level of ambition and plans for world domination only seen before in James Bond villains. Nineteen ninety-five, he said, was going to be his year. He was on the hoardings alongside the top-of-the-range Audi A4 with the slogan 'They're both the most powerful in their class'. 'If you see either of the above, exercise due caution' read the advert. He was in every magazine and every newspaper you picked up at the time; he had made it off the sports pages. Wannabes on the gossip pages of the tabloids said how they had packed in some pop star or other for the new king of the ring: 'Naseem has made me feel like a woman again. Our life together is so pure. It's so real.' My female friend had read the stories. A deal had been struck with the Joe Bloggs clothing company. They were preparing the Naz collection. A fan club had been set up in Sheffield. A lot of young girls were joining it. It was suddenly much harder to get to see him. He was being sucked into the maelstrom of commercial success. Naz's brother, Riath, explained, 'We are building an empire around him. He is twenty-one now, and basically he doesn't have to work another day in his life or fight another fight to be financially secure for the rest of his life.'

Naz might have appeared to erupt onto the national scene, but fourteen long years went into preparing him for it. He spent his childhood and his adolescence in Brendan Ingle's gym in Wincobank. He grew up one hundred yards away, living above the corner shop – the Pakistani shop that always stayed open, even if his father was from the Yemen. His father fell for Ingle's Irish blarney and for all the promises. This lad, and all the other boys you saw in the gym, were in Brendan's hands. The sign above the ring read 'Boxing can damage your health.' It was repeated a few steps to the left. These signs had been there since the club opened. Brendan never let them forget that boxing is a serious business. The front door of the gym always seemed to be open, as if he were inviting any lads passing through Wincobank just to walk in and have their lives transformed. There was something vaguely religious about it.

Brendan brought the young Muslim boy to all of the Herol Graham and Johnny Nelson fights. Naz's development took place in boxing halls up and down the country. Brendan wanted him to see it all: the dedication that has to go into boxing, the glory to be had, and the pitfalls, especially the pitfalls. Brendan had seen it all before. He knew what lessons there were to learn. 'I've had boxers before with great talent, but they never had the discipline. I've seen boxers throw their careers away. I've witnessed terrible performances in the ring and, when you ask them what they've been up to, they tell you that they've gone round the back of a pub for sex in the freezing cold the night before a fight. Naz, by contrast, doesn't smoke, he doesn't drink and he doesn't gamble. The hardest person to beat in the world is yourself, but to beat yourself you need self-discipline. Naz has got that singular determination to win.'

Naz won sixty-one out of his sixty-seven amateur fights, and Brendan persuaded him to turn professional on his eighteenth birthday. 'I always knew that he would be world champion and a millionaire at the age of twenty-one,' said Brendan. 'There was never any doubt in my mind.' Or in Naz's. In 1994, at the age of twenty, Naz took the European Bantamweight Title off the Italian Vincenzo Belcastro. This fight grabbed the headlines not just because of the demonstration of Naz's skill, but because of the taunting of his opponent in the final round. The self-discipline seemed to have given rise to an uncontrollable arrogance. *Boxing Monthly* reported that it had never received such a postbag of complaints about a boxer or his performance before. The tabloids were trying to make up their mind about him. They had taken to calling him 'Motormouth'. I went to interview Naz in the gym after this fight in a quiet moment after the other boxers had drifted away.

I was immediately surprised then that, away from the bright lights of the television cameras, 'Motormouth', to begin with, spoke in such a quiet voice, with his arms locked across his chest almost defensively. I asked him whether he was pleased with all the publicity that his last fight had generated. 'The publicity is what it's all about. It's all about getting bums on seats. It's best to cause a big ...' There was a very long pause. Eventually he settled for 'fuss'. '... fuss about you or whatever so people come and watch you. I was very surprised at the criticism for my last fight. I was surprised at how the people went against it. I think that they went over the top. I wasn't trying to humiliate Belcastro.'

I asked him, if he wasn't trying to humiliate Belcastro, what was he trying to do? 'You have to remember that I was very psyched up for that fight because it was a big fight for me at the age of twenty. It was only my twelfth professional fight. Everybody was reminding me that I had never gone past six rounds. So basically, I was thinking I've got all this to prove now to the media, so that's what I did. It was my big chance. I wanted to prove that I could do twelve rounds easy with a world-class fighter who was number six in the world. By the last round, I had won every round. I dropped him in the eleventh. Brendan told me just to enjoy myself in the twelfth. I came out jumping all over the place. I wanted to show everybody that I had as much energy in the twelfth round as I had in the first. I wanted people to ask where I got all my energy from. I wanted to show that I could stand in the middle of the ring with my hands on my hips and show the champion that he couldn't hit me. I didn't want to ridicule him at all. I couldn't believe it when I read the papers in the days after the fight.'

At that time, Naz was still living in Wincobank with his parents. He was born the fourth of nine children. Wincobank, he said, was very down-to-earth, and very good for keeping his feet firmly on the ground. His father, Sal Hamed, came from Yemen in 1967 to work in Sheffield's steelworks, and later bought a corner shop, subsequently owned by the Prince's sister. 'My parents are proud of me. They're proud to see their son up there. Their advice to me is to live my life cleanly and not to give in to the temptations of life. When people meet me, they say that I'm totally different to how I appear on the telly. When people see me on the telly, they see a cocky, arrogant, brash, bombastic fighter who just wants to win, but then when they meet me they think that I'm just normal.'

I enquired, therefore, whether it was all just an act, an act to get bums on seats, a big commercial front. He looked almost a little hurt, as if I were accusing him of something untoward. 'It's not an act when I'm in the ring. I can't put it on. It just comes out. It's just me when I'm in the ring. I really am two different people. It's the way I have to perform. It's the way that I've been brought up. It's not under my control. I can't think about it. It just happens naturally. When something clicks on naturally, you can't stop it. Outside the ring I'm totally different. I'm more relaxed. It takes me a little bit of time to change from one character into the other. After the fight I'm still hyped up. I come down usually the day after the fight.'

His arrogant style meant that, at the time, he was often compared with Chris Eubank. I asked Naz what he thought of such comparisons. 'I'm not flattered. Chris has tried to copy a few moves from me, but some of the moves he can't even do. For example, trying to hit an opponent while he's looking at the floor. When he tries to do it, he falls on his face. My advice to him is that if he keeps on watching me, he may learn something.'

You could immediately hear the arrogance start up, the strut coming into his talk, but this was still delivered in a low, quiet voice, with a defensive posture to begin with. Then the body language started to change. It became far from defensive, more congruent with the speech itself. 'It's a definite that I will be a world champion. I will be a world champion at four different weights. I'm so confident. I definitely will be a multi-millionaire. I'm planning to be a millionaire at the age of twenty-one and a multi-millionaire at the age of twenty-five. I'm not in this business for nothing. I'm in this business to secure my needs and my family's needs. I want my family to live like royalty.'

I asked him about the pressures of fame. Was it hard to cope with all the temptations that fame throws up? I remembered Brendan whispering in my ear earlier that morning about the temptations of the flesh. 'I've never tasted alcohol in my life, because of my religious beliefs, and it's helped with my boxing. It's kept me out of trouble. There are a lot of temptations if you've been drinking and getting up to whatever like other guys do at a certain age. But it won't happen to me. I just thank God for putting me in that position. I do know that I'm talented, but that's because I've got a gift from Allah. I've been blessed.'

It was, in many ways, funny talk to come from a boxer. You realised that what had happened was one of those unique combinations of events that occur once in a lifetime – the Irish trainer who had been around, who had almost taken Herol Graham to a world title, the Irishman who had kissed the Blarney stone, twice, and the young Muslim boy from the stable family home living yards from the gym who was discovered by accident at the age of seven, fighting his way out of trouble like Ingle himself back in the slums of Dublin. The Irish trainer who warned all his apprentices about the sins of the flesh, and the young Muslim who was prepared to listen, who didn't stray. Ingle worked with him and worked on him for fourteen years, and the skill of the lad – who could throw thirty-eight combination punches in eight seconds with eight different foot movements and ten different hand movements – and the phenomenal punching power, and the self-confidence just grew and grew. All nurtured in the hot-house of professional boxing. The cockiness just made him more interesting, just as it had made Eubank interesting – for a while. You wanted to see the Prince get hit on the chin, just to see what would happen next. After the Belcastro fight, a lot of people wanted to see what he was really made of.

After Belcastro, Naz's next fight, in August 1994, was against Antonio Picardi. I was at the weigh-in in Sheffield's poshest hotel. The hotel receptionist looked bored. 'Just follow the two gentlemen in front,' she said to me. One of the men wore a thick, red lumberjack shirt and boots. Brendan was there already. I could hear him talking. 'Let me have a word in your ear,' he said to a man in a grey suit conspiratorially. This was the real business of boxing, his arm round the shoulder of some middle-aged man. Hushed voices. Talking to the wall. The television cameras were busy, periodically flooding the hotel room in white light. The Prince was prime-time. He was what television executives dreamt about. A few young men with shaved heads sat by the wall, hollow-cheeked. They looked like extras from a film about man's inhumanity to man. They looked half-starved. But these were young men at the peak of fighting fitness. The men in the green and the mauve jackets who were having all the conspiratorial conversations looked positively obese by comparison.

A dapper, grey-haired man stood in the middle of the room by the scales. Nat Basso, matchmaker and manager, a big wheel in

the boxing establishment. He was there to supervise the proceedings. It was my turn to have my ear whispered in. 'Nat and
myself go back thirty years,' whispered Brendan. 'Now *he* was
poor. His family came over here from Russia. Why, it reminds me
of my own childhood in Dublin. He fought his way out of that
poverty.' But it was the same old tired metaphor. Everybody
fighting their way out and up. Everybody bobbing and weaving,
ducking and diving, going the full distance. Nat Basso was, after
all, in his seventies. But he still looked extremely smart and co-
ordinated. 'He did it all through boxing?' I enquired.

'Oh no,' replied Brendan. 'Through gents' tailoring. Boxing
was always a bit on the side for Nat Basso.'

It was time to try the scales. One boxer stripped out of his track
suit. He was wearing a G-string rather than the conventional
underpants. He forgot to remove his cap. His manager walked
behind him and flicked his cap off at the very last minute. They
all agreed that the scales were about right. The first boxer was
called – a heavyweight. It was the man in the lumberjack shirt.
The man next to me whispered in my ear, 'He's just a body
brought in. Just a body.' And then after a pause, 'A bit dis-
appointing. He's a bit flabby. You would have thought that they
would have trained him up a bit.'

Naz came in quietly, dressed in a grey track suit. Then he saw
the cameras. The bright light filled the room. Suddenly he was
in a jaunty mood – spinning, smiling and jeering. Dr Jekyll and
Mr Funk. I remember the song well enough. I noticed that Naz
and Brendan were wearing identical running shoes, but in
slightly different colours. Probably last year's model and this
year's model. This year's for the boxer, the man in the limelight,
the man of the moment. Last year's for the trainer and manager.
Probably a sponsorship deal, all carefully worked out, with the
manager qualifying for the remaindered stock. Everybody wants
a return on their investment. Everybody wants their pound of
flesh. Naz sat down. The lights had been extinguished. He looked
reflective.

There was a bustle of activity by the door. One small man with
a broken nose came in, followed by another, then another. The
trickle became a stream. All small and dark, their noses not just
broken, but pummelled into wide arches by fist on bone. The
noses were all disproportionately wide. It was as if they had been

stuck onto their faces by an apprentice sculptor, not yet sure of the perfect scale and symmetry of the human visage. The challenger, Antonio Picardi, and his entourage had arrived. The voice in my ear was whispering again. 'I wonder who will be paying all their wages. Yer man will need to borrow money after the fight to pay for the trip back to Italy for all of these.'

I noticed that for many minutes Naz did not even look towards his opponent. It was not that he was avoiding eye contact; he just looked uninterested. Then I saw him watching as Picardi stripped out of his track suit. It was a look of curiosity, with no discernible emotion. Not fear, not sadness and certainly not happiness. Just a look that said, 'So this is the man standing between me and my first million.' Naz knew that he had to keep on winning. His whole boxing persona – the arrogant Prince who would taunt his opponents, the man they could not touch, the maestro – depended upon an unbeaten record. Every opponent, therefore, stood in the way of the million pounds that he had been promised since he was a child, when Brendan would bring him ringside and whisper in his ear about the future.

It was Naz's turn to face the scales. He had snapped out of his reflective mood. He was on again, on camera, in character, ready for the action. 'He's going down. Believe me folks, he's going down tonight.' Naz's accent was all over the place and seemed more American than Sheffield at that moment. The Italians smiled amicably. You got the impression that they couldn't really tell what he was saying. Perhaps it was the phoney accent, I thought.

Naz pulled his track suit back on. Nat Basso announced that all the boxers would have to stay in the hotel for the next two hours because the doctor couldn't turn up to examine them until then. 'He's got a day job as well, you know,' I heard Alma, Brendan's wife, explain to one of the men in the mauve jackets. 'He's just like the rest of us, you know. He's got to work for a living.'

I was there at ringside for the fight. Naz finished Picardi in three rounds. None of his fights were going the distance. Back in Yemen they had Naz's image on boxes of tissues. 'Not even Muhammad Ali had that,' said Brendan. Some firm was making statuettes of the diminutive boxer. He was an idol in more ways than one. A few weeks later, I went back to the gym where it had all started. I had never seen it so full. 'Is Naz here?' I heard one kid ask. In the ring, professionals and amateurs were all mixed together, as always. One slight, eight-year-old boy called Darren, whose mother, Brendan told me, was a professional shoplifter, sparred with Johnny Nelson. Darren danced excitedly this way and that around him. Darren's mother had recently been away for six months. Brendan told the boys in the gym that she was away on holiday. 'I bet she comes back with a suntan with two stripes down the middle,' said one nine-year-old. These boys take some fooling. Jimmy Wood, fifty-five and a moneylender, who trains every day, including, he told me, Christmas Day, sparred with Ryan Rhodes, Naz's best friend. The jabs did not sting Jimmy as he moved relentlessly forward. They ended their short, abrupt journey in loud, deep thumps on the bone of shoulder and forearm.

Jimmy, the moneylender, had been robbed at home. 'It's common knowledge around Wincobank that I'm a quarter-millionaire,' he confessed to me. He told me that he encountered a lot of frustration in his particular job, but that boxing released it all. 'Plus, I love the competition. All these young 'uns go into the ring with me and they think that they're going to fucking bash me up because I'm getting on a bit, but they're wrong.' Ryan's jabs were leaving great red welts on Jimmy's upper arms, but Jimmy was still trying to rush him.

Two men from the *Daily Express* were waiting patiently in one corner of the gym for Naz to arrive for training. 'I'll let you take a photograph of me sparring with Johnny for a quid,' said Darren. It was 'no deal' said the men from the *Express*. 'Could you lend me fifteen pence for my bus home, then?' asked Darren, even though he only lived up the street. They didn't have the right change, so he got twenty pence, instead.

Naz was not just a hero back in Yemen. You only had to look around the gym to see that. Herol Graham had got so close and had fallen so far, and when Herol had faltered, so had the dreams and aspirations of a whole culture. It was tough out there, and it was just as tough in boxing itself. In fact, there was no way through for any of them. So why bother? But now, suddenly things were different. You could go all the way, with persistence and dedication. It was not just Brendan preaching to them any more. They could see it with their own eyes in their living rooms.

And they had all learned from what had happened. Naz would not make the same mistakes. Brendan had confessed that in boxing these days great boxing skill is no longer enough. Chris Eubank had taught everybody that. A man who had avoided Herol Graham in his prime had made millions from posing and strutting as 'Simply the Best'. So, right from the beginning of his amateur career, Naz had been vaulting the ropes, doing hand-springs across the ring, dancing and jiving about. All in order to be noticed, to stand out, to draw attention to the fifty-four combination punches he could throw in a few short seconds, but which might otherwise go unnoticed. And Brendan had the rest of these kids all practising their entrances as well. Every day you could watch them lining up by the ropes and one by one vaulting over them. He was not just teaching them everything he knew about boxing – or even the more valuable skills of survival inside and outside the ring – he was keeping the dream alive. And they all knew it.

This was all less than a month to the Prince's world title challenge. The gym was busy, but there was no Naz. The Saturday before, he was right there in everybody's front room, ringside at the Bruno fight against Oliver McCall, shouting his encouragement with Nigel Benn beside him. You could see the two of them bobbing up and down like puppets on a string as Big Frank, the muscle machine, kept grinding forward. When Big Frank landed a punch, it was as if the puppeteer was having convulsions as the two of them jumped out of their seats, their heads bobbing this way and that. You couldn't make out what they were shouting, but it did not require much imagination to guess. The encouragement is always the same whether it comes from a world champion, or the know-all in the second row. 'Work off the jab.' 'Hurt him.' London, with all its gaudy attractions, was where the action was, and Naz was soaking up his new-found fame miles from Sheffield.

But now, with just over three weeks to go, he was back home. But, he just wasn't in the gym. He had promised to turn up for some photographs, which I had arranged to be taken, but there was no sign of him. His brother, Riath, explained that he was watching television and didn't feel like training or posing for photographs. Brendan was as usual making himself busy, running around because a lift had fallen through for two of his boxers, and he was preparing to drive them down to Stoke in one of Naz's sponsored cars for a fight. It was the Peugeot. 'Naz will be here in a minute,' he said apologetically as the Peugeot raced down Newman Road. A little knot of fans waited expectantly outside the front door. One little black girl, whose nickname was Don King, had her autograph book ready. I asked the boy who was with her what he thought of the Prince.

'He's right cool. He acts a bit arrogant when he's in the ring, but he's got good talent. I like him being cocky. It's cool. I wish he didn't stand over some of his opponents when he's knocked them out, but I like the way he comes into the ring and the music. I like Frank Warren too. He lets me sit in his limo.'

They maintained their lonely vigil at the door, waiting for the Prince to get bored with the telly or even for the man with the limo to turn up unexpectedly. But it was a damp night in Sheffield, an early misty autumn, a dreary night to be hanging about outside a run-down gym.

Jimmy, the moneylender, was inside training, as always. He was standing in the ring sparring with a big Asian heavyweight who was hitting hard. I wanted to encourage Jimmy. 'Work off the jab,' I shouted and left it at that. There was no way that Jimmy was going to hurt him. He just had to stand there soaking up whatever was to come. And it was coming hard, fast and brutal.

I asked one of the lads in the gym, Michael, the sixty-four thousand dollar question: why wasn't Naz training that night? Michael just shook his head. I wasn't trying to imply that this might be Naz's fatal weakness, the crack that appears in all truly talented individuals who recognise their own talent early on. The weakness that spreads when the ego takes over and tells the rest of the individual that they truly are one in a million, and that hard work and the daily grind are only for the ordinary, the average, the mortal. But perhaps I was thinking it.

Michael interrupted my musings. 'Naz used to be in the gym every day, but after he won the WBC International Title he started training less. He used to come in for a full month before a big fight, but now he only comes in for three weeks before the fight. I mean, he's fighting Robinson at the end of this month, and he's only trained once this week, as far as I know.' It was, however, only Wednesday, so at most Naz had missed one day of training, but in this gym, where total dedication was the norm, even that was thought significant.

Jimmy had now joined us. As usual, I found my eyes being drawn to those big red welts on his shoulders and forearms. My arms almost ached in sympathy. Jimmy had his own explanation as to why Naz did not appear to be about the gym quite as much. 'He doesn't seem to need to train as much now. He's naturally fit. But I've seen him come in at eleven o'clock at night to train, when I'm on my way back from the boozer. That's why you don't see him. There's only one Naz. He's an individual. He trains at funny times, times that suit him. But he may miss the odd day because he's so good. But you have to be careful, no matter what talent you've got. If it doesn't catch up with him now, it will catch up with him one day. In my view, you have to train every day. I've no natural ability. All my ability comes from training. But I'm very tricky for my age. I can bash up some of the young lads who come down here. Ryan Rhodes is the only one I detest boxing. He's too strong. He fucks me about. He's three stone heavier than me. I'm nine stone seven, and he's twelve stone.'

Jimmy's calculations were a bit off. In fact, more than a bit off for a moneylender, a man who should be good with figures, but I didn't feel like correcting him. I had too much sympathy for a man with arms that red.

'Naz is very tricky, as well,' said Jimmy. 'He's a different man in the ring to outside it. He likes to get into that ring and think that he's the master, than he's the fucking king. He likes to think that's his fucking territory. I once kissed him in the ring. I do it to them all. I'm right fucking good at it. I like to go bang, bang, bang and then kiss them. It does their head in. Then I land the big ones. It puts them off, you see. Naz hates it. He hates me kissing him when we're sparring.'

We chatted for what seemed like hours, while I waited for Naz to arrive. He never did come. He did train the following night, and the photographer went back to the gym and caught him. The photographer asked if he could take a photograph of Naz sparring with Jimmy, the ring regular from way back. But Naz was adamant. 'Get out,' he said to Jimmy. The photographer tried once more. 'Don't tell me what to do. I'm the champ,' said Naz.

EIGHT

What really interested me most as a psychologist about boxing? Was it that the rewards of the fight game could be so great that parents would willingly put their children in the care of another for perhaps ten or twenty years? How often does that happen, except in the minds of philosophers? Children with nothing, no discipline and no drive, bullied at school or alternatively an insecure bully themselves, downright losers in almost every sense, would now be in that gym day after day, year after year and would sometimes emerge transformed through this process. Ultimate proof, if it were needed, of the role of environment rather than heredity in determining who we can become, and therefore who we are. And what goes into all of that shaping from a psychological as well as a physical point of view?

I loved Brendan's stories about him and Naz walking the streets of Wincobank on a Sunday evening for three hours or more whilst formulating their mental strategies, conspiring how they were going to take over and dominate the boxing world. Or Brendan's stories about how he would throw stones at Naz's window at six o'clock in the morning to get him up to train before the Sheffield air got too polluted with the fumes and the smoke. 'Naz always hated running,' Brendan liked to say, 'he always hated it. I had to persuade him almost every day to get up and out.' I loved hearing Brendan's accounts of how the human brain works, and the way that he would argue that the laterality of the cerebral hemispheres, which he had recently discovered for himself, essentially supports his training methods that went back years. 'You see,' Brendan would start, 'the right-hand side of the brain controls the left-hand side of the body and the left-hand side of the brain controls the right-hand side of the body. The wiring is all over the frigging place. When Naz was working up and down those lines in the gym, it was putting in all those little connections into his brain. When I had him box orthodox, southpaw, square on, sideways, switch – the five different ways that I taught him – that put in more of those wee brain connections to bamboozle his opponents.' I loved hearing about Brendan teaching somersaults over the ropes and giving singing lessons in the ring and advice on how to deal with the world's media. And I suppose that I was fascinated by how all of this intense effort affects the development of a human being.

I could see the changes taking place in Naz over the years. I suppose that I was sometimes there at the right times to witness the changes in his behaviour and personality, produced by all that intense physical and psychological coaching and by all that incessant attention. Brendan and everybody else would be making him feel special, preparing him for greatness from the age of seven, scripting him in what he should say, in what he should think. He is, after all, the only man that I've ever met who said that he supported both Sheffield Wednesday and Sheffield United. All against a backdrop of a northern city in steep decline, a city of which he is immeasurably proud, but a city sometimes more than a little seedy around the edges, the edges that many boxers inhabit.

I have a copy of a videotape which contains an edited version of the fights that have taken place in a nightclub and have been captured on CCTV. The tape is for the amusement of the doormen and selected VIPs of Sheffield's top nightclub. Some of the fights on the tape have been kept because they are very violent; some are kept because they are considered amusing or embarrassing in some way. They all have their own labels. 'Come On Big 'Un', 'The Fanny Kicker', 'Beer Bottle Blues'. I play one now and I can see Naz, as a very young face in the crowd – too young to be allowed into a club like this, but it's his night off. He's enjoying the action, which occurs in the doorway of the club and then spills outside. The rest of the crowd are all slightly intoxicated with that somewhat loose smile of inebriation, but not Naz, who was just out chillin' with his friends. He stayed focused even there. I remember him telling me about being introduced to this 'brand-new, beautiful drink' by a friend of his. I was waiting to be shocked by the clean-living boxer. The drink turned out to be

Coke and blackcurrant. 'But I break it up with pineapple, lemonade and orange juice,' he added, as if this might somehow impress me.

In the video, he's watching something that's taking place just outside the club. He's laughing at somebody's misfortune.

'He kicked me in the fanny,' some girl is saying as she turns towards the bouncers with her hands covering her crotch. 'And now that cunt over there is acting all innocent.'

The man she is pointing at looks innocently at the bouncers. 'I did fucking nothing,' he protests, 'fucking nothing.' You can just make out Naz in the doorway of the club, hanging out for a better look. He is in hysterics with laughter.

Later that night, he would have got some advice from Paul in the toilet about how to psyche himself up before a big fight. 'Just imagine that your opponent gobbed right in your mouth. You wouldn't like that, would you?' Or Mick, the bouncer, would have kept him company for an hour or two reminiscing about his own fights or about how he had broken six jaws, only one of them in the ring. Or perhaps he and Mick would have a laugh about the girl barred from the club now, but captured on video for posterity.

In 1994, when I interviewed Naz in the gym in Wincobank, he was still living with his parents above the corner shop. He was just nineteen years old and was preparing for greatness. He was busy practising a new entrance to the ring, a more eye-catching somersault. 'Get your arms straighter,' said Brendan, 'get a bit more spring into it.' Brendan had a great idea at the time that the Arab Prince should make an entrance on a flying carpet, courtesy of Paul Eyre's Carpets, who were big in South Yorkshire. Ali Baba comes to boxing. It was all being mapped out on a little scrap of paper on the dusty steps at the side of the ring. In the drawing, Naz was sitting cross-legged on the Paul Eyre's carpet. Naz pointed at the drawing. 'Where's the fans, Brendan?' he asked.

'Oh, that's them down there,' said Brendan, shading the bottom of the page with the thick lead of the pencil. It was just a great black smudge. 'There's hundreds of them just waiting for "The Prince" to arrive.'

'Draw us a few more, Brendan,' said Naz.

And Brendan shaded a bit more of the page. 'Is that enough

for you? Or do you want a few more, you greedy beggar?' asked Brendan, and they both laughed.

'How do I get down off the carpet?' enquired Naz nervously.

'Oh, we'll worry about that a bit closer to the time,' said Brendan. He folded up the bit of paper and put it in his pocket, and left Naz and me to it.

We talked about his boxing and that morning, when he talked about what he was capable of in the ring, I watched a transformation before my very eyes from a quiet interviewee with an almost defensive body language for much of the interview to someone altogether different. I almost felt like commenting on it to his face. The newspapers had already started calling him 'Mr Motormouth', and I think that at the time he almost took it as a compliment. 'I look at the floor, and I snap the punch out and I hit their face and my opponents think, "How does he do that? He's not even looking at my face." It does their heads in.' He wasn't the champion of the world just yet, but he was already sounding like it, rattling on and on. His new repertoire of body language, which emerged towards the end of the interview, reflected every nuance of his now confident speech. It was like a persona that he was trying on in front of me, and he realised that it fitted comfortably.

In my later interviews with him, there was no sign of that earlier, quieter and more defensive Naz. The other side of his character seemed to have taken over completely. He became Mr Motormouth personified. He thought that this style suited him. He seemed to assume that he was mimicking the verbal style of his hero, Muhammad Ali. 'And he was the most famous man in the world, and it didn't do him any harm,' Naz would say. But nobody was telling Naz that he wasn't coming across like Muhammad Ali, or if they were, he wasn't listening.

The 'talk' was, of course, one of the ways that the fight game had changed over the years, ever since the young Cassius Clay had gone bear hunting in 1964 with his bus with the famous writing on it, which read 'CASSIUS CLAY ENTERPRISES. WORLD'S MOST COLORFUL FIGHTER.' Then there was his poetry and his famous lip, which can still make you smile with its playful innocence:

Clay comes out to meet Liston
And Liston starts to retreat

If Liston goes back any further
He'll end up in a ringside seat.
Clay swings with a left,
Clay swings with a right,
Look at young Cassius
Carry the fight.

But as Norman Mailer commented before the first Liston fight, if Clay won the heavyweight crown then 'every loudmouth on a street corner could swagger and be believed'. Being a loudmouth was no longer a good indication that you couldn't fight as well. Some could do the talk *and* the walk. But there was, of course, good psychology underlying Muhammad Ali's approach, and this was really quite new to the sport. His harassing of opponents in the weeks before the fight unsettled them. His playing the fool in the face of opponents who demanded and expected respect confused them. As Ali himself said at the time, 'Liston thinks I'm a nut. He is scared of no man, but he is scared of a nut.' Ergo he is scared of me. Some have suggested that Muhammad Ali's never-ending verbal tirades were designed to convince himself as much as his opponent of what could happen in the ring when the two of them were finally alone. It was an extremely effective way of staying focused; there were no secret doubts in his head because all of Ali's thinking was articulated in the speech itself. Or at least that's how it might have appeared to an opponent. Naz had learned much from Brendan, and through Brendan much from Muhammad Ali, about the psychological side of the pain game. He had learned to damage his opponent long before they ever got anywhere near the ring. He had learned to stay focused. He could do the talk and he knew that it was effective, but it was different to Ali's, despite what Naz himself seemed to think. There was no real humour in it, in spite of all Brendan's efforts to get us to see it as funny. As Naz outlined, without any trace of humour, what he was going to do to his opponent, Brendan would be circling in the background, repeating 'the cheek of the lad', as if this might somehow alter how we perceived him. 'Ah, he's only young. It's bound to go to his head.' I sit with some of Naz's more recent quotes in front of me and I think to myself that Ali was never like this. 'I don't mean to sound horrid, but I knew there was going to be a stretcher involved somewhere along the line.' Or, 'When I'm in that ring, I just want to do some damage. It's terrible to say, but that is what I want to do. I've got to wreck something. I've got to wreck it completely, like tear it up.'

He was doing the talk, but what kind of talk was it? It didn't endear him to that many sports writers, that's for sure. But young people loved it; my son Sam thought it was impressive, a bit like the talk in the World Wrestling Federation videos. It was that 'kick-ass' attitude of Naz's that he liked; it was that confidence, which the boys themselves, of course, didn't possess as they went through the turmoils of adolescence.

But then again, the talk didn't necessarily reflect his underlying personality. It was just more behaviour that he had learned to be displayed especially in the build-up to a fight. It was his way of getting bums on seats, of coping with the stress. It was his way of winning the war. It was strategic, but it was a strategy that particularly suited him. After he became world champion, I went down to London to interview him for the BBC. This was a world away from the world we knew in Sheffield: an exclusive apartment in Mayfair, the Merc outside, and fawning looks wherever we went. He seemed comfortable in this new world. He was spending weeks at a time down there away from Brendan and the boys in the gym, but he was thriving on his new fame – twenty years old and champion of the world. He was recognised everywhere. He was in a reflective mood that night I went to see him. It made a nice change. It gave me an opportunity to discuss with him how he had got there, the story so far, this unique combination of the world-weary Irish trainer and the talented young Muslim, from just up the street, who could really punch. I reminded Naz of the familiar old story about how he and Brendan had met on that fateful day in Sheffield. It was a story that I myself liked, it had everything, but Naz just laughed when I brought it up.

'Everybody's familiar with Brendan's story, but I don't even know if it's true,' he said. 'To tell you the truth, I think it is made up, but at that particular time in my life, it was made up for a reason. It did create a big amount of interest. It did work, and people wanted to hear this story, so obviously it did good at that time. But when the truth has to come out, the truth has to come out. I can't remember fighting three guys in the schoolyard. I don't know what it's made up from, that's Brendan's story and Brendan will stick to it. What he saw, he saw, but I can't remember doing it. I was thinking about some of my school days and I hardly ever got into any fights at school, in primary or comprehensive. Never. In the infants, there was maybe a few little tangles, but that was only as an infant. Obviously at seven or eight, you're going to get into a little bit but ... At that age, of course, fights are over anything. You can have a little kid looking at you, and you're thinking, 'What is he looking at?' and you could walk over, or he could walk over and you could bump into each other and obviously you could start a fight. It was over anything, but I definitely remember most of my school days and I hardly ever got into trouble. No fights or anything. I never got excluded, never got expelled.'

We were talking just a month after Naz had taken the world title from Steve Robinson in September 1995 at Cardiff Arms Park where the crowd had chanted, 'Hamed, Hamed. Who the fuck is Hamed?' But far from upsetting Naz, it had spurred him on. He thrived on it, he enjoyed it, and he smiled when he heard those chants. And the punch line – 'Who the fuck is Hamed?' – made him smile most of all. 'They'll soon know who Naseem Hamed is,' he said, and you could tell by his face that he meant it. All that Welsh nationalistic anger – 'Fuck off back to Sheffield', they were shouting – it merely fuelled Naz's venom. Somebody hit Naz on the head with a plastic bottle top on the way to the ring. It wasn't much of an attack, but Naz thought that somebody had gobbed on him, and he didn't like it one little bit. It probably reminded him of Paul, the toilet attendant, and his advice, back in Sheffield. And it wasn't such an odd interpretation. John Ingle, Brendan's son who worked Naz's corner that night, said that he could feel the Robinson fans spitting on the back of his head and jacket on the long walk to the ring. At the time, Naz was saying, 'Steve Robinson is only a stepping stone to me becoming a legend,' but Steve was the people's champion down in Wales, and they didn't like the idea of being walked over, quite literally used as a stepping stone, in this sort of way.

Naz never did have any doubts about the outcome of his world title challenge. He was in Brendan's gym, St Thomas's, in Wincobank the week before the fight with a teeshirt with 'All I have to do is turn up' written on the back. Brendan had forgotten his glasses that day. 'What does that say on his back there?' he asked me.

I read it to him.

'The cheek of the lad. Some call it arrogance, I call it confidence.'

And we all knew how much hard work had gone into building that level of confidence.

And here was Naz now, in his new world. I called for him at some exclusive apartment with soft gold furnishings and delicate, subdued lighting and a bulky, suspicious-looking security man sitting behind a desk. We set off in a large black Mercedes with darkened windows and drove around the streets of Mayfair calling in to a few trendy cafés and bars 'for a drink', he said, but really it was so that I could gauge his new fame. It was for me to see who he had become. 'All right, Naz, my man,' they shouted. 'How are you?'

And I looked at their faces, male and female, to see this undisguised awe in their expressions, and Naz just smiled back.

'I'm just chillin' tonight,' he said back, as he swaggered, and that's the only word for it, as he swaggered into one bar and then another. We never did get a drink, he said that each bar was too crowded or too smoky or too quiet, but we did make a lot of entrances that night.

'What's it like, Geoffrey,' he asked me, 'to be out with someone so cool?' He made the 'oo' sound go on for ever. He was lapping it all up.

I assumed that he was joking or being slightly ironic. 'Very nice,' I replied regardless, in an uptight, non-chillin' sort of way.

We went back to my hotel room and sat on the edge of my bed because the room was too small to contain two chairs, and I asked him about the Robinson fight and what it was like to be the champion of the world, and he talked with all of the confidence and authority of a real world champion. In truth, I suppose that I wanted to attempt to unpick a few psychological threads from this great cloak he now covered himself in, to get some hint as to what, if anything, lay below this heavy mantle of projected self-belief, these volumes of words and those quite humourless predictions. What did it all hide? Or was all this confidence and self-belief just layers of an onion, densely packed all the way to the core? What was the outcome of all of those years of dedicated training? What had he become?

I began by asking him whether there was ever any doubt in his mind that he might beat Steve Robinson in Cardiff that night.

'No, from day one I knew I was going to be in there with the perfect style. I knew basically that he was there to be taken by a flamboyant twenty-one-year-old who was ambitious and strong at punching out. It was tailor-made for me, and on the night of the fight I showed it. There was quite a bit of animosity in the crowd. Somebody spat on me on the way to the ring, but I held my head up high. I just walked in there and took it off him.'

I wanted to know how important the psychological battle before the fight was. When does the battle really commence between two fighters? Is it at the press conference? Or even before that?

He smiled at my question; he sensed a professional interest on my part. 'I showed him in three or four press conferences before the fight that I was definitely there to take his title. He made out that he was the strongest featherweight in the world and that he had boxed the likes of Colin Macmillan. Everybody said that he was going to lose on other occasions, and he came back. But I wanted him to know that this time it would be different.'

I asked if Robinson had anything in his psychological armoury to frighten Naz at all? Was there anything that he could have done to intimidate him?

'There was nothing whatsoever he could have done. I knew that the only thing that Steve had was a good defence. A good fighter has to break that defence up and take him out. I controlled the fight, I dominated it. I was so happy, I was smiling, I was talking. I did everything I wanted to do.'

What was he saying to him during the fight itself?

'He turned round to me in past press conferences and said that he was the strongest featherweight in the world. I was telling him in the fight, "You're not the strongest, Steve", and hitting him so hard that he couldn't understand it. So mentally I was breaking him up. Physically it was happening at the same time, and he just fell to pieces at the end of it. I caught him with one clean left hook, which was the last shot of the fight. This shot was so perfectly timed that his legs just gave way.'

John Ingle had told me that he could tell by looking at Steve Robinson at the weigh-in for the fight that he had already lost the psychological battle. I wanted to know if Naz could sense that as well?

'I could sense it all right. I'd seen the look in his eyes. But I also said to him, "If we're both confident that we can beat each other, then we should put both purses in one pot and let the winner take all." So Steve started thinking about this, and he was mumbling a little bit, but then he said, "Well I'll leave it to my manager", and I knew straight away that he'd gone. I didn't even have to look in his eyes after that.'

But had *he* ever been frightened before a fight?

'No, I've never been frightened before a fight. You should see me in the changing-room beforehand – I pack it out with my friends, and then slam some music on, whatever music I'm into – rag or jungle, swing or soul, hip-hop, rap, whatever it is, whatever my mood desires before the fight. We'll be having a great laugh, and I mean a great laugh. I'm talking about laughing, giggling, cracking jokes. This is five minutes before the fight. As long as I've got bandaged up and oiled up, I'm happy and ready to go. As soon as they say, "The television is ready, you're on", I become a different person. I'm blind to all the guys around me then, and that's it, everything finishes. I'm ready to walk out and I'm ready to do the business. There is nothing else in my mind except to go out, blank everything out, get into that ring in style, and take an opponent apart in style.'

I then asked him when he was last frightened of *anything*.

'To tell you the truth, I hardly ever get frightened as in "frightened". I could never say that fear really gets to me. I'm not one of those fighters like Nigel Benn who says "I thrive on fear". I walk through fear. It's not one of those things that happens to me. I'm one of those very confident people who just forgets about fear, and gives it to somebody else. I get into that ring and I walk round, I hear my music and then I start buzzing.'

This has always struck me as being a little odd. Even Muhammad Ali had confessed to being truly afraid in the fight game, on at least one occasion – before his first fight with Sonny Liston. 'That's the only time I was ever scared in the ring. Sonny Liston. First time. First round. Said he was gonna kill me.' And then there was Floyd Patterson, who talked freely about his fear, more freely perhaps than any other boxer in the history of the sport; not necessarily the fear of getting hurt in the ring but the fear of losing a fight. 'A prizefighter who gets knocked out or is badly outclassed suffers in a way he will never forget. He is beaten under the bright lights in front of thousands of witnesses who curse him and spit at him ... The losing fighter loses more than just his pride and the fight; he loses part of his future. He is one step closer to the slum he came from.'

But Naz said that none of this applied to him. He 'forgets' about fear and 'gives it to somebody else', as if it were a counterfeit note that could be passed on. He concentrates on the music as his focus to help him forget the fear. How important was the music? I asked him for some clarification of this.

'The music is very important. It's got to give me a buzz. It always does in my fights. At the Robinson fight, all of the crowd were shouting for him. The crowd were chanting, "Hamed, Hamed. Who the fuck is Hamed?" And I thought to myself, "Wicked, I can't believe this. They'll find out who Hamed is after the fight."'

Naz confessed that he had borrowed the tune for his entrance, 'Hot Stepper', and the front flip over the ropes from Ryan Rhodes. These great trademarks of the star came from his younger acquaintance. I asked what he thought that trademark front flip does to his opponents. This flip was part of the routine that Brendan made all his boxers practise in the ring, part of the confidence-building exercises. But surely, it must be very effective in a competitive fight. I thought of David Remnick's description of how Floyd Patterson entered the ring in 1962 to defend his World Heavyweight Title against the challenger Sonny Liston in his classic book *King of the World*. 'He bent through the ropes and into the ring, but he did it stealthily, nervously, with quick glances all around, like a thief climbing in a window on the night he knows he will be arrested at last. He was in a terrible state. His eyes flicked around the ring. Rarely had fear been so visible in a fighter's face.' Brendan always knew that the way a boxer entered the ring could leak a lot of information about his internal emotional state. The flip over the ropes was the greatest mask of them all. The fighter could be churning up inside and his opponent would never see it. Plus, it required concentration and hours of practice to get it right. It distracted the fighter himself from what was going on inside.

Naz recognised its importance. 'Well, if somebody did it to me,

I'd think, "Well, that is a confident man. I just hope he can back it up."'

I asked about his boxing heroes. Who was the greatest fighter of all time?

'Muhammad Ali. His style, his charisma, how he got on, how he became a national figure, a world figure, what he did to the sport in general. Not just for boxing, but for all sport. I think he's been a credit to sport, not just boxing. I think he's made sport what it is today.'

I was, therefore, interested to know how he felt when he saw clips of Muhammad Ali today, with Parkinson's disease.

'Well, obviously it is very sad what's happened to him. I do feel for him, but I can honestly say to myself that I know for a fact that his Parkinson's disease never came from boxing. I think he got Parkinson's disease because God gave it to him. I think what is written for a man is written. I think that it only happened to him just to show people that he was human, that he was the same as everybody else. So I reckon that it was just written to him from God.'

So did Naz think that everything that had happened to *him* so far had been written by God?

'Yes, definitely. I've got so much belief in God, and I think God's got so much belief in me. The way I've been brought up – I've had the best upbringing a child could have, and I take my hat off to my mum and dad so much for the upbringing I've had. I am religious, but I like always to keep my religion personal and private to myself. I think religion is a personal thing. But I think God has given me such a gift.'

Although Naz had never lost as a professional at that time, he did lose as an amateur. So what exactly happened?

'I lost about five or six times as an amateur, but I could definitely say to myself that I never walked out of that ring a loser when I'd lost. I always knew in my heart that I'd won. I only lost because the judges didn't like my style and they went against me. I never really lost a fight as an amateur, and the guys that I did lose to, when I boxed them again, I beat them easy. But there was one lad who beat me and then retired at twelve. I can't remember his name. I was only about eleven. But I never stopped smiling. They couldn't understand it. They'd say, "Why is he actually smiling when he's lost? Isn't there any way we can get this guy down?" This is what they were thinking. I'd be looking at them, knowing what they were thinking, and I'd be smiling at them. I'd walk out of that ring smiling because that was the best thing to do.'

Because it would have been a sign of weakness not to?

'Exactly. It would have been a sign of weakness. I knew that, even at the age of eleven. When I got back into the changing-rooms, I'd still be smiling and laughing because I knew that I'd won. It didn't really affect me in any way, but it did dishearten a lot of kids, and a lot of kids did retire because they were getting robbed in decisions.'

I asked him how he might cope with defeat today?

'How would I cope with it? I would cope very well with it because I remember losing as an amateur. There are guys who lose and they're a flop after that. They can't take it. Mentally they can't be very strong. If I ever lost, I'd just come straight back. I'd let nothing dishearten me. Remember, I've been blessed by God. I walk through fear.'

Brendan had obviously done a good job with a seven-year-old and his intensive physical and mental routines. This was powerful stuff. And I watched Naz's career with interest almost as much because of his psychological power as because of any physical skill. I have another image of Naz in my head, though, from a few years later. Before the fight against Billy Hardy in Manchester, I bumped into Brendan and Naz in the steam room in the Livingwell leisure club in Quay Street in Manchester. I didn't know they were going to be there; I just walked in on them. They were pleased to see me. Naz was stretched out on the bench as Brendan was giving him a rub down. I sat across from them watching Brendan work his way across Naz's back, down his thighs, kneading the toned flesh. There was such a level of intimacy between the trainer and the fighter that I almost felt like leaving. It was like walking in on a couple. That's the only way that I can describe it. They were like a couple. The fact that I had just turned up made it seem more significant to me because I had to imagine this real intimacy between them going on all the time, when the observers and the journalists weren't there. Naz was very relaxed before that fight. The only thing concerning him, I learned later, was that the early pay-per-view sales, of which he was receiving a proportion, were low. But there was a level of animosity in the fight because Hardy had called him a kid, like Freddy Cruz had done before him. Naz's opponents were made to pay for cracks like that. The fight against Hardy lasted ninety-three seconds. Naz still had the aggression. Naz's first full punch broke Hardy's nose, and the veteran went down for a count of seven. A left hook then put him down for a six count. The image that the world remembers is of Hardy's legs rolling right back with him. The fight was stopped half-way through the first round. It was a brutal, short, sharp contest, or rather a brutal no-contest. But when I remember this time in Naz's career, it is that image in the steam room that springs to mind first, that intimacy between fighter and trainer. When they split up so acrimoniously after their seventeen years together, I always thought about that night in the steam room and felt very sad.

And the wins kept coming after Billy Hardy, even without Brendan it seemed, but you wondered for how long sometimes. And Naz still had his critics, but he still answered them. As Clinton Van Der Berg wrote in the *Sunday Times*, 'Although Hamed had won thirty-three fights in a row, most of them by devastating knock-out, criticism had attended almost every success. Too old, too slow, too small, said the naysayers of his opponents. Give him a live one like Bungu, Barrera or Morales.'

He got Vuyani Bungu first. The South African Vuyani Bungu had been knocked down just once in thirty-nine fights over a thirteen-year period and had defended his world title thirteen times. He was a hardened veteran, but some said he was getting close to the end of his career. He fought Naz in London's Olympia Arena, a venue that had once housed Bertram Mills' Circus. An appropriate venue, some of Naz's critics were saying, because Naz was responsible for bringing an element of circus to the boxing ring. Naz arrived on a magic carpet (probably not one of Paul Eyre's carpets that night but a carpet nonetheless) high in the air. All those years of sitting on the edge of the ring in St Thomas's and planning the great entrance on the magic carpet had been realised. Somebody must have worked out how to get him down off the carpet at last. Naz somersaulted over the ropes and swaggered across the ring like he had been taught to do. Years of practice had gone into this with Naz and all the waifs and strays and YTS boys and girls in Brendan's unique confidence-building exercise. Bungu, on the other hand, was led to the ring by an

Imbongi whose rattling and shouting seemed to amuse the VIPs and high rollers of London. But Bungu's years of experience had not prepared him for Naz, leaning forward, ducking down, with his hands down, switching stances, keeping his opponent guessing, taunting him, bewildering him with his unorthodox style and his power, and finally taking him out with a left to the jaw in the fourth round. As one writer put it, 'For Prince Naseem Hamed, boxing is one part agility, one part power and one part psychological warfare.' Bungu fell for each of these components in turn, and was counted out for the first time in his career. And how did Naz react to this great win in front of the world's media?

'Bungu's been unbeaten in eight years. What have you got to say now after all the shite that's been flung around?'

Bungu, on the other hand, made a dignified exit. He made no excuses but said quite simply, 'I don't know what to say. I was beaten by the better man.' He retired a month later.

Naz's next fight against the American Augie Sanchez in August 2000 won him few favours. After the fight Seth Abraham, Senior Vice-President of American cable television network Home Box Office, who was broadcasting Naz's fights in the States, publicly expressed his frustration at the quality of some of Naz's recent opponents. He had urged Riath, Naz's brother and business manager, to throw a little more caution to the wind. His words obviously hit home, and a match against Marco Antonio Barrera was the outcome. At stake was the International Boxing Organisation (IBO) Featherweight Championship, but, of course, it was more than that. At stake was Naz's whole boxing reputation. Was Naz a truly great champion? This was going to be the ultimate test because everybody knew that Barrera himself was a great fighter. He was the genuine article. A hush descended over Wincobank and all of Sheffield. Brendan, now the abandoned and sometimes understandably bitter trainer, said that it would be an enormous test for Naz. And you could see in his face that he was happy about this.

I thought that I detected a slight change in Naz's demeanour in the run-up to this fight. But this might just be with the benefit of hindsight. In every interview that I ever conducted with him, he always said that he wanted to be the 'greatest', just like his idol, Muhammad Ali. But now he had tempered this by saying that he wanted to be 'one of the greatest'. It might have looked like a small linguistic variation on the same basic theme, but I thought at that precise moment that it might have been indicative of something altogether more profound. It seemed like a broader view, a less egocentric view, a hint of some maturity beyond the brash talk that had characterised him up to this point. Or perhaps the very first sign of uncertainty in Naz that I had ever detected.

Naz understood that this was the fight that would ensure that he got the recognition and the respect that he craved in the States, if he could do what was expected of him, that is. You still have to do the business, no matter who you are, that's the beauty of boxing. What did Naz say at the time? 'Getting inside that ring with that bell ringing is the loneliest place in the world.'

As I've already explained, Naz starts the fight long before he gets to the ring. For him, the psychological battle is well under way before he somersaults over those ropes. The weigh-in would be a crucial part. Naz would have been looking at Barrera's face for those micro-expressions of fear and uncertainty. Don't ask Naz to describe them. He can't do this in any detail, but he knows what he's looking for all right. He's seen those fleeting expressions on many of his opponents' faces on the eve of battles like this one. They are gone in the blink of an eye but Naz can clock them. I've seen him do it live. I sometimes need a video playback facility to see the same things, and I'm supposed to be the trained observer. Then, when he senses this fear, which few others can see, he goes in for the kill.

But perhaps he didn't see them before the Barrera fight; there is always that possibility, perhaps he just didn't see them with Barrera. And where would that have left Naz, up against an opponent who wasn't beaten before he had even started, who wasn't going to be bullied in the ring by Naz? I watched Barrera's face on my video. I looked for those small signals of apprehension and fear and saw nothing of the kind. I listened to his words, 'With all this talk about how he is going to knock me out, and all the things he's been saying, tell him to get himself prepared well because after this fight, he'll be dreaming of Marco Antonio Barrera.' There was something very manly in this, not over the top, not hysterical like some fighters, just quietly confident, just warning Naz to get well prepared, like a man talking to a man. I saw nothing leaking from his facial expression except perhaps brief signs of positive emotion, of expectation perhaps.

I watched films of Barrera and Naz training for the fight. Naz was training for six weeks in a luxury villa in Palm Springs that had once belonged to Bing Crosby. Barrera was training in a public gym in the hills in California. There was something awfully significant about this. Naz had really taken off, he was a superstar now, he was a friend of Michael Jackson, a buddy of Robbie Williams. He had left Brendan Ingle and Mick 'The Bomb' Mills flogging Viagra outside a toilet in a nightclub in Sheffield and Jimmy the moneylender with the big purple welts on his arms. He had left the gym with the wooden floor where it had all started, marked out in strange circles and shapes to teach the science of boxing, well behind. He didn't need any of this any more. He was living the life of luxury now. I can remember him using this phrase from years ago. 'Brendan,' he would say, 'we'll be living the life of luxury one day.' And so Naz was, he and his brothers and his fitness trainer and his physiotherapist and his nutritionist and his coach. A life of luxury is fine, as long as you never forget what a boxer is paid to do in that, the loneliest place in the world. He has to conquer pain, with both mind and body, to feel that pain, to take that pain, and then to control every single cell of his being to stop that pain being revealed, to kill any expression that might tell his opponent exactly how he feels at that precise moment in time. He has to be able to extricate himself from those soft, luxurious surroundings and do all that.

Naz sounded confident enough. Asked whether it was going to be a tough fight, he replied, 'Yeah, it seems to be a very, very tough fight on paper, but I'm very, very confident, cool, calm and collected that I will dispose of my opponent. I will take him out in style.' You could imagine why he was feeling confident because in many ways Barrera seemed to be tailor-made for Naz, with his tendency to push forward throughout his fifty-five professional fights straight into those big punches of Naz's, coming in from either side. That is the way the reasoning would have gone.

But there was always something about the surroundings that suggested that things might not turn out according to plan. The surroundings seemed to hint at this new aspiration for an easier life by Naz, for a life without pain, for a life away from the likes of a famous Mexican fighter preparing himself in an ordinary public gym. Maybe it was the private jet to take Naz's entourage to Las Vegas. Maybe it was Naz's insistence on flying his private hairdresser in from Los Angeles for the pre-fight trim. Maybe it was that Naz picked green goatskin gloves because 'goatskin gloves are the best gloves to taste. They've got the best taste in the world when it comes to getting smashed in the face. And I want green because green is the Muslim colour.' Or maybe it was the way that he changed his mind about the green goatskin gloves at the last minute and demanded the yellow gloves instead, the gloves that Barrera had already selected. Maybe it was his brother Riath witnessing all the hassle and all the expense of sending someone all the way to Mexico to monitor and oversee the goatskin gloves being made and then commenting that 'But now he's a prince and whatever the Prince wants, the Prince will get.' Maybe it was that last sentence going over and over again in my head that got me worried.

I just couldn't imagine Brendan tolerating any of this. It would have been a different life of luxury if he had been there. There would have been no private jet and no special hairdresser flown in the night before and no loss of focus over a pair of gloves, that's for sure. For the last two weeks of training, Naz was joined by his new trainer Emanuel Steward who watched over sparring sessions between Naz and two Mexican boxers, brought in to reflect Barrera's particular fighting style. By all accounts, Steward wasn't impressed with what he saw; Naz's punching was wide and poorly controlled. Steward later complained that Naz had only sparred a total of twelve rounds in preparation for the fight. The Hamed entourage flew on to Las Vegas by private plane. Naz's wife Alicia and their two sons arrived the night before the big fight, but as custom dictates they spent the night apart from Naz. Naz said that he was ready to do the business – and what business that was. He was getting six and a half million dollars for this fight.

But as John Rawling wrote in the *Guardian*, 'From the moment Barrera and Hamed arrived at the arena in weather more Manchester than Nevada, it was clear that the occasion carried a hint of the unexpected. And once Hamed's preposterously overblown ring walk was over, it was obvious that Barrera was in no mood to be upset by the enormity of the event.'

Naz's ring walk was something special. He was called to the

ring by a mullah and he had 'Islam' written on the back of his shorts. HBO, who were broadcasting the fight in the United States, were apparently not at all keen on this display of Naz's religious heritage. His entrance was forty-five minutes behind schedule because he felt uncomfortable with his gloves. He abandoned his usual somersault into the ring. I could feel my nervousness and my son's when I saw this. I think that I knew then what was going to happen. That flip was just too important to all the lads from Wincobank; it was part of their psychology and Brendan's. It was only ever abandoned in very special circumstances, to get an extra edge, and that's not why it happened that night. Once Naz was in the ring the commentator said, 'To honour his father and family heritage, he has requested to say a few words.' A translation of what Naz said is 'Allah is the greatest, Allah you are the only God. Mohammed is your messenger, peace be upon him.'

The pattern of the fight was fixed in the early rounds, with Naz looking surprisingly clumsy as he tried to land one of his classic power shots and being punished by Barrera throwing three-punch combinations. Naz looked awkward. He wrestled Barrera to the floor in the second round. It reminded you of Herol Graham at his worst, but any messy wrestling by Naz in this fight was met with a foul back again. Barrera was slipping and blocking Naz's punches, and he had a strong, durable chin. Naz's unguarded style did not work against Barrera's pace and strength. Rather than charging forward and creating openings for Naz, Barrera stood his ground and kept his guard up. His longer reach enabled him to attack Naz without seriously exposing himself. Perhaps even worse from a psychological perspective, Naz's taunting made no impression on Barrera. Whilst other fighters had seen an infuriatingly untouchable opponent, Barrera saw only an unguarded chin, which he attacked repeatedly. It was Barrera who toyed with his opponent and Naz who was lured forward. Naz's team decided in the later rounds that the only way to win the match was with a knock-out, but Barrera's guard was too good for him.

Kevin Mitchell wrote in the *Observer*, 'Hamed rarely inconvenienced his opponent. He ran out of ideas after a poor start and only occasionally landed blows of any hurtful consequence. Barrera took Hamed's boxing away from him, upsetting his rhythm by refusing to accommodate him in the close-quarters showdown most of us had expected.' After twelve rounds, the judges unanimously decided that Barrera was the winner. It was a crushing defeat. Barrera took the IBO title, and Naz's long winning run was over. But much more importantly, Naz's cloak of invincibility had been stripped from him, and we all stared long and hard at this small, bruised Arab man in front of us with nothing left to hide behind.

I had watched my son's face at the end of the fight. He didn't understand how Naz could have lost. He also couldn't comprehend the fatalism that started to emerge in Naz's interviews after the defeat, in a man who had always seemed so confident, so in control of his own destiny. He had always said that he wanted to see Naz knocked down, roughed up a bit, hurt. But he didn't want to see him lose. There was something in Naz's success that was almost iconic for young people. My son asked me if I knew it was going to happen, as if this might help. I explained to him that Naz probably had trouble making the weight. I told him that I always thought that Naz had never been the same fighter since he left Brendan's gym. I told him that Naz and Brendan once went through everything together, and that it must be tougher on your own.

I suppose that I was shocked by Naz's defeat, as if I had been suckered by his talk, as if I had not really heard the critics who had argued that somebody with such a weak defence could never be considered a true boxing great. Wayne McCullough from my native Belfast, who himself had been beaten by Naz, commented that 'Before the fight, I said Naz was not the man he was when he was with Brendan Ingle, that he was not as elusive as he was. But I thought his power would sort Barrera out. It was incredible.'

But I was even more shocked by Naz's reaction to his defeat. He said after the fight, quite simply, 'Well, that's just the way it goes ... I tried so hard to knock him out, it's not that I relied on that power, it's just that I wanted to knock him out so bad. I'd trained so hard. And it happened. I suppose it's just the way it's written.'

There was real fatalism in his understanding of the outcome of the fight, as if he couldn't alter or change his own destiny, and with that fatalism went a certain emotional neutrality. He wasn't mad or angry, and he certainly didn't seem desperate to get back into the ring. He almost seemed indifferent to the whole thing. 'I'm nowhere near as sad as I thought I would be, simply because the kid won the fight, and if that's what's written for me from Allah, it's written. I give him the fight, basically, not that I give him, he won the fight, he won the fight clearly in my eyes. I didn't box to my best ability. I would honestly say that credit is due to him, and I feel that I'll be back. What more can I say?'

But there was no call for a rematch. Naz, as Kevin Mitchell in the *Observer* starkly put it, just walked away from Las Vegas and from boxing:

Now, like a lonely, neglected old relative, he trains in solitude at his tiny gym in Sheffield, where there is a small ring and a shower for one. The rest of the time he plays golf – occasionally with estranged friends from his fifteen years at Ingle's windswept academy. Details about contracts and earnings have always been closely guarded secrets. It is thought Naz has made £30 million from the ring, but the truth is difficult to detect and is certainly not contained anywhere in Riath's assertion that his little brother, a fallen idol at just twenty-six, is 'happy'.

Nabeel, another of Naz's brothers, commented acidly, 'Let's hope England likes him a bit more now he's lost.' But you doubted it somehow. The recriminations were also now flying. His trainer Emanuel Steward was reported to say that he didn't like the way things had gone in training at all. 'It was all about stroking his ego. He surrounds himself with people who tell him exactly what he wants to hear. When I asked them if they watched Barrera's fight with Jesus Salud, they said, "We don't need to see that fight. We got others." They showed him old tapes where Barrera wasn't looking so good to build Naz's confidence. Then it was sixty-five thousand dollars a month for Bing Crosby's old house in Rancho Mirage. What's that got to do with boxing?'

I wanted to discover the truth about how Naz felt for myself. After all, he had told me he would cope well with defeat, but what was it really like now that it had finally happened? What had happened to him psychologically with this defeat? I needed to finish my psychological story. So I rang Naz's press agent for an interview. I told her who I was and how I had written about

Naz from the very beginning of his career. I told her that I was the first to do a major piece on him. 'I'm sorry,' she said eventually, 'Naz isn't talking to anybody, no matter who you are.'

I rang eight times in all, over weeks and then months, each call a little more embarrassing than the last. There was no positive response to any of the calls. Naz, it seemed, had just disappeared. Brendan kept ringing me every Sunday regardless. 'He's just a poor little rich kid now,' said Brendan. 'He's been ringing up Johnny and the other lads from the gym; he wants to be their pal again. But they don't really want to know him.' Brendan seemed happy at their response.

'Do you know something?' said Brendan. 'Kevin Mitchell from the *Observer* rang me the other day and he asked me if Naz were to beg me to train him again, what would I do? And I says to Kevin, "I'll tell you what I'd do, I'd say no frigging way." Not after what he's done to me. It's not just about money, it's that he killed our dream. I always said that he was going to be bigger than Muhammad Ali. I spent eighteen years with him convincing him of that. I spent eighteen years, day in day out, morning, noon and night, building that dream in his head. He was going to be bigger than Muhammad Ali, greater than the greatest man on the planet and all of this in a kid from Wincobank with sticky-out ears and a big nose. That was the dream, and Naz took all that away from me. Do you think I could go back? No way,' said Brendan, 'no way.'

And even though he was at the other end of a phone line, I could picture his face, and I can tell you that it had a look of the most terrible sadness imaginable.

NINE

Journalists always said that Brendan's blarney was important in Naz's early career. But this was a bit more than the blarney that I had witnessed at first hand. There was something profoundly psychological in Brendan's approach. Something unique and different and true had been achieved in this Northern city neglected by a central government that seemed not to care about its citizens. This was concrete evidence of what people could accomplish when they worked together with the kind of dedication that the rest of us cannot even imagine let alone emulate, a micro-society of souls striving for something beyond the individual. And when money, greed and the need for a reattribution of the origin of their success finally drove them apart, that fine, fragile thread of world-class success seemed even more dazzling and beautiful to the naked eye.

I could see my son looking around at the other VIPs at the Johnny Nelson fight, but really he was looking for the Prince himself, the boxer who had connected with his generation, the embodiment of success, fame and money, like a pop star or a film idol. And okay, he had one flop behind him now, but he still had that aura around him that marked him out to his young fans. But it was the actual process that my son needed to see, the process that he and Brendan had gone through. That was where the magic lay, and my son had missed it all, as had all the others who had come to see the star, fully formed and radiant in the full glow of the media. I felt almost privileged for a second that I had been in Sheffield at the right moment, with time on my hands, to witness the whole thing and to say, 'I was there. I know what really happened.'

I looked around at the other VIPs at Johnny Nelson's fight. A WBO official sat in the row in front with black boot-polish hair. He was talking to an MC, the one with the very familiar face from the television. The official had thick gold jewellery clanking on his wrists. Hair like that on a middle-aged man, jewellery like that on a man with a lined face had nothing to say to my son. Two boxers talked each other up in the ring. I couldn't see who they were. They were over at the far side in the glare of the cameras. 'I've got four belts here,' one said.

'A few more fights, and you'll bring more to the table,' the other replied.

Or was it the same one? Their voices sounded the same from where I was sitting. Just hungry voices, but they sounded big. They were men who were going to be big names one way or another.

I'm interested in the construction of reputation in this kind of world: how you get it, how you hang on to it, and how you market it when you're never going to be the undisputed champion of the world. None of this is that easy, no matter what they tell you. I had recently been to see somebody else with a big reputation to see just how this other process worked. He wasn't what you might call world class, but he was still making money out of what he had got, which, in his case, was to be certified criminally insane.

It was a sell-out. I was just too late. Pete, the manager of the club, looked me up and down. 'No tickets left. Sorry.' He watched my expression drop slowly to the floor. 'But I'll tell you what, I'll squeeze you onto the top table with Mad Frankie and the comedian. How about that?' We were standing in Pinegrove Country Club in Stannington, Sheffield, a country club 'for the ordinary working man', Pete had explained. A place where Naz used to come for years to have saunas and to play on the fruit machines. It was launching its series of 'Gentlemen's Evenings' with Mad Frankie Fraser. 'A man who needs no introduction, really,' said Pete. 'Even though he's never been to Sheffield before. But the Krays, Jack 'The Hat' McVitie, Mad Frankie. He's a bit of all our lives.'

I was told to get there early, so I found myself in the foyer of the club making small concentric circles around the floor, the way that you do when you're on your own and waiting. There was me and this short, roundish man with a perm, who was wearing a yellow jacket with a matching Bart Simpson tie. The punters were arriving in good time. In walked Glyn Rhodes, 'more professional comebacks than Frank Sinatra', and some of the lads from his gym, the boxers marked out by their lean, mean faces, followed by the friends and hangers-on, who were almost flabby-faced by comparison. I hadn't seen some of the boxers for a few years, but they all nodded. Then in came some older businessmen, some with blotchy skin and paunches. 'The corporate sector,' said Pete, who had joined me. Then groups of young men in their early twenties, laughing and pushing each other. Up here for a nobble.

Then I saw him. A small, dapper man, the build of a bantamweight still in training. He was instantly recognisable, even though I had claimed that I had no idea what he actually looked like. The man in the yellow jacket recognised him, as well. 'Hello, Frank. I'm the comedian tonight. I've never worked with you before, but I'm really looking forward to it.' Frank shook his hand. Mad Frank paused for some photographs, so I followed the comedian to the top table. We sat in silence for a few minutes, just the two of us. So I asked him if he was nervous, just to break the ice. 'No,' he said, shaking his head. 'I've been in this game far too long. I used to be on *Tiswas* and *The Comedians*. You remember them, don't you?'

I told him that I intended to write about the evening, so he asked me to write his name down, and I printed it carefully in my notebook. The only problem was that I misheard it as 'Ian Sludge-Sleaze'. I thought that it was a curious name, but I wrote it anyway. 'No, no, no,' he said. 'It's "Ian Sludge Lees", not "Sludge-Sleaze". "Sludge" is in quotes, like Jim "Nick, Nick" Davidson.'

'Or "Mad" Frankie Fraser,' I added. But the comedian didn't laugh.

Mad Frank and his minder took their seats beside us. Frank started on his first course, and I was mesmerised by how he ate. It was so delicate. A few of the punters at the tables in front of us threw quick glances his way, but they were glances of curiosity, fleeting, information-collecting glances that were not meant to catch his eye.

I asked Sludge whether he would be telling any jokes about

Mad Frankie that night. 'No,' he answered almost in a whisper. 'I sometimes kick off with a few jokes about the main speaker, but not tonight. Tonight, Gary Glitter's going to get the hammering. Here's one for you. What's silver and sticks out of a pram? ... Gary Glitter's ass.'

I glanced over at Mad Frankie but he was still in a world of his own. 'I'm sure that you could get Frank into a joke, if you tried,' I suggested. 'What about him that time with the axe? That could be very visual.'

'You leave the jokes to me,' said Sludge, turning slightly away, as if he wasn't sure what side the crazy man was sitting on. The boxers were passing a dainty blue mobile phone amongst themselves. I pointed this out to Sludge. Some good observational humour. Sludge grimaced again.

It was getting noisier in the room, the noise of expectation. There was a lot of laughter coming from the table just in front of us. 'They all want to be the comedian when they're pissed,' said Sludge. 'They all think they can do my fucking job.' I watched them glance at Mad Frankie in that almost curious way, and I thought that the same was probably true there as well. After a few drinks, some of them might think that they had what it takes to be that famous, that hard.

'Hey,' shouted Glyn from the next table. He beckoned me over and tossed a pile of photographs onto the table. It was Glyn and a friend, both grinning away, with their fists posed below the chin of a round-faced black guy with goggly eyes. A man past his prime. 'What do you think?' asked Glyn. I flicked quickly through the pack until I eventually recognised him.

'He's put on some weight,' I said cautiously. Marvellous Marvin Hagler and Mad Frank, both faces to be seen with. But why exactly? I asked one of Glyn's friends why he was there.

'I've only come for the stripper,' he said. With the background noise, I thought he said 'slipper'. I started to write down 'slipper'. 'He's not the fucking comedian is he, Glyn?' he asked.

I returned to the top table. To get things going, the MC asked us to toss two quid into a champagne bucket 'for a good cause' for a quiz about Mad Frank's life. We were given sheets of paper with 'true' and 'false' written on them. The prize was a copy of Mad Frank's book, twenty-four cans of lager and a cassette player. I decided this was going to be easy. I was just going to watch Mad

Frank's reactions, like a thousand police officers before me. His body language would tell me the answers. I watched him surreptitiously to get some baseline information about his behaviour. He was gesturing delicately as he spoke to Sludge. He neatly cupped his hands and then parted them to illustrate some point before returning them to the cupped position again. It was a gentle movement made with quite delicate hands, at odds with that nose, which was fractured, cracked and bent, a nose that hinted at an altogether different personal history.

We all had to stand for the quiz. When you got an answer wrong, you had to sit down.

'The first question is . . .' began the MC, '. . . is it true that Mad Frankie Fraser has been certified insane three times?'

I watched Frankie smile quietly with pleasure. I held up my bit of paper with 'true' printed on it.

'That is true!' said the MC. 'Frankie Fraser has been certified insane a total of three times.'

I watched Sludge bite his lip. Perhaps he was thinking of working Frankie into a gag, but was now having second thoughts.

'Is it true', continued the MC, 'that Mad Frankie Fraser has served forty-two years in prison?'

I knew this one. I didn't even have to look at Frankie – Pete had told me. I was right.

'Is it true', asked the MC, 'that once, when Frankie was released from prison, he was met by his son driving a Bentley?'

I looked at Mad Frankie again. His eyes were reliving the moment. He was smiling again – happy days. I confidently held up 'true'.

'False,' said the MC. 'His son met him in a Roller.'

Mad Frank laughed even more.

'Is it true that Mad Frankie has been shot in the head?'

Even though I was out of the game, I wanted to play along. I was looking for a sign in his face, a glimmer of the horror if indeed it were true. But there was just that quiet laugh again. I thought that it must be false, but I was wrong. These questions were sorting out the men from the boys all right. One man eventually won the armful of lager and got to shake Mad Frankie's hand.

We were on the main course. Waitresses were hovering behind us. Sludge was looking worried. He saw my look of concern. 'I had a load of chicken chasseur tipped over this jacket the first time I wore it,' he said. 'You have to be on your toes at functions like this.'

I leaned across the frightened Sludge to Mad Frankie and introduced myself.

'Ah, you're Irish,' said Frank. 'My mother was Irish. You know what they say, don't you? If you meet somebody and their parents or grandparents aren't Irish, then don't bother with them.'

'Why not?' I asked.

'Because they're liars,' said Frank, and we both laughed.

I was having to lean right across Sludge to talk to Frank. 'Why do they call you Mad Frankie?' I asked. I could feel Sludge wince quite distinctly next to me. I watched Frankie's gestures rise in his body. He reminded me of a slim Alfie Bass, for some reason.

'Well,' he said, 'when you've been certified insane three times, it's bound to stick.'

'Nothing to do with a temper, then?' I enquired.

'Oh no,' answered Frank. Why I found this reassuring at the time I don't know.

'What about being shot in the head? What was that like?'

It was an odd sort of question, but he answered politely. 'Well, not so bad,' he said. 'But if I hadn't been drunk, it would have killed me because when the bullet went in I was all over the bleedin' place.'

He asked me where exactly I was from, and when I said Belfast, he told me that he had been to a top IRA man's wedding in Belfast. He had met him inside. Frankie loved Belfast, and we were now getting on great guns. I could hear the conversation from the boxers' table about some boxer with bite marks all over his nose having to take a fight at the last minute. 'Aaaagh,' said Glyn's friend, mimicking the horror.

Meanwhile, Frankie was passing me chocolate liqueurs. 'My girlfriend's mum made the balaclavas for the Great Train Robbery, you know,' he said. 'The eyes weren't level. She got a bit of stick for that, I can tell you. I should have been on that job, but I was red-hot at the time. Red-hot.' He started telling me about all the celebrities he had met, 'Frank Sinatra, Lucky Luciano.'

'Rocky Marciano,' repeated Sludge helpfully.

'No, Lucky Luciano, the Mafia boss,' said Mad Frankie. 'Sinatra

117

always had a thing about gangsters. He was born on the twelfth of December, by the way, and I was born on the thirteenth. He had a thing about birthdays and that always gave us a little bit of a bond.'

'Oh,' said Sludge, confining to memory this little nugget about Old Blue Eyes himself.

Frank's minder got some paper out for him, and together they made some notes. 'In case he forgets,' said the minder. 'He is seventy-six, after all.'

The audience were offered a 'comfort break' before he started. 'That means you can go to the toilet,' said Sludge.

After the break, Frank rose to polite applause. He told us about the life of the criminally insane. The forty-two years inside. The eighteen strokes 'and all the trimmings' on his 'deaf and dumb'. He told us that he preferred the cat-o'-nine-tails because it was across the shoulders. It was more manly than getting it on your bum. 'I did have some laughs in Broadmoor,' he said with a smile. And throughout his speech, he stressed that the violence was only ever directed against other villains and that it was never, ever directed against 'the lovely, ordinary people like you here tonight', except when they were prison officers or prison governors.

He had cut an ear off and flushed it down the loo when he was inside. 'I knew that they'd never find it.' He had 'done' people with an axe. 'I bought that axe in Harrods, I wanted it back.' He had led riots and been on hunger strike. 'I was a glutton for hunger strikes,' he told us. You found yourself waiting for the punch lines. 'The police say that I've killed forty people,' he said. 'Well, I always say that I like even numbers.' That got a big belly laugh.

The table in front were lapping it up. You could hear them repeating the odd word or phrase: 'ear', 'axe', 'shooter', 'Ronnie', 'Reggie', 'even numbers', and shaking their heads in disbelief. From the top table, I could see the faces of the corporate sector, hanging on his every word.

Reggie Kray, we were told, was 'a smashing fellow'. 'He rings me twice a day. When he gets out, he'll be the celebrity of celebrities. That's why they won't release him. He'll be red-hot. Red-hot.'

After he finished to rapturous applause, there was a question-

118

and-answer session. It was remarkably specific at times. 'Who killed Freddie Mills?' asked one.

'Who shot Ginger Marks?' asked another.

'Who's Ginger Marks?' asked Sludge.

'No idea,' I said.

'Who was the hardest man you ever met?' asked a voice from the back.

'Who was the most evilest man you ever met,' said one huge, fat man just in front of us, with saliva all over his fat, wet lips.

It was like somebody else's story. That was the problem. It was hard to think that the man with the impeccable manners did any of this. They queued up for his autograph. 'Mad Frankie Fraser,' he wrote with my pen. He thanked me every time he handed it back. He invited me to his next birthday party. Meanwhile, I noticed that the table in front, with its row of empty champagne bottles in silver buckets, had got noticeably more boisterous, fuelled by all the drink and all the stories from Mad Frank. One young man, who had shed the jacket of his suit, raised his boot slowly to the level of the table and playfully kicked his massive friend on the side of the head. It was more a tap than anything else, just to provoke him. They were both glowering at the next turn, the man with the blond perm. But Sludge, with his tales of Gary Glitter, Eric Cantona and other living legends – except of course Mad Frankie Fraser and the Krays – soon had them eating out of his hand. They were two old pros at work that night.

And then it was time for the punters to pay their ten pounds for their photo with Frank in the foyer. This was a brief interlude to reflect. Glyn tried to help me out. 'It's all about credibility,' said Glyn. 'You and the hardest man there ever was.'

But what about all the nasty, vicious violence? I directed this question to one businessman queuing for his photograph. 'It was all a long time ago,' he said with a nonchalant shrug. 'It's history.'

'So Gary Glitter himself might be back here one day?' I asked, and on that note, and without saying another word, the businessman turned his back on me and left me quite alone. Alone and staring at this long, snaking line of 'lovely, ordinary people' stretched right across the foyer of the club.

TEN

At the Johnny Nelson fight, the MC stood in the middle of the ring, which was bathed in the white glare of the television lights. 'Ladies and gentlemen,' he began. 'Welcome to World Championship Boxing in Sheffield, England.' I nudged my son to indicate to him that this was the big one. He sat forward in his seat. The MC started to introduce the celebrities who were ringside. Most were ex-boxers who were now commentators for Sky, until he got to 'Yorkshire's favourite son'.

'That's Naz,' I said to my son. I still wanted to see him. 'He's here. I knew he would be.'

'Mr . . .'

I turned and winked at Sam.

'. . . Paul Ingle.'

A short, bloated man in a baseball cap with unsteady eyes and slow, deliberate movements got to his feet. I have to confess that I hadn't recognised him. He was on the front row with his girlfriend. Six months or so earlier, he had been knocked unconscious in Sheffield and had been rushed to hospital for emergency surgery to remove a blood clot in his brain. This was the other side of boxing, and it made me feel very odd.

Coincidentally, a few nights earlier, I had talked to the gastroenterologist who had fed Paul intravenously during the weeks he lay unconscious in Hallamshire Hospital where they had operated to relieve the intracranial pressure from the blows to the head. This doctor was my squash partner, but he was also a keen fight fan, and he had talked about the mixture of emotions that he had felt at the time, including his surprise: 'I didn't expect a boxing match to end like this.' His excitement: 'He was a class boxer, and I was going to participate in his recovery.' And his

horror: 'Despite all its skill, grace and beauty, it's all about inflict-
ing damage on your opponent.'

Paul's career was over. The doctor put this quite bluntly. 'His
brain is like an eggshell that's been broken. It can't take any more
damage. It's as simple as that.' And then he had paused and said,
'I never want to see boxing banned but I would like to see
professional boxers wear headguards. It would prolong their
careers, for a start. It was so odd to see a boxer whom you admire
lying in front of you like that. All I remember thinking was that
he wasn't as big as I thought he would be. The television makes
everybody look big somehow. He seemed much more vulnerable
in real life.'

I watched Paul's slow, unsteady movements and thought of
the doctor's words. My son interrupted me. He sounded irritated.
'So Naz isn't here, then?' asked Sam.

'It doesn't look that way, does it?' I replied slightly impatiently.

Johnny Nelson's opponent, Marcello Dominguez, entered the
ring behind his manager and corner man. The corner man had
'Topper' written on the back of his track suit. There was some
writing on the back of Dominguez's shorts, which I always think
is a good sign, as if it might indicate that at some point Dominguez was going to be face down in the ring allowing the cameras
to read the message. Dominguez's eyes were glazed over. He had
a look that would frighten me. His nickname was 'El Gordo' ('The
Big One') but he seemed awfully small in comparison to Nelson,
who had now entered the ring. Dominguez's record was thirty-
two wins, three defeats and one draw. Two of the defeats were
against the German-based Cuban Juan Carlos Gomez, 'The Black
Panther'. But since his last defeat, he had won his last six fights
and was the WBC and the WBO number-one challenger.

I could feel Sam's tension rise as he watched these two men a
few feet above him in the ring. There is something about that
moment which I think is different from any other sport because
you know that in boxing quite literally anything can happen. I
felt my eyes moving of their own accord towards Paul Ingle. I
suppose that I wanted to get some hint as to what he was feeling
at that precise moment. His head was tilted a little back because
he was looking up from the front row. He was looking up at the
fighters with a kind of childish awe. I don't know what I was
expecting – perhaps fear, perhaps a rerun of the trauma, perhaps

a flashbulb memory of great intensity with sadness and anxiety written on his face. I wasn't sure what. I stared over, distracted by his expression, until his girlfriend noticed my intrusive regard and, feeling quite embarrassed, I averted my gaze and looked away towards the action.

I think that the problem with Johnny Nelson is that he is a lovely guy with a classically proportioned body. He seems too nice and too pretty to be a boxer – rather like the young Clay. I am always worried that he is going to get hurt. I feel for him, and it reminds me of those afternoons in front of the black-and-white telly watching the wrestling. Every wrestler in that ring had a role to play: good guy or bad guy, pretty boy or brute. The old women would attack the brutes with their handbags. Johnny would have been a favourite with the old dears. They would have been trying to thump El Gordo, the brute, short and squat with his big, beefy shoulders.

The Argentinian group all stood in the ring with their hands behind their backs. I thought that they were admiring Johnny's physique. That's what it looked like to me, like when Sonny Liston first saw Cassius Clay close up and realised, perhaps for the first time, how tall and athletic-looking he really was. Johnny had his hair in plaits. There were little rolls of fat over Dominguez's shorts. He looked a little plump. You can always tell the ugly brute in boxing. There's always one who doesn't look quite so fit, and you think to yourself, 'I know what role he has to play tonight.' Johnny was hitting his gloves together as if he were trying to work himself up into something resembling rage, but it looked as if it wasn't working. He was chewing gum but managed to display a hint of anger as he was introduced to the audience, but the expression faded quickly, as if the strategy simply hadn't worked.

I suppose that I find the first few seconds of a fight more exciting than any moment in any other sport, when you are just trying to predict who will come forward and who will back off. All human psychology is in those moments. They have studied films of each other. They have watched each other in the flesh. They have tried their little experiments: not blinking right in the face of the other, private wagers, honest threats, sideways glances. They have drawn their conclusions about each other's character. And here they are, ready to put it all to the test, with a little fat bloke with unsteady eyes and unsteady movements in the front row as a reminder of what can happen when you get it wrong. Johnny didn't once look Paul's way during the introductions, although he had clocked one or two faces in the crowd. And then Marcello Dominguez came forward with a slight smile on his face and great haymakers that swished through the air.

'He's come to fight,' said the voice behind my right ear with huge disappointment, and I watched Johnny's expression to see if he were trying to imagine what effect one of those wild, arcing punches might have on him. I think he was imagining it because he looked as if he were trying to suppress his expression of vivid imaginings. Dominguez was here to fight.

Round one ended, and my son and I slumped back in our seats more or less simultaneously. The blonde card-girl was up first. 'Get your tits out,' somebody shouted from the audience but her smile never wavered.

'She's got nipples like raspberries,' the voice behind me said. 'Nipples like big fucking raspberries.'

Round two started with the voice behind me shouting to Johnny to get his jab working and also commenting that somebody was 'a strong bastard'. I knew whom they were referring to. At the end of the round, the black card-girl smiled because she got more wolf whistles than the other girl.

In round three the voice behind me was non-stop. The plastic chairs were too close together for me to look behind comfortably. It was just an anonymous commentary on the fight, a commentary for VIPs like us. 'He's going to take some knocking over this kid. It's the classic: the boxer and the fighter. Johnny is the boxer; the other guy is the fighter. I bet he's knocked a few out with those haymakers. He's a fucking wild man. If I was in the fucking pub, and somebody came at me with those eyes, I'd fuck off out of the place.'

I watched my son, not blinking, taking it all in, and I studied Paul Ingle, with his eyes wide open, tracking across the ring.

Every time Johnny was pinned up against the ropes, they vibrated with the force of Dominguez's forward momentum. Every time a punch landed anywhere, a little cloud of sweat rose into the air.

'Some of the Argie's punches are a bit south of the border. Keep them a bit higher, mate,' shouted the voice in my ear. In the sixth round, Dominguez was deducted a point for a low blow. 'I felt that in my bollocks,' said the voice. 'I really felt that one. Just imagine how it made old Johnny feel up there.'

The end of the sixth could not have come sooner. 'I would give all the money in my wallet for ten seconds with that ring-girl,' said the voice.

'How much have you got in your wallet?' came the voice from beside him.

'I don't fucking care. I'd give the fucking lot.'

It was odd that his friend had not commented on the ten seconds, merely the amount.

The seventh round changed the tone of the voice from behind; it was cracking under the strain. 'Get nasty, Johnny. Get fucking nasty with him. Put the fucker to sleep.'

My gaze was drifting towards Paul Ingle again, who was watching like an infant focusing on a mobile. Only his eyes made any movement – there were no surrogate movements from his arms or fists, unlike the man sitting behind me whose fists were jabbing the small space between the chairs. Johnny's punches seemed to be landing gently on the great slab in front of him, who kept coming forward. It again reminded me of Cassius Clay in that first fight with Sonny Liston. My father, my brother and I were up in the middle of the night in the front room in Legmore Street. My father and brother both died suddenly and, in my brother's case, tragically, although in reality there was nothing less tragic about my father's demise. I have only a few images of my life with just the two of them, the three men of the family together. The middle of the night, watching Clay and Sonny Liston, is one of them. My father was a gentle man. We watched Clay tame the great bear in the fifth round with what looked like gentle, soothing punches, tiring Liston, who had not boxed as many rounds in his previous two years as world champion. 'How could those punches do all that?' I had asked incredulously.

My father smiled. 'They're a lot harder than they look.'

But above, Johnny's jabs looked like mere touches, more to measure distance than anything. 'Take his fucking head off, Johnny,' came the voice. 'Step in. Bang him.'

I could see Brendan in the corner, making himself busy as usual, hollering instructions so loudly that the referee stepped in and threatened to deduct a point from Johnny if he continued.

In the tenth round, Brendan was silent but anxious. His hand was over his mouth. His gestures were doing his talking for him. They were beckoning Johnny forward. Only the occasional 'come on' escaped from his mouth. Brendan's gestures came in great flurries as vigorous as anything Johnny was throwing. I watched the heads of the boxers, especially Johnny's which was rolling this way and that, always on the move. In the twelfth, one of Dominguez's haymakers connected. Brendan waved Johnny forward. Paul Ingle rolled his chewing-gum round in his mouth. Johnny got the unanimous verdict and the applause.

It was a decent enough fight, although Johnny never did get nasty the way the punters would have liked. Away from the cameras, I watched Johnny hug Dominguez. There was real affection in the movement, perhaps the strongest emotion shown all night by Johnny, and it was a positive emotion rather than something like hate or anger.

I looked at my son, Sam, who looked relieved that it was all over so painlessly in the end. I had an image of my brother and my father sitting on the floor in front of the settee, a few inches from the electric fire. I have so few images of just the three of us together, and I felt both sad and elated at the same time. I looked at my son and winked. He smiled back at me with an open, excited smile, and then he looked back towards where the action had been, having witnessed close-up what Norman Mailer has called 'the ultimate expression of masculine courage', on a warm balmy night in a leisure centre in Sheffield, with his dad, the way it should be.

'How much would Johnny Nelson get for that fight?' he asked. I wasn't surprised that he wanted the experience translated into pounds and pence. It's the way teenagers think nowadays. 'A million quid?'

'Nothing like that, I'm afraid,' I said. 'Why do you ask?'

'I was just wondering,' he said. 'I was just wondering.'

ELEVEN

At the end of the fight, Brendan came over and hustled my son and myself out of the VIP area and into the changing-room where the boxers were all dressing or standing around joking, and waiting to go on. They all said 'hello' to me as soon as we entered, and looked pleased to see me. They all knew my name. That was important to me on that night of all nights. I could see the look on my son's face. He was obviously impressed. 'You remember Geoffrey?' Brendan said to his boxers rather unnecessarily. 'He was the guy that Mick Mills used to take down to the gym on a Saturday morning and punch holes in.'

They all laughed. They had all read *On the Ropes*. They had ordered copies from me directly.

'That was a great book,' said Johnny Nelson. 'Are you planning any more?'

'I'm not sure,' I said. 'It depends on what comes up.'

'How's *Big Brother*?' another one asked. I recognised him, but I didn't know his name. He had shaved his head since I last saw him, although why that should have made me forget his name, I don't know. He hadn't fought yet. He was punching the air. 'Did you meet Brian and all the rest of them? I loved Brian. I thought that he was a real scream.'

Brendan looked over at me. 'I didn't know you did that crap,' he said.

'Oh, he's a star now,' said Johnny, who was sitting on a wooden bench drying his long, smooth, muscled thighs. 'He's the world expert on body language. Didn't you know that? He can read all of us here like a book.'

I caught my son's eye again. I could see his pride in his dad.

He was trying to disguise it, but you can't fool an expert like me, not as easily as that.

I stood there chatting away, as some of Johnny's slightly embarrassed female fans were led in one by one for Johnny to sign autographs. 'Oh, I hope your towel doesn't slip,' said one tubby blonde, with a black bra that you could see through her white blouse which was struggling to close over her ample chest.

'What does old Johnny's body language say at this precise moment?' said the shaven-headed boxer, who was laughing away in the corner.

I tried a knowing smile but didn't answer.

'I'll tell you what it says,' said Brendan. 'It says I'm the frigging champion of the world and I did it all because I listened to Brendan and I never forgot what he taught me – all he taught me about social and personal skills, all he taught me about the science and the art of boxing, all he taught me about right and wrong.'

He looked over at me, and then back at the champion of the world, who was still writing on his fan's programme, and then he continued. 'And his body language also says that I am going to be a great champion and that I will never forget what Brendan did for me, unlike some people that we all know. Isn't that right, Johnny? Isn't that exactly what your body language is saying right now?'

Johnny stopped writing, smiled and nodded. 'Whatever you say, Brendan. Just whatever you say.'

STORY 2
THE EDGE

'The artist, like the idiot or clown, sits on the edge of the world, and a push may send him over.'
OSBERT SITWELL

ONE

I suppose that I'm fascinated by the fact that, in this world of constant joking and wisecracks and humour, things sometimes happen. 'Things', I love the way I just wrote that. As if 'things' just happen by themselves, violent things that are hardly provoked at all and often little understood. Perhaps I'm more like Mick and the boys than I sometimes think. They are always talking about 'things going off', as if events are not really under anyone's control. But then again, perhaps they're not. This is another tale from the shadows of boxing, a different sort of tale. It's not always the *other* person who ends up in difficulties, as you will see – sometimes the fly on the wall ends up in the ointment too, like the ant in the ashtray.

We were sitting in a darkened, smoke-filled room. We had positioned ourselves towards the far wall, where the smoke hung low like thick cloud. We had picked our seats carefully, not to be near the fug of smoke, but for other reasons.

He was already there in front of us – the hard nut that was going to do him. Mr Big, we were calling him already, and we hadn't really seen him close up yet. Big Lenny had suggested the name. He knew a few Mr Bigs. This was just another one. We were waiting for the others to arrive at the drinking club. We knew that there was going to be some serious violence that night. We had heard all about Mr Big, and what he was capable of.

'Serious violence' – I laugh when I catch myself saying it. It kind of slips off the tongue like other expressions worn down into cliché and euphemism. It slips between your fingers like a bar of wet soap: hard to get hold of, slippery, evasive. It sounds like police argot. Loitering with intent, affray, serious violence.

131

Important-sounding words that make something out of nothing to help the police out in their bureaucratic travails. Lenny liked using the expression. It became worn and smooth in his large horny hands. He threatened punters with it, the ordinary punters. 'Slippery fuckers', he called them. 'All of them.'

So what did we really know about what was going to happen that night in the club? We knew that somebody was going to get done that night. We knew that, and that's about as serious as you can get, even by Lenny's standards. I knew who he was. I had been told his name and a bit about his background. He did security work. He had been a sort of journeyman boxer some time in the past. Lenny told me to put all the personal stuff out of my head. 'It won't be relevant to what's going to happen tonight,' he said. 'Forget it.'

I checked the time by glancing at my watch. I wasn't as surreptitious as all that. I brought my arm up steadily against my body and pulled the sleeve of my jacket back slowly and carefully. But I could see the muscles of Lenny's eyes almost clench. 'Patience,' he whispered out of the corner of his mouth. His bottom lip was all extended. 'Patience. Just try and relax for fuck's sake. You're making me nervous.' He stressed the first syllable of 'nervous' rather than the word 'me'. I noticed that. I like to think I'm a good observer of people.

He started to light up another cigarette. The match lisped twice across the sandpaper, and then crackled into life. It sounded loud and intrusive in the tension-filled room. This action made me nervy, but I didn't comment on it. The privileges of power, I thought to myself, privileges that he negotiated for himself through that mouth of his, and those large horny hands with their misshapen and swollen knuckles. 'I've got knuckles on my knuckles,' he would say, and the lads would all laugh. 'It takes years of careful nurturing to get them to look like this.' Lenny had been a boxer but never made the money that he said that he had been promised. He had to make his own way in the world.

I was somehow accountable for everything that I did in that room, but he wasn't. It seemed unfair, but that was the way he had made it.

We sat side by side. We knew roughly what was going to happen that night in the drinking club. We had been warned. Or rather, I had been warned in the first instance. Lenny had invited himself along. I don't know how he had got it out of me, he just had. 'I'm game for anything,' he had said. 'Anything like this, that is.' And he had laughed, which I had thought was curious. In anyone else, I would interpret it as a sign of tension, but not in him.

I was waiting quietly for what I knew was inevitable, not the murder itself, but for the wave of revulsion to hit me. It wasn't the victim I was concerned about. It was me. I had to watch it all in front of Lenny. I was like a child on a seashore in a storm, watching the tides roll towards me. It was a violence that could not be stopped or turned back at this stage. There was an inevitability about the whole thing. I glanced at Big Lenny. His bulk almost reassured me. I was new to this game. I was the child here.

I watched the calluses on Lenny's hand move towards his mouth and saw the ash of the cigarette glow in the half-light, like a red, pulsating ganglion. The thought occurred to me that this is all we are – a collection of pulsating nerves that could be extinguished by a guy like the one over there, the guy sitting at the bar with a beer in his hand. Not a care in the world. Or perhaps a guy like Lenny. Carefree individuals, careless with other people's lives.

I had once asked Lenny if he had ever killed anybody. It was half a joke, designed to flatter him. It was the sort of question that I thought might break the ice one cold night outside his club when he had stopped me from going in. He liked to stop me sometimes just for the nobble. 'Just for the nobble,' that's what he always said. Just in case I was taking too much for granted. So I had to hang about outside with him and the lads, stomping up and down in their overcoats, keeping themselves warm, keeping themselves amused at my expense. Men with big stiff necks that hardly moved. They had to swing their shoulders to turn my way to view my discomfort.

'All that fanny in there, and he has to stay out here with us,' said Lenny, laughing still. He moved me to one side with a slow, sweeping movement of his large hand, with the blistered palm held towards me. 'Good evening, sir. Good evening, madam,' he said to a couple arriving at the door with gold clanking on their unnatural winter tans and a curious synchronicity in their appearance.

Big Lenny, the official greeter of the great movers and shakers in Steel City. 'Nice to see you again, young sir,' he said to a man with biggish hair and a tight, over-used grimace of a smile, who glanced at me and pretended to shiver.

'Oooooh,' he said to me. 'Fucking freezing.'

I stood in the cold up against the wall, attracting superior, haughty looks from those that were allowed to enter the club without having to endure the indignity of the knock back. The bouncers periodically rotated towards me and laughed. This was early on in our relationship.

So I asked my question about killing. And why shouldn't I have done? I assumed that it was the kind of thing that Lenny and his friends talked about out there in the cold with all that social intercourse going on behind those gold-flecked doors, in the perfumed warmth of the club.

'What?' Lenny said, the quick delivery sounded like a bird squawking. He didn't sound the 't'. It came out like 'whaaaa'.

He came over to me slowly with this bewildered expression. 'Whaaaa?' he squawked again in my face. He was so close that I could smell his minty breath. He was always very particular about this. He sucked on Polo mints more or less continuously when he was working the door. He would some-times have two or three in his mouth at the same time. You could hear them rattle against his teeth when he was preparing to talk, when he was thinking of something witty and barbed to say. I was waiting for them to stop.

'I'm a fucking professional,' he said eventually, spitting excitedly on the word 'fucking'. 'I've been dealing with wankers for years. No, let me put it another way. I've been dealing with wankers, shitheads, tosspots, assholes, cretins, wankers.' He paused momentarily for breath and then repeated the last word again. 'Wankers, who think that they're big men because they're out with their mates, guys who are acting big because they're out with their bit of stuff. I served my apprenticeship dealing with pissed fuckers, guys as high as a kite, druggies, cokeheads and speedfreaks. I've had to eject lefties, righties, rejects from Khomeini's Iran up in Steel City because they got chucked out after the revolution, Arabs, Eyeties, Frogs – once a whole team of Frog footballers in their official fucking jackets. I've had to fight Paddies, Pakis and Chinks. I always judge it right. "No unnecessary force" is my motto. Do you understand me?'

I said that I did, but I had watched him knock drunken punters spark out – his words not mine – spark out down concrete steps. Paddies, Pakis and Chinks spark out in puddles of their own making. Deep-red and black puddles streaked with vomit and piss. I had watched ambulances take them away across town, with Big Lenny and his friends waving goodbye. Big Lenny was rarely even picked up for anything. He got on well with the local CID. They seemed almost to admire each other in an odd and unhealthy kind of way.

'I nearly joined the police,' Lenny would say.

'You're better off out of it,' Cliff, the Inspector, would say when he was on duty in the club where Lenny worked, late, late at night. 'It's all hands behind your back stuff. It's shit, really.'

Lenny and Cliff always liked to share a joke. 'How can you tell the copper who's off duty?' Lenny liked to ask. 'He's the one drinking halves.' That always got a laugh. The coppers on duty got their little perks. Everybody knew that. They got their pints from the side of the bar where the notice read 'staff only'. It should have read 'staff only plus, of course, all the coppers out for the night'.

So Lenny had nearly joined the police, or so he said. But had he ever killed anybody? I still didn't know. But he was looking forward to the action that night in that smoky room where we were both waiting, with me trying to keep myself calm and composed. Ready for anything. I was taking my lead from him. Every time he put his cigarette to his mouth, I felt my finger move towards my mouth, and I nibbled my nail in a sort of synchronous movement with his smoking. I wasn't biting my nails. I never have. 'Nibbling' is really the wrong word for it – there were no ragged edges. My nail just wiped across my lips, which closed in on it. There was a lot of hand-to-mouth contact.

My copying of his movements made him edgy. It's not supposed to do this, from what I've read. But it was as if he could sense a shadow following him in the dark. I could see it in his face. A momentary stillness kept crossing it, as if he were waiting to see what would happen to the shadow when all of his tics, tremors and smaller, more significant movements had dampened down. Like Lenny's well-muscled boxer dog on the street, when

135

it has seen that piece of white, furry flesh flagrantly wandering along all carefree and provocative. The hard, muscled body that moved perpetually would suddenly become quite still. Listening, waiting, fixed on its target, all senses attenuated and strained. Quite still.

I had seen the dog many times. Lenny often brought it with him when he visited me. He called it Butch, but he pronounced it 'Bootch'. It was just one of his little jokes. It sounded effeminate. 'Bootch, come here,' he would shout on the street, extending the 'oo' sound, just to watch the faces of the passers-by. It was a little dig at nobody in particular. A little warning salvo. 'Just a nobble' is what he called it. 'Just a fucking nobble'.

I thought that his dog had very poor eyesight. Poor eyesight and very short legs for something that was meant to be a pedigree boxer. But you couldn't mention either of these things. Lenny was proud of that animal. Butch seemed to think that anything white was a cat, and therefore a potential victim. It could hardly discriminate. Litter, a plastic canister and, last winter, a snowman – they were all cats as far as 'Bootch' was concerned. Anything white, and the dog would stand quite still and its breathing would start to diminish. Sometimes it would crouch there on its hind legs, its big bollocks swinging from side to side like a pendulum oscillating, winding down slower and slower. Watching for signs of movement from the snowman that never budged, or the scrap of newspaper that might be lifted up by the wind and thrown across the street, causing Butch end-less excitement in the process as he tracked his victim's every movement.

I stopped biting my nails, and I could see Lenny's body return to life again. I was nervous; I admit that. I could feel my nerves jangling away inside me, the adrenalin careering through my body towards my extremities, which felt a little numb. My mouth was dry, almost salty to the taste. I could feel myself flicking the roof of my mouth with my tongue. This action was making a soft clicking sound, like a dog gently lapping water from a bowl. Lenny told me to be quiet.

I was trying to stop myself displaying my nervousness in front of him. I sat with my fingers interlocked to stop them from trembling, to stop them leaking any nervous energy. My fingers rubbed the bones of my thin, smooth knuckles, and then tried to find sanctuary in the crevasses at the base of my fingers. I crossed my ankles so that at least one of my feet would be off the ground and therefore not tap on the floor with that irritating, incessant, dead giveaway beat. I kept staring straight ahead at the door, so that Lenny would only ever get a side view of my face. That would be less revealing, I thought. I wouldn't leak anxiety or fear from the side of my face quite so easily.

I tried to keep my jaw relaxed. I tried to let it hang open, gaping and wide. I had thought about keeping it taut so that when the violence did come, there would be no change in my facial expression. But I didn't want any comments as to why I was sitting there beside him, grimacing. He might think that I had indigestion, or something worthy of comment. I couldn't bear him making some kind of crack about it. I was too tense to laugh or smile or make any jibe back, the way that you must do if somebody plays that sort of game. I had been around Lenny long enough to know that this is how you must respond if somebody makes a crack. Never let an insult stand, that's what he always said. Always give as good as you get. If you don't you're a nobody. A fucking nobody.

I had learned this the hard way. One night, Big Lenny saw some punter saying something to me in his club. I had brushed against the guy's arm and spilled a little of his drink. The club was packed. I had just swayed his way with the crowd and knocked into him, and some lager spilled out of his full glass as he bent forward for a sip. It was no big deal. Nothing to get excited about. 'Fucking clumsy wanker,' said the guy, with wet running down his chin. He said it quietly, almost below his breath.

'Sorry,' I replied. 'Sorry about that.' And then I tried to walk away. Lenny, standing by the pillar with mirrors on each side, watched me walk a pace or two and then caught me by the arm. He pulled me in close to his chest so that I could smell the sweat and the aftershave, which he sprayed himself with for free in the gents' toilets.

'I think that I must be fucking hearing things,' he whispered in my ear. 'I must have spent too many nights in noisy nightclubs. My hearing must have gone. Or perhaps it was all those years in the steelmills. That must be it. That must be why my hearing is completely fucked. What did he just say to you?'

'It was nothing,' I said. 'Nothing.' I tried to sound casual, carefree.

'Oh, all right, then,' said Lenny, and then he pulled me closer, until I was nestling on his chest. 'What did he say to you?' Lenny held me just by my elbow and squeezed harder on the nerve, literally squeezing the truth out of me, like juice from an orange. He always liked to say to his CID pals that if they had the same freedom as he had, they would get the truth out of the bad guys a lot quicker. They always talked about the bad guys. I often wondered who these bad guys were, as the CID wandered around the club on duty drinking their complimentary pints, talking to Lenny and the lads on the door about the bad guys. The guys in dark corners, the guys who worked rival doors, perhaps. Bad fuckers.

'He said something like "fucking clumsy", I think,' I replied.

'No, he didn't,' said Lenny. 'He didn't say that.' It was as if he was scolding me. 'He said "Fucking clumsy wanker".' And just in case I didn't get it, he made a wanking movement with his forefinger and thumb in a tight, sordid little trembling movement, like a bottle being shaken.

Lenny said that he would sort it out for me. I watched the reflection of the man's face in the mirror on the pillar as Lenny approached him. Lenny had shown me this trick. You can watch all the comings and goings that way without ever being noticed. Lenny spent a lot of time looking in tinted mirrors.

Lenny said something to him.

'Eh?' he said.

'You fucking well heard,' said Big Lenny, stepping closer.

'That fucker knocked my arm,' he said, pointing at me. 'That fucker with his back to us. That guy over there. The one who is deliberately ignoring us.'

'What did you say again?' said Lenny quickly, pointing at his ears, tapping them, as if he was indeed deaf from the small number of years he had spent in the steelmills and the large number of years he had spent in clubs like this.

'That fucker knocked my arm,' repeated the man. 'That cunt over there.'

'Right, that's enough of that abusive shouting in here. You're out.' Lenny grabbed him by the throat and pushed him back against the wall. 'Walk quietly,' he said.

'Oh fucking hell,' the girlfriend said. 'Don't batter him, for fuck's sake. He's staying with me tonight. I don't want any blood on the pillowcases. My fucking mother will kill me when she gets back from her boyfriend's.'

'Take it easy, for fuck's sake,' said the guy, whose chin was now dry through all that pushing and shoving and rubbing and heaving. 'I'm going to come quietly.'

As soon as he turned to walk, Lenny got both arms around his neck in a smooth, continuous movement and pulled him backwards until only his heels were touching the carpet. Lenny walked backwards towards the nearest fire-exit with the man gurgling away in front of him, like a helpless baby.

'Don't make him sick, for fuck's sake,' said the girlfriend. 'He'll be up all night puking. He's used up all my paper hankies already drying himself.'

The DJ spotted the crowd parting to let this unlikely triumvirate through. Lenny, and then the man, and then, a few paces behind, his girlfriend, who suddenly realised that their big night out was coming to an end. It was trouble all right. 'Door staff to lower cocktail bar, quick! Alpha priority. Door staff to lower bar. Alpha rating. Alpha! Get a move on, lads.'

The rest of the doormen bustled through the crowd. Lenny was shouting instructions to his team. 'Get that fucking blonde bird,' he shouted to Becksy. 'She's in on it as well.' She had taken her white stiletto off and was trying to hit her boyfriend in the face with it. Lenny was strangling her boyfriend with one arm and trying to shield him with the other.

She was irate. 'You've ruined our fucking engagement celebration, you selfish cunt. You self-centred fucking twat. My mother was right. You're no fucking good.'

I watched Becksy grab her from behind and move his hands up across her sides and then onto her large breasts, pinning her arms to the side. 'Come on, love,' he said. 'Calm down.' He was saying this in an almost seductive way, as if he were trying to chat her up. His hands stayed where they were.

Her boyfriend was kicking and screaming now. His face white with anger, saliva all around his mouth. Big Norman thumped him on the nose. That's what they did when they wanted to make the punter really angry. It was the chin to pacify them; it was the nose to gee them up, especially when they were already restrained and when Becksy was getting a feel. I heard the crack and then, after a long, long pause, the blood started to pour in a stop-go movement like clotted cream down his white shirt.

I heard the door of the fire-exit being kicked open and the blonde screaming. Not in anger, but in pain. Somebody must have popped her. Perhaps it was the boyfriend. I couldn't make out what she was saying. I pushed against the crowd who were all shuffling as they tried to get a better look. I watched their faces which were unconsciously set in anticipation, their eyes widened to take in the entire spectacle. I stood quietly on my own in a small, deserted patch in the middle of a busy nightclub. The DJ winked down at me.

Lenny came back in to find me. He stood beside me, his arms folded across his chest. He looked pleased with himself. Another little lesson. 'You caused all this,' he said. 'You know that, don't you? You set all this in motion because you don't know how to act. You can't let cunts like that insult you. Otherwise they'll shit all over you. And then they would get carried away and start to think that they could shit all over other people as well. And then where would we all be?' He said that I owed him for his help that night and on other nights.

I shrugged my shoulders. He made a 'hmmmmph' noise and walked off, smug and satisfied. 'The Enforcer', he liked to call himself sometimes, from the Clint Eastwood film. The enforcer of the rules of social etiquette and social division in this fading northern town, with the unemployed blowing their dole on one night in his club and pretending to be something that they were not.

He left me alone to ponder. You had to give as good as you got. As good as you got. I didn't know how. There were rules, I knew that. They were complex, intricate rules, like rules of grammar. These were rules of interactional grammar specifying precisely what was and wasn't permissible in response to an insult. The rules constrained the topic, the structure and even the intonation pattern to be used in any response. That's how I thought about it. You can see that I'm an academic. I had worked this out for myself from the hundreds of examples that he presented me with. I had built up somewhere in my head a large corpus of his insults and now I had worked out the rules.

Lenny always said that the point was to see how far you could go without causing real personal offence. Right up to the brink. He was good at it. I had watched him trading insults hundreds of times. As quick as a flash, the insult would be slapped back in the face of the punter plus interest. No obvious pause for reflection or planning, no perceptible delay in its delivery. Like tennis, but that's too middle-class an analogy – back and forward, thwack, thwack, as smooth as you like. Until the other guy faltered. Until the other guy blinked.

He could anticipate what was coming. That was his secret. It was uncanny to listen to sometimes. That degree of anticipation.

He seemed to have lots of these insults stashed in some internal store, ready to be modified slightly and then pulled out to be used. It was as if a major part of his social life consisted of these little semi-automatic routines for everyday use. He enjoyed these confrontations. He liked taking people to the edge and leaving them there, and when it all tumbled over the brink, he liked that too. Perhaps he liked that best of all. Perhaps that was his secret. There was no real brink, as far as he was concerned. 'You do whatever is necessary,' he said. I have always thought that he lived a complex and dangerous but ultimately very orderly life.

I didn't want to get into this routine on the night of the serious violence, so I decided against assuming a taut, grimacing face that would not be affected by any gore or any killing. I kept my jaws slightly apart, my mouth slightly open. 'That's a good lad,' said Lenny. 'Stay loose, for fuck's sake. Hang loose.'

I wasn't accustomed to serious violence right in front of me. Right on my lap, so to speak. Big Lenny, on the other hand, had worked on doors for years. He was used to it. He always said that he had seen everything. He said that nothing could surprise him any longer. He had once been a boxer, albeit a poor one. 'My wages depended upon me being a hard, tough guy and putting up a good show, but losing in the end. That's what those boys in London wanted to see. A big brute like me taking a good fucking beating and not diving for the floor like some of the cunts you see as soon as the other guy goes anywhere near them. I've seen fucking everything.'

There was a weariness about how he said it sometimes, so that you just had to believe it. But the weariness was part of the act. I knew that he loved it all. He had been attacked with bottles, hammers, coshes, knuckle-dusters, penknives, Stanley knives, machetes, screwdrivers, beer crates, shoes, stilettos, briefcases, metal files, doors, chests of drawers, wardrobes, cars, vans, fans, fan heaters, electric fires. The list was unordered and virtually endless. 'Try to name one object that I haven't been attacked with,' he would say.

His one joke about the list was that most of the weapons used against him were once dangerous tools of work before the politicians got going, and started closing down British Steel, and then started shutting the mines. They had taken the hammers, the Stanley knives and the screwdrivers off the violent punters. The politicians had disarmed them. They had done all that for law and order in Britain. But the punters weren't disarmed, of course. They were just using other things now. Now, according to Lenny, it was all instruments of leisure that they wanted to fight with: pens, women's combs with the ends sharpened, bottles and camping knives rather than Stanley knives. That was what Thatcher and New Labour had really done for law and order in this country; they had confiscated the work tools from the violent punters and given them sharpened combs to fight with instead. Lenny said that the types of weapon men and women used in fights in and around Sheffield were a good index of the economic climate in the North of England. Better than any of those made-up economic statistics from London, anyway.

I was thinking about this joke of his. It helped me to relax a little. My jaw had gone a bit wobbly for the first time. I could feel it move. I thought of some of his other jokes. He had told me one night in the club where he worked that he had been attacked with parts of an animal. He used this in a guessing game to pass the night away outside the clubs where he worked.

'What part of an animal was shoved in my kisser?' he would ask. The other doormen would all have to guess. All the doormen in Sheffield knew the correct answer. It was part of the knowledge, part of knowing the score around here.

I knew the answer, but it didn't make me one of the guys in the know. Clearly not. You needed other qualities as well.

The story goes that one night, on a door in Chesterfield, Big Lenny had had a load of pigs' feet pushed in his face by a butcher's son during a fight. He told me that he had made sure that he got the address of the shop where the man worked off another doorman, and he had hand-delivered the dry-cleaning bill to the man responsible the next day.

'Big greasy stains,' he had told me, 'up and down my dinner jacket. Big greasy fucking stains. They were even on my bow tie. I went round there the next day in my suit and tie and I made sure that he paid up there and then. He asked me if I would take a cheque. The nerve of some people. "I only deal in cash," I said. "I am an integral part of the black economy of this country. Go fuck yourself." He had to go and nick the money out of his dad's till to pay me.'

And what was this butcher's son doing with pigs' feet in a nightclub? That was my response to the story. That was just my natural, automatic response. None of the bouncers ever asked him. It's funny that. They just accepted the story as it was, but I always thought that it was the logical thing to enquire about. I mean, what was somebody doing with pigs' feet in a nightclub? Was he taking them home for his supper? Had he got them from the kitchen of the restaurant? It's not that I didn't believe the story, it was just that I wanted to understand it better. But it was the kind of response that might be expected from a hanger-on, a man who didn't quite know the score, a muppet, a man like me.

'Fuck knows!' is all Lenny ever said when I asked him. He would get annoyed when asked, as if I were querying it. I just couldn't help myself. I suppose that it was because of my education.

'I think that they were for his supper or something. I never asked him. It never came up in the conversation, fucking muppethead.'

Lenny always laughed when he told the story about the pigs' feet, when he wasn't asked, that is, about where the pigs' feet came from. The story, like Lenny himself, had done the rounds. Night after night in the frosty air outside different clubs, you would hear this and other stories. They were embellished over time, but not too much. Doormen liked the raw urgency of the genuine article, a story that was not too well crafted or contrived. They could tell the real thing, even if sometimes the logic was just left hanging there.

Our night waiting for the action to unfold in this drinking club would be a story one day, I thought at the time. I hoped it would make more sense than some of the others.

Lenny had been hardened by his years on the doors, and they had made him opinionated. These were my conclusions, anyway, based on what I knew about him. He said that he had always been like that. Always hard, since his father, who had come over from Dublin, had been laid off work and had taken to the drink. 'We were the first wogs in this country, the first proper nig-nogs, before they started picking on the blacks,' he said. 'My dad went to some digs and there was a sign outside this real shithouse of a place saying "No dogs and no Irish". They painted "Irish bastards go home" on our backyard wall in bright-green letters. They wouldn't dare write it on the front wall.'

Lenny often managed to find something positive in even the most depressing of situations. 'Fucking cowards, you see. They wouldn't say it to your face or try to get the paint out at the front of your house.'

Door work, he always said, had just firmed him up a bit, and confirmed all his prejudices, of which there were many: Paddies like a good fight when they've had a drink, but they don't bear grudges when they've sobered up; Pakis like to use knives; Southerners won't fight unless they've got plenty of backup; women are just as bad as men in fights, just as vicious and just as nasty. He treated all troublemakers in the same way: an armlock with his big, deep forearms, then a sideways or backwards drag along the floor, keeping them off balance at all times, their toes just skimming the surface of the dance floor, then a gratuitous smack for their trouble and, finally, a push out onto the street for them to become somebody else's problem.

'Get fucking shot of them,' he would say. 'As quickly as possible. Just get shot. I want a quiet life and these people are stopping me having it.'

But I had never seen him so nervous before. I started thinking that what was about to happen might be too 'tasty' even for him. 'Tasty', that's a word he liked to apply to violence. When I had told him in the wine bar about what was going to happen in the club that night, he had offered himself up immediately. 'Nice and tasty,' he had said at the time. 'Just the way I like it.' And I swear I saw him lick his big, fat, cracked lips as he said it. I can't explain that action. I thought that it might be a conscious act, a deliberate attempt to show me how hard he really was. So I asked him to repeat the action, right there in front of me. Casually, like the way he might do it.

My logic was impeccable. If it was at all conscious, or if it was deliberate, then he should be able to repeat it on request. If somebody gives you the V-sign, for example, the fingers, then they know what they're doing. It's a conscious, meaningful act. We know exactly what it means and, therefore, it's repeatable. On the other hand, if somebody just gestures as they talk, and the gestures are just those apparently vague movements that go along with everyday speaking, then you can't repeat them. They're subconscious, and you might not even know that you've been moving at all. You've just got a vague sense of something going on, but not much, nothing definite.

That was my logic. I didn't explain the logic to him. I'm not that daft. I just made my request as casually as possible.

'Repeat what you've just done,' I said to Lenny, as he finished licking his lips and smiling that night in the wine bar. I said it in a friendly sort of way, with a gentle, amusing laugh in my voice, so that he wouldn't see it as a challenge.

'Repeat what?' said Lenny with this look on his face. It was a blend of an expression, really: half-incredulous, half-sneering. It was a common expression for that big face of his.

'What you've just done with your facial apparatus,' I replied.

'What?' he said. 'What fucking facial apparatus?'

'Look, just try to do what you've just done,' I said. 'For me. Go on, just try. Repeat what you've just done and say the words too. That might help you.'

So he made a stupid face, part-innocent, part-surprised this time, and said, 'Nice ... and ... tasty', pausing after each word to watch my response. He had remembered what he had said all right, but there was no licking movement. None at all.

So it wasn't conscious after all, I thought. He really does lick his lips like that when it comes to considerations of violence. Or else he had seen right through my test. There was always that possibility. There are some things that are very hard to understand in people. Even for me.

I watched Lenny slowly pull on his cigarette, the cigarette nestling in the cup of his hand. He was concentrating hard on the scene in front of us. The man in the leather jacket with the girlfriend was sitting to the right of the bar away from the door.

We were watching them at a slight angle, but we could see most of his face and a good part of hers too. His girlfriend was blonde. Her curls bobbed a bit whenever she spoke. She was wearing a black leather dress. You could see that she was sexy even from that angle. She was sort of protruding out of the dress. She was the kind of girl who might elicit comments from any man that she passed in a club. The kind of girl who provoked trouble, Lenny would say. He had her placed immediately in a number of logically interconnected categories: prick-teaser, trouble-starter and potential headache. You could see it in his face; all that categorisation was immediately obvious in how he looked at her. His own girlfriend wasn't that attractive. He said that he preferred it like that. 'Then you don't worry who's fucking her when you're out at work,' he always said.

He needed to provide a quiet commentary on the characters in front of us. He often did. He always talked about people behind their backs and even to their face. He talked about them in the third person right in front of them. 'Look at this loser here,' he would say. 'No brains, no fucking brains or he wouldn't be standing in my face provoking me like that.'

And then sometimes that big knuckled first would shoot out. Wham, bam, thank you, ma'am. 'Don't say you weren't warned,' he would say. But they weren't warned. They were discussed, but they were never, ever warned. That was how he survived.

Lenny took a drag of his ciggy. 'She's the kind of bird', he started, 'that is always responsible, always fucking responsible for guys kicking off in clubs.' He turned his head slightly towards me to check my response. 'Always.'

I nodded back quickly and surreptitiously.

'If you banned birds like that from clubs, my job would be a lot fucking easier,' he whispered.

'Yeah,' I said. I said it so quietly that it sounded as if I was just breathing out.

'A lot fucking easier,' he repeated.

'You know this,' he said, emphasising the 'know' and leaning towards me, looking eager. 'In fact, you've probably got a fucking theory for it. Guys only fight when they've got something to fight over. Something like that down there. It's the fucking caveman in us, isn't that right? Some bollocks like that. We want her in the fucking cave with her legs wide open and the dinosaur meat on the fucking table for afters.'

'Yeah,' I said. 'It's something like that.'

The man in the black leather jacket and the girl in the sexy dress were talking intimately. They were leaning towards each other, both leaning about equally. I think that can be important. Equality of lean, that is. It seems to me to be more significant than the lean itself. He was looking at her straight in the eyes. I could see that without knowing exactly where she was looking. His eyes had a fixed focus; they weren't all over the place. That can be significant too. His hand was on top of hers on the bar. We couldn't hear any words, but we could see that he was doing most of the talking. I looked around the bar area. Lenny's eyes followed mine. There was a painting of Winston Churchill on one wall with a cigar in his hand. Lenny noticed it as well.

'What's this place called, by the way?' asked Lenny quietly, wishing to display his vigilance. 'It's not Churchill's by any chance, is it? Or Winston's?'

I said that I wasn't sure. Sometimes you miss details like that. It was just a smoky drinking den, that's all I knew. And we were there watching all the action in it.

The conversation we were focusing on was becoming quite animated. The man was gesturing a lot. I don't think that he was annoyed at her; he was just involved in what he was saying. Lenny nudged me. 'He's getting keyed up about something. Look at his hands,' he said. I did. I would have noticed them anyway. He was making a series of short stabbing beats in the space in front of his chest. They were emphasising the words, coinciding with the stresses of each sentence. They were quite violent. But that's a very loaded word. Brisk, baton-type movements, that's about as neutral as I can get, although that sounds a little artistic. Like a conductor's baton. The movements were neither violent nor artistic, just brisk.

'He's an aggressive sort of guy,' said Lenny. 'Look at the way he's talking to her. You need to keep an eye on aggressive guys like that in clubs. Guys who are always stabbing the air with their fingers.'

But then, the short, sharp stabbing movements stopped, and his hand rested peacefully on hers again.

'What is he now?' I asked. 'Has he changed his personality?'

'He's just taking a breather,' Lenny whispered. 'He's still an aggressive cunt, but he's just worn himself out, that's all.'

She leaned forward and kissed him. I looked away. I couldn't help it. It felt intrusive to watch. I felt embarrassed. Lenny just kept staring, taking it all in.

'Well, what I always say is that fucking is a lot better than fighting,' he whispered. 'Better for them and better for us. Better for all of us. And better to watch,' he added.

I glanced back. The man in the leather jacket was ordering some more drinks from the barman, an elderly man with grey hair and false teeth that didn't seem to fit properly. You could see that whenever he tried to smile. We were close enough to the action to be able to make out that level of detail.

'How many drinks has your man had?' asked Lenny. 'I hope that you're keeping count. You're the clever one. You keep the tally. That might be important.'

It was then that the door opened and in came another man with two companions.

'Oh, oh,' said Lenny. 'We're on. Is that him? Is that your man?'

I looked through the smoky haze. It was hard to make anything out over by the door. The light was bad over there, but I thought that it must be him. It was about time that he arrived. I had never seen him before.

'Yes,' I said. 'I think that's him.'

'He's a big fucker,' said Lenny, looking at his height and his shape in the doorway. 'A right big fucker. They both are. This is going to be very tasty,' said Lenny.

I looked out for the lip licking, but none came. I noticed that my lips had gone very dry. My hands were clasped together tightly and I could feel that my palms were moist. I rubbed them together in a vain attempt to dry them. The room felt even hotter. The adrenalin was making me feel a little queasy.

The three men sat down at the bar a few feet from the couple. I noticed that the girl in the sexy dress looked round at them almost immediately. We got a better view of her face. She was very pretty.

'She's fucking tasty, as well,' said Lenny. 'Did she smile at any of them?'

'I don't think so,' I said.

'But they've noticed her and they know her,' said Lenny. 'You can see that in their faces and their little sly looks at each other. They knew that she was going to be here. They've found her, their looks tell you that. And look at the guy in the leather jacket's face.'

We could see him clearly. His expression had changed, I admit that. It changed quickly, and the new expression that had taken over his face stayed there without any perceptible movement. We both noticed the change even from that distance.

Lenny exhaled some air in a long, blowing motion. 'Phoooooooow. He means business. That look says, "Don't fucking mess with me or my bird." I think that those three guys are too pissed to notice. That's the problem with drink. That's why people get into so much trouble when they're pissed up.'

'Do you think that he's consciously saying that with his expression? Or do you think that it's more subtle than that?' I whispered.

'How the fuck should I know?' replied Lenny. 'I'm just telling you what I see. I'm an expert on that, and I can tell you that his look is saying ...'

'Signalling, do you mean?' I said, interrupting him. 'Do you mean signalling?'

Lenny turned to look at me. He was scowling. 'All right, fucking signalling, then. He's signalling that he wants these three fuckers to fuck off and leave him and his girlfriend alone,' whispered Lenny. 'You see my reading of it is that the one in the grey suit, the one nearest the tasty bird, has fucked her – probably when the guy in the leather jacket was away on business or something. The guy in the grey suit knows her intimately. You can see that from his body language. He's not facing the bar, he's facing her, and look at how wide apart his legs are. 'He's saying, "Come and climb on top of this, baby." She doesn't want to give the game away. That's why she won't even say "hello" to him.'

I noticed that the two men in the dark suits were in exactly the same posture as each other: arms folded, legs tucked under the counter of the bar, head slightly rotated. But the other one, the man in the grey suit, was in a quite different posture to them. He had orientated himself exclusively towards the blonde in the sexy dress, who was clearly with somebody else.

'Just wait for the sparks to fly,' said Lenny in a hushed voice. 'Just wait. It's pretty obvious what's going on down there. The guy in the grey suit has fucked her. That's why he and his pals have come tonight. He wants a bit more of what he got the last time. Your man in the leather jacket doesn't know about this, but he suspects. That's probably what they were talking about earlier. That's why he was getting so hot under the collar. He was going to give her the third degree and then your man walks in with his pals. Well, that tells him all that he needs to know, doesn't it? And his face tells me all that I need to know. Just look at that face now. He could murder the three of them.'

I looked at the facial expression of the man in the leather jacket. I had never seen an expression like it. Not in books, not in film depictions of violence, not on the street, not in any club that I had ever been to. It was a prolonged stare over his girl-friend's shoulder at the man in the grey suit. It was the immobility of the expression that was so new and so dangerous. It was beyond the myth of film, which prefers faster, more fleeting images that are meant to say it all. She could see it as well, directed out past her, not changing or flickering or altering or transmogrifying into something else. She reached out her hand to stop him moving, which seemed like an almost contradictory action given that there was so little movement from him. It was a look that meant business. The imminent action of this dangerous man seemed to be signalled through the very immo-bility of his expression.

I thought of Butch for a second. It was just a mental image of Butch, from the back, tracking a scrap of paper tossed in the air by the wind. It was like Butch's pose before he struck. Quite still until he pounced.

The man in the grey suit smiled back at the man with the immobile face. A wavering, sideways smile, almost a real smile of enjoyment with the muscles around the eyes working over-time, as if he was really enjoying the whole thing. Enjoying the situation.

'He's fucking pissed for a start,' said Lenny. 'He must be. Get yourself ready. It's going to kick off in a second.'

It was an odd exchange between two men who did not seem to know each other. One had hate written all over his face in this long, uninterrupted stare, and one looked as if he hadn't a care in the world. They looked at each other for perhaps a full minute. No words were exchanged. It was all done through that set of looks, a whole world of meaning somehow contained within them. It was like children in a staring game without the effort. That was what was so odd about it – it all looked so effortless. There were few blinks that we could see.

Then I noticed that the man in the leather jacket seemed to be trembling. That, at least, was my perception of it.

'He's trembling,' I said in a whisper.

'He's shaking with anger more like,' said Lenny. 'Trembling, my fucking arse. That's a fucking shake not a tremble. A tremble is gentler than that. He's going to blow in a few seconds.'

We sat there in the darkened room, waiting. I sneaked a last glance at Lenny's face. I had never seen him concentrating so hard. He didn't notice that I was looking. That was unusual for him. I felt afraid, I have to admit that.

Then something started to happen. Not suddenly, but slowly and deliberately. The man in the grey suit began to talk to the man in the leather jacket. We couldn't hear what he was saying. Then he made a small gesture. His right hand was outstretched with the first two fingers together. Then the fingers started to make a claw, then a fist. Two fingers together dragging behind the others. He seemed to stop talking. Then he reached his hand out again. Lenny nudged me. The hand settled on the back of the girl in the leather dress and moved slowly in a gentle, smooth arc down the back of her shiny leather dress onto the top right-hand side of her backside. You could see the disbelief on the man in the leather jacket's face. It was just plain disbelief turning to horror. He had seen the hand moving towards her and had to guess where it had now settled. I had never seen a face like that before. The horror turned in slow motion into murderous rage. I almost have to invent the categories as I go along. Murderous rage. That's about as extreme as I can get.

His hand went up inside his coat.

'We're on,' said Lenny. 'This is it. This is what we're here for.'

I saw the blade. It didn't flash in such a darkened room. I recognised it from its outline, its fragile shape. He pulled it out of his coat. Not a Stanley knife. Something longer and wider. Lenny would recognise it, I thought. He could give it a name if he had to. But he wasn't talking. He was watching too intently to be disturbed or distracted by the hum of talk. The other man's hand pulled away from the girl in the dress. He must have been drunk. The action was too slow to help him. His stool tilted backwards as he retracted his hand. He fell back onto the floor. The man in the leather jacket stumbled on top of him. There was no pause. He stuck the knife in. It went easily through his jacket. The other two men bolted for the door and ran out onto the street. The door, banging against its frame, let some raw light into the corner, and you could see the wide blade going in, not once but three times, in a fluent movement with what seemed to be very little resistance.

You could see the blood spurting in a thin jet, marking the temporal boundaries of the stabbing movement, like commas between clauses. I suppose that because of my education I sometimes think in terms of text and the printed page. Lenny wouldn't have seen it like that.

The girl in the leather dress was mouthing a scream, but it was quite silent as far as we were concerned, as if the horror of it all had taken all her breath away. The barman with the false teeth had somehow disappeared. Lenny later claimed that he was so perceptive that he saw the man's teeth fall out as he ran. We couldn't see where he was at that moment in time. Lenny just said that he had got offside quick without his teeth.

Lenny and I were rooted to the spot. The man in the leather jacket took his time. He got up slowly and dusted himself down, although why he dusted down a leather jacket covered in blood I will never know. It was just a little act that seemed to say that everything was cool, everything was okay. There was no dust, and you can't remove blood with a slight brush of your hand. It was not a functional act. Signalling, that's the word for it. He was signalling that everything was cool. Then he led the girl out. The girl who was the cause of all the carnage, according to Big Lenny and his theories of human behaviour out there in the urban jungle of Britain today.

I noticed the time. I don't know why I looked. I just did. It was five minutes past three. In the morning, that is. The man in the grey suit lay there. His body made small, quiet, convulsive movements for about three minutes. I felt myself timing them. Blood formed a darkening patch on his suit. If you blinked, every time you opened your eyes again there was more dark there. It didn't seem to be flowing from anywhere. It was just that the stain kept getting bigger. The blood had trouble soaking into the carpet and dispersing. A pool was forming. It was getting deeper. You could see that the man was badly hurt.

Lenny turned around in his seat. He made that blowing noise again. 'Phoooooow. This is fucking serious stuff. I can't believe I'm sitting here watching this as calm as you like.' I motioned for him to stay where he was. I was telling Lenny not to move.

The man was lying there still bleeding. The stain was spreading. His movements were becoming more slight and quiet.

'Is he dead?' I looked at Big Lenny. I asked again to get some response. 'How do you know when he's dead, Lenny?' Lenny just sat there immobile, almost transfixed. 'I can't believe we just sat through all that.' I could hear my voice now as if it wasn't me who was doing the talking.

'He's a fucking goner all right,' said Big Lenny eventually. 'He's well and truly fucking gone.'

'Did you see it coming?' I asked, but there was no answer. 'Could you see it coming?' The question emerged with a staccato rhythm, like stones hitting a window with a light 'tap . . . tap . . . tap' with gaps in between.

The man in the stained suit was quite still now. We had watched a death right in front of us, with no words that we could hear. A life terminated in and through silent action. Hardly any words had been spoken between the protagonists. It was life and death negotiated through the silent language of the body, and I was meant to be the expert on that silent language. That was the scary thing.

Lenny and I were still stationary.

'I could see something,' said Lenny. 'But I didn't think that it would be a knife in the belly like that. There was so much blood. I can't get over the amount of blood that comes out of a belly. Look at that fucking carpet. It will cost a fucking fortune to get that clean. Look at the fucking mess. Who owns this place? Do you know who actually owns the club? He's not going to be very pleased when he turns up. It will cost him a fortune to get the whole thing cleaned.'

I almost laughed to hear Big Lenny talking about the carpet-shampooing bill after what we had just witnessed. Perhaps it was his way of dealing with it. On the other hand, perhaps he really cared about these sorts of things. I got up and pulled out my hanky and wiped my forehead. I was feeling hot, as if I had been out for a short, fast run. My heart was beating quickly. I think that I had seen enough. I looked at Lenny. He was still watching the man lying on the floor. I couldn't remember the man's name at that moment. I had been told it, I just couldn't remember it. I had made no effort to remember it. It would have made the whole thing too personal, I suppose, just as Lenny had warned. He was just the man in the grey suit. A man whose hand had wandered in a sleazy after-hours drinking club, or a man who had been playing away with somebody else's girlfriend, depending upon your point of view, depending upon how much you were prepared to read into things.

Lenny saw me looking this time. He tried a smile. 'I can't fucking believe this. I didn't think it would be quite like this. It's funny if you're not involved in things. It seems different. I wouldn't stab somebody anyway. It's not my fucking style, I'll tell you that for nothing.' Then he went silent, as if he might be thinking.

There was silence in the room. I felt myself sniffing and it sounded loud. Just enough to break the solemn silence.

'Can we play that last bit again?' asked Lenny. 'That last section. Can we rewind the tape? And then I might pick up a bit more. Just one more time?' I said that he could watch the whole thing again if he wanted to, and leaned back in my seat glad that it was all over. He leaned across to the video recorder and pressed the rewind button. The tape whirring into action almost made me jump. He started to rise slowly without taking his eyes off the screen.

'You might be a man worth knowing after all. Not such a fucking muppet-head as I first thought,' and he gave me a great relaxed wink, and I swear that he licked his lips for the second time that night.

Sometimes I think that we are all psychologists – those who get called upon to analyse behaviour professionally, like me, and those like Lenny who just have to do it day in, day out for a living. Lenny should not have been in that editing room with me but, of course, the point was that he had just invited himself. He had realised that there was something on my mind when I had been sent the tape on the recommendation of a colleague, and he had managed somehow to work out what it was and invite himself along. At some level, I thought that his presence might be useful. I am, after all, no matter what I say, an experimental psychologist, more used to behaviour in the psychological laboratory than in dark, dirty clubs like the one on the screen. This was his patch. He understood how men and women behaved there better than I ever could.

Of course, Lenny wasn't finished with me that night. He said that he wanted to borrow the tape, the 'ultimate snuff movie', he said, but I explained that this was quite impossible. 'We'll see,' he said. 'We'll see.'

TWO

Sheffield, they say, is the biggest village in England, and Lenny used this fact to his advantage. There was no hiding from somebody like Lenny in such a small town, where everybody knew everybody else. I learned this quickly. Sheffield, I should also say, was somehow not what I had expected. I remember when I first moved there, to become a university lecturer. I was glad to get away from the pretences of Cambridge, which was always going to be difficult for a working-class boy from Belfast. People had always told me I should be so proud to go to Cambridge. 'Imagine, someone from your background,' they would say, and I would stare back at them, trying to work out just what exactly they were referring to. My mother had some reservations. 'I hope it doesn't turn you into a snob,' and she would drawl longingly on the first letter of that last word. She didn't want a snob in the family, but she did want a nob with social grace and education. She wanted me transformed, but not too much. It was always going to be a difficult balance to maintain.

'And don't show yourself up,' she warned me before I set off.

'I'll try not to,' I said.

Trinity College was all I expected and more – magnificent courts, young men dressed in short, billowing black gowns with unfamiliar accents, eccentrics, bells, port and cheap beer. I would walk round the perimeter of Great Court and through the hallowed cloisters of Neville's Court, thinking, often aloud. That was part of the great Cambridge experience – drawing attention to yourself through idiosyncratic behaviour, but my thinking aloud was quieter than most. Byron had kept his bear in Neville's Court, and whole issues of the college magazine were devoted to trying to ascertain exactly which room he had lived in. Wittgenstein had eaten his pork pies (apparently he liked them) in these same cloisters. And here was I. Great ontological questions would rear up in front of me. 'What is existence?' 'Why are we here?' Or more specifically, 'What is an ordinary lad from Ligoniel in Belfast doing walking through the cloisters of Neville's Court at midnight with a half-eaten pork pie in his pocket?'

The social side of college life was problematic. But I didn't feel out of my depth mixing with the cream of English society because, quite simply, I didn't mix with them. They dominated the Senior Combination Room sherry scene. I dominated the Baron of Beef pub. My best friend at Trinity was a working-class lad from Glasgow, and I went all that way to meet him. Great socialist ideals could have pulled me through. Even normal middle-class aspirations would have helped, but I had none of these – just good exam results and my own natural embarrassment.

My idea of a revolutionary act was to go to dinner in hall dressed in a gown and afterwards go to the Midland Tavern, a reggae club off Mill Road full of West Indians, where, wearing a teeshirt, I would dance all night and fit in with black culture, which was alienated and self-contained in that twee town. Well, didn't Roddy Doyle write that the Irish are the blacks of Europe? And what about the wee Ulster Prods loved by nobody? Why, we must be the real blacks of Ireland. I didn't hate or resent the Old Etonians or the titled students. I just felt that I'd nothing to say to them. They would sit in clumps over dinner and laugh and joke and guffaw, and I would sit, often alone, staring at the portrait of Henry VIII which dominates Trinity dining room. Henry had a large and fat face, but I knew every part of it. I knew it better than my own.

Those privileged students had been reared on polite conversation. I came from a different social background. In the art of conversation I was still at the talking-by-numbers stage. And anyway, I didn't share their sense of humour – I could never laugh like that at those sorts of things. I envied them only because they had so much in common with each other. Becoming a Trinity man didn't pull our past or our present together. Belfast and Belgravia were never further apart.

But I tried. Cambridge was renowned for scholarship and sport, so I did both. It thrives on competition, so I competed. I got a Ph.D. I played for the university against Oxford in badminton, and I eventually became college badminton captain – all the things that the successful student is supposed to do. But they were hollow accomplishments for I never did become either a snob or a nob. Any changes were really just cosmetic, and when I had had a few pints, the make-up would start to run.

I had been reared with a certain prototype of how a man should behave, and this prototype seemed often to be clearest and to clash more forcefully with that of the Old Etonians when I, and they, had been drinking. Alcohol made them tease each other and play pranks and develop self-important poses, and, in some cases, even surrender to the amorous feelings that they had about each other. It did no such things to me; it made me macho. I had an image of how men behaved with drink, and I stuck to it. Education wasn't going to change that.

One incident in particular sticks in my mind. It was the first year I attended the College Badminton Club formal dinner. I had just won the college singles tournament and was to be presented with a trophy. I was also captain elect. It should have been a great evening. The dinner started well enough and the alcohol flowed. I had to make a speech. It went quite well, and the alcohol continued to flow. I was presented with the trophy. The alcohol didn't dry up all night. The dinner finished late and thanks to Trinity's hospitality, I – and everyone else – was inebriated.

Now a famous tradition at Trinity is the Great Court run, depicted, if inaccurately, in the film *Chariots of Fire*, in which young men attempt to run round the perimeter of Great Court whilst the college clock strikes midnight. (In *Chariots of Fire*, the run seems to take place at midday.) It is a very difficult feat because the path is cobbled in parts, and its turns are very sharp. It is an impossible feat if you've been drinking.

But that night, alcohol had made me invulnerable, or at least less vulnerable, so I stripped off my dinner jacket and rolled up my sleeves. Gut determination and single-mindedness honed and narrowed by alcohol would pull me through. I was sure of that in the way that you are when you're bladdered. Part of this great Trinity tradition, however, also seems to be that those with rooms overlooking the route should throw water onto the contestants. This makes both the contestants and the cobbles slippery.

That night, the Badminton Club minus their dinner jackets and a few keen souls in proper running gear lined up for the run. We waited in silence. I kept thinking of William Wilson from the *Hornet*, the barefooted centenarian who appeared from nowhere to beat all the modern, high-fibre, super-carbed, high-tech athletes in the Olympics. I was going to show the nobs. The clock chimed and we sprinted off.

I got to the first bend, and then my head struck the head of the person immediately to my right. It wasn't anybody's fault. We were both drunk, and unfortunately alcohol was pulling our bodies in different but converging directions. There were two loud cracks: one as our heads collided and one as my head hit the cobbles. I got up feeling very confused.

I was, however, aware that (1) I had just been hit on the head with something; (2) my head was sticky; (3) some wet substance was trickling down my new dress shirt; (4) that substance was red; and (5) William Wilson probably didn't drink anyway.

I staggered back to the bar to pick up the badminton trophy, which I'd deposited on a windowsill for the duration of the race. But surprise, surprise, it had gone. A typical public school prank. But I wasn't having any of it. One person, who was obviously of upper-class background, was smirking. I grasped him by the lapels. 'Where's my fucking cup?' I whispered in his face. Now, I had seen this done a thousand times in Belfast, but I had never tried it myself before. The secret, I understood, was to say it as quietly as possible to make it more threatening.

He looked at me in a truly horrified fashion. 'But I don't know,' he replied in that upper-class high-pitched squeal of his.

'You fucking lying bastard,' I said. I raised my fist, but then my badminton partner intervened. He had played so many games with me that he could anticipate my every move. I tried getting him off me, but thankfully God in all His wisdom made the upper classes (and I use the term loosely) substantially taller than the lower classes, and I failed to push him off. I resorted to the sort of abuse I'd heard outside pubs in Belfast, but he didn't take any notice. I suspect that, by this stage, he couldn't make out what I was saying anyway since my accent during the course of the evening had become progressively stronger and less decipherable to those around me.

I returned to my room that night bloodied and scarred. I had lost my trophy, my dinner jacket, which someone had also pinched as a prank, my veneer of sophistication, but thankfully not my self-respect. It was obvious to me, even with all that alcohol inside me, that I could never become a fully-fledged Trinity man. I could, perhaps, be a Trinity man in the lecture theatre or on the sports field, but not, unfortunately, in the college bar.

The exams, the competition and the work were within my grasp, but the pranks, the laughter and the self-conscious, self-important poses were not. I resorted to violence only because it was the coherent alternative. From cultured Cambridge collegian to boorish Belfast brawler in one short step, but neither persona was really me. I wanted to be somewhere in between, but that was the most difficult position to maintain. It has no internal coherence or consistency. There were no models around, no one to imitate or copy. Or so I thought.

Young men can be amorphous, malleable things. With my second-hand Moss Brothers' dinner jacket, which cost a fiver from Oxfam, and my Trinity field colours ties, I almost started to look the part, even if I didn't always act the part. But parents are less amorphous and less malleable. They are fixed in old, familiar shapes, which are obvious to anyone who glimpses them. I always feel for working-class students when their parents visit them at university; you can sometimes see the mixture of emotions in their faces – pride and shame in almost equal measure. The strain shows visibly.

By the time I got to Cambridge, only my mother was alive, but she visited me with a very close aunt and uncle. Together they formed this strange and completely unmanageable triumvirate. If they had felt the slightest hint of shame from me, they would never have forgiven me, and I would never have forgiven myself. And yet here I was, trying to acquire an education, to assimilate some taste and desperately to escape from my past. And here they were, spectres from my childhood coming to haunt me.

At my insistence, they came to visit out of term-time, in July. It was the twelfth week, which is an important week if you happen to be a working-class Protestant from Belfast. They all wore sunglasses. My uncle had made an effort – he wore a suit, but it was a thick woollen suit, which had got crumpled on the drive to Cambridge from Chippenham where my aunt and uncle now lived. He looked to all the world like a big Irish farm labourer dressed for the local hop. My aunt was his alter ego and antithesis. She was small, grey, wizened and had a permanent cough from smoking sixty a day. The cough, once it started, bent her double. My mother was dressed in her bargain nylon slacks and top. Her hair was teased up into a Gina Lollobrigida style *circa* 1962, but was going thin.

I wanted to keep them out of sight and keep them sober. But the plan failed somewhere along the line. My uncle insisted on visiting a pub he had heard about in the east side of Cambridge, a part I had never been to, 'Laudate dei', but then he sank twelve pints quickly with everyone else sinking the equivalent in whisky or Carlsberg Specials. It was the twelfth week, after all. They then insisted that we should go into the centre of Cambridge for lunch. We parked on Sydney Street. My mother kept up. She trotted along beside me, her sunglasses over the edge of her nose. My uncle trailed some distance behind before slumping up against the wall of Heffer's Bookshop.

Now Cambridge likes to boast a few eccentric tramps and professors, but the sight of a large Irishman nailed to the wall with drink in the middle of the day turned more than a few heads. His big, thick woollen suit was making him sweat. His face was red, his hair tousled. His words were short and to the point. 'Geoffrey, where the bloody hell are we going?' His words made me sweat. My aunt, bent double with her cough, remained at the end of Trinity Street shouting instructions all the way up it. She said she wasn't going to bloody well move until I found a proper place for us to eat. My uncle lost his sunglasses.

We eventually got to the Whim in Trinity Street, which was a good choice because they sold sausages, which was all my aunt ever ate. My mother kept her sunglasses on throughout the meal and asked the waitress if she sold Carlsberg Special. Thankfully, they weren't licensed. My uncle ate his meal in silence before eating my aunt's. I didn't say a word, not even to practise my polite conversation.

As we left, I spotted my college tutor. He looked at me in his usual way and then at my guests. It was just a fleeting glance, but it said everything – contempt and pity intertwined. 'Never aspire, boy,' it screamed in my face. I hung my head. 'Who was that nice man?' my mother asked as we walked back to the car. 'Your tutor? Why didn't you introduce us?'

I knew that I would fit in more easily in Sheffield. I could keep some of myself there. My brother had been in Sheffield with some climbing friends off and on before I ever got there, so somehow I always associated the city with him. We had a family connection with the place, just as Old Etonians had a family connection with Cambridge. But the connection with Sheffield was the rocks in the Peak District and climbing, which my brother did professionally. In other words, nothing really to do with the city at all.

The day that I left Cambridge was one of those golden autumnal days before the greyness of the Fenland winter. I left with all my worldly possessions packed into my little brown Triumph Spitfire: my suitcase which would not close, my sleeping bag unfurling before me, my rucksack, which was not designed for any Alpine peak, not quite fastened, a large, green screen print of an almost-human figure on a Martian landscape painted by an art school friend blocking the back window, two briefcases – one leather and one a poor shiny vinyl which slipped and slithered on the passenger seat at every turn. I was virtually invisible in the middle of all my clutter as I left my wife, who was also from Belfast, behind to work in Heffer's Bookshop; she was to follow me north later.

I drove out past Fitzwilliam and then Girton, past students with long, slender legs, tanned from late holidays in Thailand, who were cycling in for lectures at the very start of the new academic year. All were travelling in the opposite direction to me. I drove away from Cambridge until there were no more long, golden limbs on bicycles. I passed green fields that were empty and quiet apart from the cawing of crows in the copses, and later I passed Happy Eaters and Little Chefs and traffic that flowed and ebbed and eventually tapered onto a single line north. It was like driving away from the light, despite all the discomfort that I felt there. That's how it seemed at the time. On along a straight unwavering line to this grey northern city, greyer even than Belfast. The landscape was changing again. Then I saw it coming into view. Rows of terraced housing on grey hills stretched out in front of me. Giant blocks of flats appeared from nowhere. A city built on seven hills, like the Eternal City, with all the terraced houses looping around meandering hills at the end of the dual carriageway.

The road seemed to stop quite abruptly, expiring right in the heart of the northern city at the flats that dominated the view. This was the great, mythical North. I drove around the round-about twice, unable to find my exit. A car tooted at me. I could feel my face flushing with embarrassment. My left hand rose in a placatory gesture. I mouthed 'sorry' in an attempt to explain I was new to the North. I tried to explain, in that instant of distant contact, my working-class roots, which were written over with some half-acquired genteel Cambridge code. The car drove right up behind me. I could see the driver giving me the V-sign as he took the next left. I waved back. I know that it was a stupid gesture, but it was automatic. I knew that he hadn't waved at me. I just couldn't stop myself. He had made a kind of waving movement, so I had waved back, even though his wave had involved just two fingers.

I had to find my way to my digs. I followed the signs to the university and passed an exhaust garage on the left. It was on the map that the university had sent me. The exhaust garage was represented by a little red drawing. 'Pass it on the left,' the map said. It was then that I saw her.

I pulled up at some lights and she was standing on the pave-ment. I thought that she was waiting for a bus. She dipped her head in a smooth, practised swing so that she could look in without really seeing me. It was as if she wanted her eyes to be at the right level to make contact. I assumed that she wanted to ask me for some directions. I was starting to prepare 'I'm sorry, I'm a stranger here too', ready for when I got the window down. The only problem was that it always got stuck. I was trying to get the window down. She suddenly straightened up as if to say, 'It doesn't matter.'

She didn't actually say that, but her nonverbal communication said it: her posture, her gesture, even her facial expression. I had already studied nonverbal communication for three years at Cambridge so I knew what I was seeing. Body language in popular parlance. Not necessarily female body language, but body lan-guage in general. I mean that I study the code rather than the person, which is the way that I think it should be. Body language without the body, if you like.

It turned out to be important when I watched behaviour in the world of boxing, where small nonverbal actions often said a good deal more than all of the torrents of talk that boxers were encouraged to use.

The last time I saw him, I talked to my brother excitedly about my work on body language. He laughed at some of my accounts of what I did, but I loved that laugh, even when he was laughing at me. When I was younger, I would say stupid things just to make him laugh out loud like that. Stupid but plausible things. Things that I really might have meant.

In church, he had explained to me all about Advent, Epiphany and Lent and how they were reflected in the crimsons and golds on the pulpit. So I asked him what colour the church used for Hallowe'en, and he laughed so loudly that the woman behind asked us both either to shut up or leave. The next Sunday, I asked him the same question again, the very same words, hoping for the same response. But it didn't work the second time around. I can still feel the disappointment in the pit of my stomach.

I was still trying to get the window down. She had stepped back. She was wearing a thin cotton top – too thin and flimsy given the chilly autumn weather. I saw her skirt for the first time and her long, thin, white legs without tights. The skirt was very short. She had big, black bruises, which had started to turn blue, on her pencil-thin white legs. 'Hi,' I said. 'Can I help you?'

'What?' she said in reply.

She was frowning heavily. She was quite pretty, but her eyebrows were knotted. There were deep creases across her forehead.

'Um, can I help you in some way?'

'What are you fucking on about?' she said.

I could feel myself going red. First the tooting and now this. People seldom ever tooted at me, and as for this! Everyone back at Cambridge was so pleasant to each other, even when they were pretending to be so distant that they hardly recognised you. They were still cordial, even with their studied indifference.

'Would you like some directions or something?' I said.

I had guessed that she didn't want directions, but I couldn't think of anything else to ask. I felt that I had to ask something.

'Fuck off,' she said, and she turned her back and walked off.

I could feel that gesture starting again – that wave of mine. I was signalling, but to nobody in particular.

She glanced back at me. 'Go fuck yourself, you time-wasting twat.'

'Okay,' I said quietly, almost inaudibly. 'Thank you.'

So this is the North, I said to myself that day.

I was looking for the house where I was to lodge. 'Edelweiss' it had said on the letter I had received from the landlady. I had laughed when I saw the name. It was an Alpine flower and an old song whose tune I unfortunately couldn't get out of my head. 'Edelweiss, Edelweiss.' I repeated those words over and over again, but I couldn't remember any of the other words to the song. The house was university-approved accommodation and it was near where my brother had once stayed. I had an image of what it was going to be like there. I saw myself in an airy attic – impossibly airy, in fact. Air coming in from all sides. It would overlook some recognisable view, a dark mill perhaps with dark, northern fumes pouring into the night sky. It's odd entering a strange room for the first time, knowing that it's going to be your new home, knowing that in the near future others will enter the room and perhaps see something of you in it. I opened the door carefully and switched on the light. There was no lampshade so the light was harsh.

My eyes, temporarily blinded by the raw light, moved instinctively towards the fireplace. There was an electric fire with a note on it, which said that it didn't work, and a gas fire next to it. I noticed that there was a fire extinguisher to the side of the electric fire. Somebody cautious had lived here. There was a blue rug in front of the electric fire – the fire that didn't work. I thought that it should have been in front of the gas fire, if the previous occupant was being logical.

There was a wooden desk to work at, with its top drawer hanging at a jaunty angle. Opposite, there was a Creda Corvette water heater beside a sink and a bathroom cabinet with a silver fish motif that had a large protruding mouth and an elaborate tail fin. I couldn't work out if this was for decoration, or merely a joke, an ironic stab at the kinds of people who might find this sort of thing sufficiently decorative to display in a prominent position. I was trying to form a mental image of my predecessor.

165

It was clearly a man, who was quite possibly more ironic but less, can I say, rational than myself.

There was a Polarfrost fridge in the corner. I thought that it sounded like a good make. I opened the fridge door and I could see rust in each of the bottom corners. Somebody had tried to brighten this part of the room with a McEwan's Lager teddy bear fridge magnet. I didn't see this as ironic, just sad. It wasn't the airy attic of my imagination or the kind of room that my brother might have entered.

The room had been tidied before I arrived. There was a poster rolled up beside the litter bin. I unrolled it. It was the early Human League. I thought that I had left my student days behind me, but clearly not yet. I had been fortunate up to that point in terms of accommodation, but then again, this was the North. I had had a poster of the young Chatterton on my wall in Cambridge, his hand outstretched, the poison taking effect. I thought that it might not be appropriate for here. I sat down hard on the bed, and it squeaked. I imagined the landlady downstairs listening to me intently. I moved up and down several times to see what would happen to the noise. The bed springs creaked in rhythm.

I glanced out of the window and saw a gang of lads, laughing, smoking and joking away. It was as if they sensed me looking down at them. One of them looked straight up at the window of the room with the bare lightbulb hanging from the ceiling. We made eye contact. I could feel the menace in his eyes.

I moved around the room getting my bearings. There was a little blood on the pillow. It was very old, almost black. I looked at it carefully and tried to scrape it off, thinking about whether it had come from a nosebleed or something else, perhaps more violent. Or from sex. You couldn't tell. There was no personal history written into it. It was a sign rather than a signifier. What I mean is that it told me something, but I don't know what. Perhaps it was from somebody old before the house was divided into bedsits. Perhaps it was part of the final scene of the old, retired previous owner, before the new landlady and the students and the room full of beer mats, tatty posters and fridge magnets. Perhaps it was, therefore, a signifier of evolution and change. Or, on second thoughts, maybe it was just a sign of violence. You really couldn't tell. This was my new home.

At nights, I would squeeze out past the bin, which stayed permanently in front of the house, with its lid lying insolently open, leaving that sweet, sickly smell of refuse in the air, and go for long runs along the wet, greasy roads that dropped down to the east of the city. It was a strange world down there. The factories were coming down. Piles of blackened rubble, brick and metal would be constantly moved around in those dark, depressing spaces, and I would be huffing and puffing on my way past, trying to remember each detail from my last run, like a historian, like somebody who cared about the trajectory of all of this destruction. Concrete blocks hanging from metal rods like corpses hung out as a warning. Improbable spiked chimneys. Gouged, pockmarked concrete blocks. Sometimes the front façades of these factories were all that was left. You would run along deserted streets, like long dark tunnels, and then into a lit-up area with sex shops and saunas and a few Asian men hanging about on the street corner. They didn't see many joggers up there on long, wet nights. 'Hey, you're running the wrong way,' they would shout after me. 'You're running the wrong fucking way.' Cambridge, with all the young sportsmen jogging out towards the sports fields of Grange Road seemed like a long way away.

The irony was that my brother died in a climbing accident within a year of me moving there. He had been to visit me only once. He had come to the psychology department and talked and laughed with the other lecturers, and then he had turned to me and said quite simply, 'You're not like them. Do you know that?' He had meant it as a loving and thoughtful compliment. And I knew what he meant. Within five months of his death, my wife, whom I had married as a student, had an accident when she fell beneath a train and lost an arm. My life had changed for good.

I thought of my brother a lot. I would often have clear images of him. They would come from nowhere. His walk is one of the easiest things for me to recall about him. I just have to close my eyes, and there it is. It is a slightly lopsided walk, lower on the left, for some reason, with a real spring in his step as if he is floating above the ground. But I can visualise him and his walk clearly only from the back. It's funny that. He always seemed to be walking away from me, never coming towards me. He never stayed anywhere too long. Climbing great sharp, jagged rocks, scaling snow-covered mountains that petered out somewhere in the clouds above some distant, foreign land.

I could still feel my brother's presence in Sheffield, and every time I saw something that he had described I felt sad and cheated. I remember seeing my first coal mine, an image that stands out in my mind because my brother had talked about mines and the social history of the North. I could see the mine appearing in the distance, but even from that somewhat oblique angle I could recognise it. It was silhouetted against an iron-grey sky. It was quite flat, a sharp outline, two-dimensional like a picture. Self-contained and framed by green fields with muddy tracks through them. Flat, dark features against the grey scenery. Old, strangely familiar shapes. Shapes from my past.

As I looked closer and closer I could see that the real mine was more untidy than in any pictures I had seen or any images that I ever had provided for me. There were more bits and pieces left around the place. More debris. More mess. There were wagons parked, probably containers waiting to be loaded. But they were carelessly parked. They almost looked abandoned.

I had this one thought. My brother would have seen it like this on one of his visits: the silhouette, the familiarity, the flatness, even the unexpected untidiness. My eyes were seeing it for the first time. Just as his had done before me. We were united again. Briefly. We were together. It's pathetic how some people try to deal with death. I suppose that was how desperate I was at that time, as I tried to come to terms with my brother's death, a brother killed by his sport, or rather the love of his sport. Climbing for him always came first. Back home in Legmore Street, he would climb around the yard walls, his feet never touching the ground. He was a climber, he always said, not an electrician, not a spark, which is how he served his apprenticeship.

He had left to go on an expedition, and had not returned, and now there was not one night when I did not see him briefly in my dreams. At first he would talk to me, and we would walk together through strange and unfamiliar landscapes, but recently he seemed always to be walking away from me, or leaving buildings that I was just entering. And in those buildings, there would always be cages and wheels, and sometimes there would be fire and the closing curtains of blackness. Sometimes there was to be no comfort.

It was a climbing expedition to the Himalayas. He was climbing Nanda Devi, the Goddess of Joy. He was near the summit when he fell, that's all we heard. I remember two telegrams arriving simultaneously, one from my Uncle Terence saying 'Serious accident to Bill. Ring home.' I can't remember what the other telegram said. It was from my mother, and it was probably more vague. 'Ring home' perhaps, but I don't know. The face of the telegram delivery man is just a blank in my memory. It is only his hand reaching out towards me that I can visualise – the movement from the bag, the two telegrams like playing cards spaced out in a hand in front of me as if I could take my pick. But I had to read both, and one was more serious than the other.

By this time, my wife had joined me in Sheffield, and we lived in an old coach house that was infested with rats in the loft and which crouched down below a leafy road that led towards the university from the rich suburbs, where the men who had run the steel industry of Great Britain had once lived. I remember my heart pounding as I went to the public telephone to ring home. The question was forming in my mind as I half-ran along that road. 'How serious?' I was almost rehearsing it. I can remember my relief that there was nobody in the phone box. It was a Sunday morning, and the streets were deserted. I can picture the red phone box now as clear as day on that Sunday morning. The sun was shining. I can remember the angle of the box changing, which suggests that I might have been jogging, but I half-walked, half-ran along the road. I must have been running towards the end when I got near the telephone box where I rang my mother's number. As soon as a quiet voice that wasn't my mother's answered the phone, I knew exactly how serious the accident was. If he had only been injured, my mother would have been there on the other end of the phone, angry with him and angry with me. I had prepared myself to hear her rage. She always hated him climbing. She just never saw the point of going out into the country loaded with all that equipment. That's what she always said when the three of us were sitting in front of the fire. 'I don't really understand it. I don't know why you got interested in that bloody nonsense.' But there was just some other woman's voice, and then a long silence, and then my mother's voice drowned in sobbing. 'He's dead,' she said. 'Your brother's dead.' The breaking of the bad news was as straightforward as that.

We had a service in the house without Bill ever returning home. His body lay below a pile of stones on a Himalayan hillside with a few details of his life scratched with a stone or an ice-pick on the side of a grey rock. A few of his friends who had served their apprenticeships and stuck with their trade came to the funeral. Some had moved on: one was now a fireman in Belfast with stories of smoke-damaged bargains to be salvaged from shops that had been blown up in 'the Troubles', one was in insurance. Both were now good, sound businesses to be in in Belfast. The old house was too small, and the crowd of friends and neighbours congregated on the pavement and on stairs. In order to see them all you had to pan around like a camera, which I suppose I was in a way as I tried to imagine what Bill would have thought of the turnout, and the emotion displayed for him that day in September.

Bill's wife of a few months was there, and she slept that night with my mother in the front bedroom. Bill would have laughed with embarrassment to hear about that. I would have loved to see his face at that very moment. 'She's really middle class,' he had told me when they first met, and I liked the way that he had used the word 'really', as if to say he had really landed on his feet. 'I've told her about the old house,' he said, 'and she says that she understands that it's not very modern or nice, but I don't think she does,' and we both made a face, like kids do when they're dreading something but they want to show it. And now she was here without him to supervise her experiences. I laughed on my own at the thought of that. But I don't suppose really that it was much of an actual laugh.

He didn't leave much behind. He had a diary that I was allowed to look at before it was taken away from me. 'It'll just upset Geoffrey,' my mother said, and then she complained that I never got the clothes back that I had lent to him. She cried for months on end every time I rang her, just as she had done for my father, although I had to listen to that from the back bedroom. But she always said that the loss of a child is the hardest thing to bear. Her 'wee son' is how she referred to him. Her wee son. She never seemed to take in any of the details of his death, and even years after she would ask me what country Bill had died in. Or she would ask, 'How did he fall?' Or, 'How long was it before they found his body?' But she didn't really want the answers.

After he died, the name of the house I had lived in – Edelweiss – started to upset me greatly. I hated anything to do with Switzerland or mountains, snow, rocks, crampons, Tibet ... the list was almost endless. I thought of Alpine peaks and him beneath the ground, beneath that deep snow. And I thought of the seasons changing around him and the snow melting. I guessed that there would probably be white mountain flowers in the spring out in Nepal, erupting through the brown earth made damp through the snow melting. And I imagined him lying there quite still, not motionless but quite still, a stillness like sleep.

These were powerful and painful images, which I tried unsuccessfully to control. But that is the ultimate legacy of death, I suppose; areas of the mind and areas of consciousness become out of bounds. My mother missed him badly. Whenever I was home, she would often burst into great gulps of lugubrious, self-pitying tears that took her breath away. The room smelt heavy with whisky. You would see her reaching out for the glass that had been knocked over, lying on its side up against the settee. He had been taken from her. I wanted to tell her that he had also been taken from me, but I don't think that she would have been that interested. I would try to talk with her as she drank, and I would see her glance at me, a glance as vague and grey and unformed as twilight. A glance that never seemed to connect with anything within me. It was a glance into the distance where he now was. I knew how she felt. I just didn't show it, I suppose. So she lay there in that front room of ours late at night, drinking and sobbing, saying his name over and over again, as if it might help to say it. She would wait up for him all through the night. Sometimes, you could hear what sounded like real conversations. You would hear her voice rising to ask questions and sometimes you would hear the downward intonation of an assertion in her voice, as if she were telling him what he must do. Perhaps she was warning him.

One night I came in late and found her lying in front of the television, which was still on despite the fact that the programmes had finished hours ago. The crackling set illuminated her face. She was half asleep and she came to slowly, annoyed to be woken up so late, or so early. She started to sit up. Still half asleep, she started talking to me. She told me through those bleary, watery eyes that she wished it had been me who had

171

slipped off the mountainside that day. She wished that it were me who had plunged that fine, bright morning in snow-covered Nepal into the hallowed sanctity of pontifical death.

But it was just the drink talking. I don't know what prompted it. She was probably just confused in the middle of the night. And in the morning, I am sure that she never remembered saying any of it. As she tried to wipe a drink stain out of the carpet, she told me that she must have fallen asleep in the living room. She was rubbing furiously at the red carpet. It was never mentioned again. But she had sobbed it out at me that night, like it was the painful truth, like it was hard to say. I had lost my brother, and then I felt that I was in danger of losing my mother through her grief and her anger and her willingness to turn on those left behind. Every time I thought of a boxer killed in the ring, I thought of those left behind, not united in their grief, but like this, like my family, tearing at each other, trying to forget. It was like what Naz had said about forgetting fear; there were worse things to try to forget. I thought about Paul Ingle's family and how they might be feeling, how they might be when the drink takes over. They weren't cosy thoughts.

My mother sought to find my brother in old, tear-stained photographs which showed him when he had a gap in his teeth and thick eyebrows, in the days before she started plucking them for him. She always tended him when he was a boy: plucking his eyebrows, fixing his tie, smoothing his hair. I never got that attention. She said that I didn't need it. My tie was always straight and my eyebrows managed to grow in a fairly controlled way all on their own.

My brother and my mother were always very close. I was closer to my father – as my mother always reminded me – who died when I was thirteen. It felt solitary after that. I enjoyed my own company when I was young, I think. My brother and my mother were the sociable ones, and he grew up to be a climber, a sport that depends on others, although the morning he died, he was climbing Nanda Devi quite alone. With the exception of bad-minton, I have always been attracted to solitary sports: marathon running, squash, boxing, sports for which you don't need to depend on another soul.

I think that there were indications of this even when I was young. I would take my scooter every night up to the park gate, regardless of the weather or season, and count the strides to get to the third railing past the gate, the one with the rust covering its base. My brother and his friends would sometimes watch me on my scooter at night up by the park, under the street lights where the bats would flap and swoop through the black night air. Occasionally, he and his friends would hear me riding along, counting out loud the number of strides on my routine out and back. I didn't want to lose count. Sometimes, he would lay his hanky out on the park railings because he said he had heard that it attracted bats. The park keeper had told him that. He didn't want to study the bats; he just wanted his friends to get close enough to them to at least touch them with their sticks. A violent touch, of course, but it was the touch rather than the violence that was crucial. The touch would be a demonstration that my brother and his friends were in control. It would be evidence that they understood how bats could be drawn down from their meaningless zigzagging forays across the black night sky. A dead bat would have been even better. That would have been a permanent demonstration of their success, of their superiority in this regard. But they never came near to that. There was never any waxy, festering bat carcass to look at in our house. None that I can remember, anyway.

I would make that journey on my scooter again and again. My Uncle Terence said it was like training. He had been a boxer; he knew what he was talking about. I have always been attracted to the idea of boxers rising at 5.00 a.m. every morning to run in the city, whilst the air is cleaner. I like the solitariness of boxing. My brother hated it. He said it was pointless risking your life like that in a ring where somebody is out to hurt you deliberately.

I would ring my mother up just to say hello and tell her that I was in Sheffield, and for a moment she would be confused as to which son it was that was calling her so late at night. Sometimes she called me Bill by mistake. I didn't bother to correct her. I let her have a conversation with her other son for a change. I thought that it might do her some good. I thought that it might be good for her to have her son back for a while. You could hear her coming round on the phone, her mind slowly trying to remember what it was that was blackening and shading her days. She would sound shaken, a little confused.

Sometimes, I thought that she was getting confused more in

general as she was stuck in that room day in, day out with the dog-eared photographs and the swirly red carpet still soaking up all the drops of drink that she spilled.

I, on the other hand, wanted to move on with my life, to leave all this mourning behind. I was sure that Bill would have been proud of me in Sheffield, with the rock faces of Stannage Edge on the outskirts of the city which perhaps still has his impression on the wet, grey millstone grit slabs. I wanted to feel his presence.

Whilst my mother still sat tending Bill with her old photographs of him on her lap, I was now away, making a life at university, in the biggest village in England. My mother wasn't sure if I was a swot or not – Bill had always said that he knew people who worked even harder than me. He said that he was too pretty to study and, whenever he worked in our bedroom, he told us that he would have to dismantle the mirror on the dresser so that he would not be distracted by his own image.

Lenny always said that I was from a privileged background. 'Cambridge and all that,' he remarked. 'Fucking Cambridge.'

'Not as privileged as you think, you know,' I said.

But he didn't believe me, not then and not now.

THREE

How did I first meet Big Lenny? Steady Eddie in his own words when he wanted a favour. The man with knuckles on his knuckles when he didn't. The man with the mouth. Gob on legs. Mouth on a stick. The big fella. The man to know. That's an easy question to answer. It's hard to forget meeting somebody like that. He always liked to say that nobody ever forgot him and nobody ever forgot their first meeting with him. Everybody met him the same way, though – on his terms. He liked to know the score, to know what was happening in that city where everybody knew your business. I suppose that a psychologist might know something that he didn't. There was always that small possibility. I had been going out in Sheffield on my own, and he had got to hear about this psychologist who was out and about. He said that he had never met one before so he invited me along to meet him through this barman that I had got to know.

'I've a friend who wants to meet you,' the barman, whose name I didn't know, had told me. 'He says that you might be able to help him.'

'I'm not a clinical psychologist,' I had said.

'That doesn't matter,' said the barman. 'There's nothing really the matter with him anyway.'

It was wet that Thursday night. There was a wet, damp mist. The street was empty, even the gang wasn't in its usual place. I carried an umbrella and took a bus into the city centre.

'Tell me when we get to town, please,' I said to the driver, a man with a thin face and a faint moustache who looked very gloomy.

'We're in town now, luv,' he replied.

I couldn't tell whether this was a joke or not. His manner confused me.

'The centre of town, I mean,' I said.

'Oh,' he said. 'Okay, luv. You want the town centre? I've got you.'

I sat at the back and shook my umbrella. A couple looked round to see what was causing the flapping noise, as if they thought that some large, mad crow might have found its way onto the bus and was frantically shaking its feathers. Then they went back to staring out of the window, which had rain running down it in rivulets. I was the last to get off the bus, and the driver tipped his imaginary hat at me. 'Have a good one,' he said. He sounded wheezy. He was smoking and blowing his smoke through the open window.

I glanced back at him as he looked out sadly at the wet, empty streets. I watched the bus shudder off slowly. I walked up and down the same street a couple of times as I tried to find the club. I turned the corner and saw dozens of people queuing in the rain. It was as if all the people in this deserted city had congregated in this wet, lonely place. I joined the back of the slow-moving queue. Girls in light summer dresses bobbed up and down in the rain for warmth in front of me. One girl with long, shiny black hair asked me if she could have my umbrella.

'No, not really,' I said politely.

'Okay, then,' she sneered. 'Stick it.' And her friends all laughed.

One of her friends was a large, wide-hipped blonde who was wearing a dress decorated with pink and green condoms that had been blown up and pinned to the shoulders. She had pictures cut from magazines of men with big, erect cocks pinned to both the front and back of her dress. I wasn't sure why. A large black man with an enormous erection stared at me every time she turned her back. He seemed to be smiling at me. It was an uncanny picture because no matter how I turned he seemed always to be able to catch my eye.

'I think I'm going to be sick,' said the girl in the dress.

'Not here, for fuck's sake,' said the one with the dark, shiny hair. 'Wait until you get inside. It's warmer in there if we have to hang about waiting for you to finish gypping.'

Every now and again, the girl with the dark hair would pretend to go down on the man with the largest cock pinned low on her friend's belly. She waggled her long, speckled tongue, a tongue stained purple with red wine, in front of the picture and made 'num num' sounds.

'I should be so lucky,' she said, when she eventually straightened herself up. I could see that she was getting quite wet, so I told her and her plumpish friend that they could share my umbrella if they wanted.

'Fuck off, creep,' she said and turned her back on me.

'I don't think that they should let creeps in here,' she said to her coterie of friends. 'What do you think, girls?' They threw me short, disgusted looks and occasionally made comments about my umbrella.

'I hope that fucking well chokes you,' said the fat girl, who was still threatening to be sick.

Eventually, I got to the door. A small bouncer with close-cropped receding hair, who was much smaller than me, stopped me. He was staring at my umbrella.

'What's that?' he said, pointing towards it with a sharp movement of his forehead, as if he were nutting someone even smaller than himself.

'An umbrella,' I replied.

'Oh,' he said. 'That's all right, then.' And he motioned me in with his head. I entered the warmth of the club and started to shake the umbrella with a delicate and controlled wrist movement.

'It's a very wet umbrella,' I said to the same bouncer.

He left his spot to stand in front of me. He was looking up.

'Don't push your luck, mate,' he replied. 'All right? Pay here and fuck off.' And he pointed to a bored-looking black girl with large, heaving breasts bulging out of a leotard. Her breasts were resting on a counter. She took my money without saying anything and nodded me in. I made my way through a long, dark tunnel with fluorescent lights on the walls that were flashing intermittently. I was struck by the loud music and by a thick, pulsating wall of people that started a few feet from the end of the tunnel. I tried to ask a doorman where the lower bar was but he couldn't really hear what I was saying. And I had to repeat it several times so close to his ear that I could see a ragged, festering scab on his earlobe. He had obviously been bitten. But by what or by whom? I was starting to have doubts about this club. He

177

pointed casually over the heads of the people with a bandaged finger. The bandage wasn't quite big enough to cover a severe bite.

'I hope that you have got a bad dog,' I said loudly, but he didn't hear me.

I set off slowly and carefully, apologising every time I made contact with a hot, almost moist, body. I made my way gingerly through the crowd until I could see the bright rows of bottles before me and the bum cheeks of the waitresses, which were lifted up and displayed with stilettos.

There was a small group at the bottom bar, where I was told to meet Lenny. One girl was quite small and perched on a stool, drinking. She had a distinctive face. I could see that even from the side. She was recognisably different. But I thought that I might be mistaken in that light with all those people crowded around, pushing and shoving. It was hard to see. She was sitting on a stool chatting to a woman with a thin, lined, tired face, who was smoking, and to a very broad-backed bouncer who had a bald, shiny head that reflected the bright, white light from the spotlight. Any other person might have avoided this spot because of the cruelty of the white light, but he looked like he had chosen it intentionally.

This one harsh white light in a world of pink and red hues made the rings under his companion's eyes look darker and made her look much older. But I could see that he wasn't bothered. This small group seemed to have an invisible bubble around them. The edges of the territory were marked by the bouncer's expansive posture with his hand outstretched on a mirrored pillar, stealing extra feet. I noticed the hand. It was enormous. He was taking up space in this club where there wasn't any.

They were all laughing. But the laugh never made him lose his guard. He was vigilant, watching everybody and everything. Every now and again, he would glance behind him, watching his back. I don't think that I ever realised until that very moment that this was more than just an expression. They didn't notice me at first. Not even him. I was at the edge of the crowd, part of it. Anonymous faces that were sensible enough not to attempt to break the skin of that bubble. I wanted to see what they were like. I strained forward for a better look. It was that which he noticed – my odd straining posture. In that sea of faces and shapes, he picked that out. That was how observant he was in this territory of his.

He seemed to laugh. He came over to me and, without saying anything, he took my arm and led me across the gap. His fingers pinched the skin under my arms. He didn't drag me over, but it was forceful enough.

'Well here he is,' he said to his friends. 'I'm Lenny, by the way,' said the bouncer. 'Most people call me Big Lenny, but you can call me Mr Lenny, if you like, or sir.'

And they all burst out laughing. Especially the small girl, who was rocking back and forth on her chair. The two women were introduced to me and then there was silence again. Lenny, Karen and Linzi all stood looking at me expectantly. Linzi took a long slow sip of her drink. Despite the volume of the background music, there was a deep well of silence.

'So this is the real Sheffield,' I said eventually. 'It's been hit hard by the recession, hasn't it?' There was no response. Not even a nod. 'Are you all fortunate enough to have jobs?' I asked. It sounded stupid before I had finished saying it.

'Well, I do three jobs at the moment,' said Lenny. 'Door work, security work and debt collection, not counting working as Linzi here's minder. That's unpaid, though.'

And they all laughed again.

'There's plenty of work up here if you're prepared to be a bit flexible. There's so much debt that there are a lot of jobs in the debt recovery business, and that's just for starters. And there's plenty of door work,' he added. 'Even the pubs need somebody on the doors now. All the pubs are getting really violent so that generates even more work.

'Have you never been in a top-notch club before?' And he gestured around the bar area at the waitresses in leotards working the tills and serving the drinks, and the men queuing at the bar, leering over the counter at them. Commenting on their bum cheeks. 'These are just the ordinary punters down here,' said Lenny. 'There's a wine bar as well. But that's just for VIPs really. Linzi will be up there later. But because you're new we thought that you'd feel better down here with the . . .'

'Ordinary folks,' said Karen.

'The more common type of people,' said Linzi.

179

'The fucking riff-raff,' said Lenny. They all spoke more or less simultaneously.

I looked around and said that there was no problem. Lenny told Linzi that it was her round. He told her to go to the centre of the bar to get served. She had trouble getting off the stool.

'I hope that you're not narrow-minded,' he said, sensing my embarrassment.

Linzi descended from her high stool into another world. She was transformed immediately from a small person on a tall stool to a midget on the floor.

Lenny bent down low and pinched her cheek. 'Ain't she lovely? I call her Bridget the Midget,' he said. 'We'll have a dance later, Bridge.' He said it very loudly as if he were talking to a deaf person or a dog. She was beaming.

Linzi came back with the drinks on a tray. I held them for her as she climbed back onto the stool again. She was more or less level with me.

'I'm not really a midget,' said Linzi to me. 'I believe the correct word is dwarf. I'm a twenty-one-year-old with a twenty-one-year-old's body, but I've just got short arms and legs. A midget has a nine-year-old's body. My mum's a dwarf as well,' she continued. 'It was my friend, Karen, who persuaded me to go to nightclubs to get me out of the house,' said Linzi. 'I know lots of midgets who never leave the house at night. I used to go on my own. My mum was really worried because she'd heard that in Australia they have competitions to see who can throw the midget the furthest. She'd seen it on TV. She was afraid that they'd start throwing me onto the stage in the nightclub. I only met Lenny because there was this guy bothering me. When they're pissed at the end of the night, some blokes think that if they haven't pulled, they might as well chat up a dwarf. I couldn't get rid of this bloke – he followed me to the taxi. Lenny had to follow him outside and sort him.'

Lenny just smiled.

'I like going out to nightclubs with Karen and there's always the possibility that I might meet someone,' said Linzi, sucking through her straw.

Another bouncer came up. 'Pulled again, Linzi, eh?' he said, touching her hand and glancing at me. 'She never fails that girl, you know. I don't know what her secret is.'

180

'It's just my great personality,' said Linzi. 'Don't you agree? Everybody tells me that I've got a super personality. And I'm a bit tipsy tonight with all this brandy and Babycham. It's gone to my head.'

The hours passed painfully slowly. Lenny left to do his rounds. 'Some of us have got to work for a living,' he said.

'Time to leave, ladies and gentlemen, please.' The small bouncer who had asked me about my umbrella had approached us. 'Have you no beds to go to?' he asked and then winked at me. I didn't like the ambiguity of the wink.

'Will you walk me to the taxi, please?' asked Linzi. 'I don't want to get bothered by all the guys who haven't managed to pull. They're always making comments to me about how they'd like to have a dwarf at the end of the night, if they can't get anything better, just to see what it's like.'

I could see Lenny coming to the door to watch us leave. 'Goodnight, sir. Goodnight, madam,' he said. He was laughing with another bouncer. I heard him say something more. I couldn't really make it out. But he was laughing a lot, probably at me, but my mother has always said that I am a little oversensitive.

FOUR

Late in the winter afternoons, after the students had gone, I liked to keep my room in the psychology department quite dark, so that my focus was on the bright figures on the screen in front of me. In the distance I could see some high-rise flats, now housing students, and at four o'clock in the afternoon, the lights would go on in the flats and I could see lives being lived, almost in miniature. But compared with what was going on right in front of me, I could see almost nothing of interest taking place in those bare rooms in the long afternoons, grey with rain. The brightness from the screen sometimes dazzled me.

After Cambridge, I continued to work on the microanalysis of human nonverbal communication, the very basis of social interaction. I liked a large, magnified image of the people I was studying, so that even the smallest movement would be sharp and discriminate. A bright image full of contrast and shape with hard edges.

He was sitting there in front of me. Quite still to begin with. Another student. They were all students. This one wore jeans and a striped shirt under a black denim jacket. I don't know what colour the shirt was. I have forgotten. I never paid much attention to them when I was trying to persuade them to go with me to take part in my study. The image was black and white. The shirt might have been blue and white perhaps, but that's just a guess. He wore glasses. I don't remember his name either. He wrote it down for me. It was hard to pronounce; I do remember that. I called him 'glasses with foot out front' for reference purposes. That was the image I had of him on my bright screen. Glasses with black rims hiding his eyes and a big black boot that liked to move across my screen as he talked. I could see his laces flicker as he moved.

I only used that title for personal reference purposes, though. He was officially subject eleven. 'Glasses with foot out front' sounded to me like an impressionist painting. Blue bowl with olives, that kind of thing. I liked that sort of title for my video recordings. The art of conversation. That was what I was analysing really. There is a lot of important detail in paintings that most ordinary people miss. He didn't look too comfortable.

The student on the screen was starting to move. His leg was pulled across his body, like a fragile, trembling barrier between him and me. His left foot was magnified in the foreground, with that gigantic flickering lace. His boot wasn't tied properly. The foot looked huge. With my hidden camera in the experimental room, I could see the sole of his shoe. A glimpse of his very sole, that was my joke. His head was tilted back at an angle looking up at the cartoon story that I had projected onto the wall for him. He had to tell me a story about what was happening in the cartoon. I used cartoon worlds as my focus. Everyone thinks that psychology is like *Cracker*. It isn't. I was studying what the movements of the hand add to the communication of meaning in cartoons. *Cracker* never considered human behaviour in situations like this. I don't think that he ever studied anything. Suddenly, the phone rang. I pressed the pause button on my video. It was Norman, the porter. There was somebody on the way up to see me. He didn't know who he was. But whoever it was wouldn't wait until I came down to fetch him, which was the rule to prevent strangers wandering around the department.

There was a loud knock on the door. And, without waiting for me to respond, the door swung open and hit the wall. Some chipped plaster fell to the floor. It was Lenny. He invited himself in.

'You didn't think that you could hide from me for ever,' he said, sitting on my armchair. 'I thought that I'd just pop in to see you,' he said, smiling. 'I was up this way anyway. I was just passing.' And then, after a pause. 'The way you do.' He looked around the room in a slow, deliberate fashion, almost theatrically. 'Do you always sit in the bloody dark?' he asked, trying to make it sound funny. He switched on the light. 'Let's throw some light on the subject, eh?'

I hadn't said anything yet. I was very surprised to see him. I didn't think that he knew where I worked. In fact, I knew that he didn't know where I worked. His eyes moved around my small office and then fixed on my screen.

'So what's this all about?' he asked, pointing at the hand movement, frozen in time on the screen in front of us. 'Do you mind if I smoke?' he asked.

I said that I did, but he ignored me. He blew the smoke towards the middle of the room for good measure. Roughly in my direction. He was challenging me, I knew that, so I responded in a way that only an academic would. 'Why don't you watch this carefully,' I said, sounding irritated. I played a tiny fragment of the tape and then paused it, and asked him what he had seen. I asked him to tell me exactly what he had seen.

'Let me see,' said Lenny, scrutinising the screen with that look of his. 'What did I see? Hmmmm. What exactly did I see?' He was imitating my accent. 'I saw a spoilt fucker, a bit on the tubby side. Is it all right to say that? Is it all right to use ordinary language here?'

I nodded. 'In your own words,' I said. 'I wouldn't want you to try to change just for me.'

'Good. Okay then.' He changed his position on the chair. 'Probably a public school boy, like you.' He pointed at me in a sharp, jabbing movement with the hand that was holding the cigarette and screwed his face up. 'A bit of a swot. A bit boring-looking, like a lot of you university types,' he said.

'Anything else?' I enquired. 'What about the gesture?' I played the short loop of tape again.

'Yes, there's definitely a gesture there. A little bit of hand movement. Yes, I can see that. He's nervous. Is that what you're after? Yes, I can tell that. He's definitely nervous.'

Suddenly, a new expression swept across his face. 'Oh, I've got it. Is he a poof or something? A bum bandit? Is that what the gesture is meant to tell me? Is he a bit on the old limp-wristed side? That's it. He's a fucking bum boy. You've devised a new technique for spotting poofs. That would be very useful for the police or the army. You could make millions from your research.'

I rolled my eyes to the smoky ceiling of my room in an exaggerated way and said that it wasn't anything to do with his sexuality. I tried again. 'What about what the gesture is saying?'

He looked again. 'Not much,' he said.

'Now listen to the speech this time.'

I played the tape with the sound turned up. 'She's eating the food,' said the overweight public schoolboy on the screen.

'Now watch the tape again,' I said. 'Now what is the gesture saying?'

'Nothing,' said Lenny. 'Except that he's a nervous poof.'

'Okay. Let me ask you a few questions about it.'

'Fire away,' said Lenny, who had obviously decided to humour me.

'He says that she's eating the food. What is she eating?' I asked.

'Something like a sandwich?' suggested Lenny.

'How big is this sandwich?' I asked.

'Pretty big,' he said.

'How is she eating it?'

'The fucking normal way,' he said. 'That's a queer fucking question. Using her fucking feet, of course. Don't be so fucking daft.'

'Okay, forget about the last question,' I said. 'You see you got some information from the gesture. You knew that it was a sandwich. You knew that it was big. Just look at the original cartoon.' I dropped it onto my desk in front of him. 'Look at what she is eating,' I said. 'You got both answers right, even though the fat boy never mentioned any of this in what he was saying. Do you see the significance of this?'

'Not really,' said Lenny.

'Look,' I said. 'Speech and the small movements of the hand work together to tell you about what is going on out there in the world. Speech doesn't give you the full picture. He never said in his speech, "She's eating a sandwich." His hand movement told you what she was eating. Look at the cartoon from *The Beano*. Look at this picture. What's Ivy eating? That's right. It's a sandwich – a big sandwich.'

'Oh,' said Lenny.

'Do you understand what I am saying here?' I asked.

He sat there looking at me long and hard and then his face started to light up as if he had just thought of something.

'Do you mean to say that you get paid for doing this? I'm in the wrong fucking game,' he said. 'I'm in the wrong fucking racket. Honestly, I'm in the wrong fucking game,' he said again.

'Okay, I'll show you something else,' I said. I led him into a less used, dustier room where there was some equipment for physiological measurement: a device for measuring galvanic skin response, a slide projector and a long mirror stretching along one wall. It was equipment for an older study, long before my time at the university.

'This is more like it,' he said. 'Is this lie detection or something like that? I can identify with that kind of work.'

I said that it was something like that.

I made him sit on a red plastic chair in the middle of the room and attached the electrodes to his large, horny hands. I explained that I was going to record his galvanic skin response to certain stimuli, which would produce a variety of emotional responses in him. Then, without telling him, I activated a video camera hidden behind the one-way mirror to film his facial expressions. He sat there with an unwavering smile on his face.

'Try to relax,' I said.

'I am fucking relaxed,' he replied.

The first image burst into life in front of him. It was a mother and a newborn infant. There was a beatific look on the mother's face.

'Aaaah,' he said. 'Am I allowed to make comments like this to show that I'm normal?'

'Not really,' I said. 'It will affect the equipment.'

'Okay then, I'll say it to myself instead. Aaaah,' he said again.

It wasn't any quieter the second time around.

'Look, you have to be silent for this experiment to work,' I said. The next image appeared in front of him. It was of a landscape, a mountainous landscape. I could feel my own emotion changing in very personal ways that few psychologists, who did not know about my brother, would have understood. I recognised the landscape. It was the Alps with Mont Blanc in the background. My brother had climbed there one summer. I had kept the postcard from him. It was one of the few things I had left of him. I would look at the signature and imagine him signing the card in the Alpine sun, his face tanned, a happy smile on his face.

'Oooooh, that's a nice picture,' said Lenny. 'Very peaceful.'

'Look,' I said quietly, 'I'm not trying to see if you're normal through what you say. Just try to be silent.'

186

The next picture was of a naked woman.

'Nice,' he said. 'I know that I'm not allowed to comment, but I don't want you to think that I'm a queer fucker like that other cunt. That's very nice. Nice big fucking breasts.' He made wet smacking noises with his lips, like a baby sucking. 'You can tell that I'm normal,' he said.

The next image was a very graphic photograph of somebody who had been butchered in some atrocity in Africa. The victim was black. It was a scene of a tribal slaughter. It was an extreme image. There was a lot of blood. His head was drowning in a deep pool of blood on a dusty track. It looked like a machete attack, deep slashes everywhere. I hadn't selected the photographs. I wouldn't ask strangers to watch this. They belonged to somebody else. They were designed to produce extreme emotional responses in people. I had heard about students viewing this particular picture and covering their eyes, shielding themselves from the horrors of life.

I watched Lenny's face. He seemed to be staring more intently at this picture, taking it all in. He didn't say anything. Perhaps he had got bored with goading me. His pupils seemed to have opened up like flowers in the rain.

The images went on and on. He sat there often smirking, sometimes staring a little more intently. He was masking as much as he could with that great irritating smile of his because he suspected that there was something or somebody behind the mirror.

'So what did you learn about me, Mr Psychologist?' he asked at the end of the sequence. 'Am I normal?' He looked at me.

I gave a gentle, cultured laugh. 'Pretty normal,' I said. 'For somebody in your profession.'

He didn't seem to like my response. 'So what did you learn through all of that bollocks?' he asked. 'That I can smile even when I see a dead body? I could have told you that if you'd asked me. It's a hard world out there, mate. I've seen more than most.'

I told him that it wasn't as simple as that. I took him into another room with equipment for playing the videotape back in slow motion. I made him sit down as I rewound the tape and found a short sequence. I played his own recording back to him. He didn't look surprised that he had been taped. He assumed that everybody deceived other people whenever they could. I showed him his face in close-up during those first few nano-seconds when the image appeared.

I explained to him that there are tell-tale signs of emotion in the human face, but that these are usually missed by observers because of their fleeting nature. I showed him his own micro-expressions. The fleeting image now ticked slowly across the monitor a frame at a time. The expressions on his face slowed down sufficiently for us to see.

'People never see these expressions of yours,' I said. 'But I can.' I was sounding almost as arrogant as him.

I glanced up at him. He was looking interested in what I had to say. He was off guard now.

I went through his performance frame by frame right in front of him, isolating the micro-expressions of disgust and surprise, fear and sadness before he managed to squelch them with his great smirking smile. That great mask of his behind which he hid so often.

He was impressed by what I had managed to uncover. He was laughing at his own slightly inadequate performance right there on the screen. His mask was not quite quick enough, not quite as quick as he had always thought. A psychologist could see through him. He asked whether 'normal' people could see through him as well.

'It depends on what you call normal,' I said. I explained that of all the groups ever tested in this research paranoid schizophrenics turned out to be the most sensitive at reading these tell-tale signs. It was as if they lived in a world where they were just too accurate at reading people.

'Just as long as the police don't employ any of those nutters, then,' said Lenny, and we both laughed.

'I'm still better than the rest at covering up, though, isn't that right?' he asked. 'I know that myself.'

I didn't answer. I felt that I had the knowledge now and I liked the way that I had somehow gained the upper hand.

'I'm still good, Doc?' he asked. He sounded unsure of himself for the first time. 'Isn't that true?'

'Not bad,' I said. I felt that I had turned the tables on him. I could be non-committal now. I could be the one with the brief, vague comments that had to be attended to. 'And wee Becksy's good too,' I added. 'I've been watching him on the door. He gives nothing away, you know.' I don't really know why I mentioned Becksy. Perhaps I felt sorry for a doorman who had a dodgy ticker, like my dad. Perhaps that was it.

Lenny nodded. 'Yeah, I thought that about Becksy, as well, despite his bad heart. Your research backs up my hunches really. Well, Doc,' he said, 'it just shows you – we've all got our fucking uses.'

And he left with that vague comment ringing in my ears that kept me wondering for the rest of the day.

FIVE

It was a quarter past two in the morning and nearly time for the changeover. One shift on, one shift off. That's how it worked. They weren't really shifts, but that's what they called them. I suppose that they thought that they were back in the steelmills. We were the late shift. Quarter-past two. I knew the exact time without looking at my watch. I had developed a sort of internal clock that worked well at night, an internal clock that ticked away in the dark. You can't keep looking at your watch in a place like this; people might think that you are bored. It was just another little trick that I had picked up along the way.

I knew the time because I sensed that the bar had been closed for about fifteen minutes. I had got a drink in just before that. You had to make this one last while the bouncers got the customers out of the club. The ordinary punters, the bouncers called them. The nobodies.

The flat lager sat in my glass. I looked down at it. The last remaining bubbles in the middle of the glass looked a bit like the shape of a map of the Philippines. I laughed quietly to myself and sipped the flat lager. I looked back inside again. The map seemed to have changed. The remaining bubbles were breaking up. That's presumably what happens to bubbles. They don't dissolve – they break up. I scanned the circumference of the glass, but there was not a single bubble left.

I was trying to fill time without looking around me, without making eye contact and starting up a conversation. I wanted to be on my own at the changeover. You hear about drinkers crying into their glasses, but I had noticed that a lot of punters spend a good deal of time staring down into the bottom of it. It's a kind of civil way of not attending to all the stuff going on around you.

190

It says to the punters out there 'Look, I'm counting bubbles. Fuck off.'

The drink tasted metallic. It does when you sip it slowly like that. That's not how lager is meant to be drunk. That's what the owner of the club liked to say to me. He'd catch me sitting with a dribble of honey-coloured liquid in my glass, more spit that lager, and make his little comment. That always made me laugh.

The two waitresses in the wine bar – Sandra and Michelle in their fishnets and leotards – had cashed up and had just finished stacking the glasses. They looked bored. They had tired expressions that rarely changed. They were too tired to change the configuration of their faces from one moment to the next. Their interaction was all very impersonal, professional they might call it. There was no eye contact, not even with each other. It was as if they were focused on the job in hand. But they weren't, and you knew it.

I had spent a few minutes looking down Sandra's cleavage and trying to imagine her stripped bare – her body rather than her soul. Every punter in the wine bar that night had probably had a similar thought. You could see it in their faces. Leers would creep across from their eyes to their mouths and then out to the further edges of their faces where they would hang. It wasn't the leaking that was important; it wasn't the fact that these feelings got out in the first place. Rather, it was the fact that these expressions, which told you all you needed to know about what they were thinking, stayed on their faces far too long. That's what gave the game away. It was all to do with time. These ordinary punters wore their feelings like tired old suits. It was like having a dirty stopover, and going out in Saturday night's clobber on a Sunday afternoon. Everybody would be able to read you like a book. Everybody would be able to tell exactly what you'd been up to.

Tired old suits, that's all that girls like Sandra and Michelle ever saw. Leers on inebriated faces, with a few faltering words. I was now better at disguising my thoughts than most, and when I did leak the odd feeling, I would notice it quickly and begin the process of burying it. Burying it alive. I was learning.

Sandra wore fishnet stockings and a very high-cut leotard. It was a come-on to justify the fact that the prices were higher up here in the wine bar. I would pay her a compliment when she was fetching a glass from the lower shelf and would watch her look up at me, smiling. The ordinary punter never got that. It was hard to get a smile from Sandra even when she was happy, which itself was a rarity. If you ever tried chatting to her, she would quite readily tell you all about her miserable home life, as long as you weren't leering at her. She lived with her mother, with whom she didn't get on. She had a little girl called Sam, or sometimes Sami, spelt with an 'i', whom her mother looked after when she was out working. Sandra would arrive home just after three in the morning to find Sami lying in bed with her sheets kicked all over the place, having fled from the monsters in her dreams. In her dreams, Sunbeam, her My Little Pony, would have sharp dark teeth and would chase her through bright-green meadows, green like the back of plastic chairs, melted and shiny. Sami's hair would be stuck to her forehead, her pyjamas wrinkled and wet. All those wicked dreams in Sandra's absence, all that kicking and running whilst Sandra served cocktails with names that might sound funny on holiday, but which just sounded ridiculous on wet nights in the centre of Sheffield during the middle of a recession. 'Sex on the beach' it said on the blackboard beside the bar. But it didn't sound quite right when you had to say it out loud. The punters just pointed up at the blackboard. 'Two of those,' they'd say. They called the club Style City sometimes. 'Two of those big yellow drinks with the straws sticking out of them, luv,' they'd say. 'Real Style City.'

The cashing-up usually took about half an hour. There were one or two stragglers left in the wine bar. Naz had been in earlier but even he had gone home. One of the stragglers was talking to Fat Eddie, hoping that somehow he'd be mistaken for a VIP and be asked to stay behind with the select few. But Lenny never made that kind of mistake. He and Becksy were working the wine bar. The final sweep, they called it. They were professionals. 'Wine bar clear,' they would shout half-jokingly when they had finished. Becksy had been in the army once, but he had a bad heart, a very irregular heartbeat he always said, which meant that he had to leave. He was always asking punters to listen to his irregular heartbeat. He missed the army and said that the lingo stuck with you for ever. Lenny waited patiently whilst Eddie and his new friend finished talking. Eddie kept looking Lenny's way as if to say, 'I'm just being polite here. Chuck him out if you like. He means nothing to me.' But Lenny was more polite than that. He waited for a suitable juncture, and then in measured tones asked him to leave.

It was only the most select of the VIPs who could stay behind. The Gold Card holders. You didn't actually have to show it. Everybody knew who we were. They called us the queue-jumpers behind our backs, and worse, much worse – flash bastards, poseurs, ten-bob millionaires – but they missed the point. We didn't pretend to be millionaires, just men in the know.

We were queue-jumpers, though. The first thing that you came across when you were looking for this particular nightclub was the queue. This place was almost defined by its queue. 'Oh, that's the club where you have to queue to get in,' they'd say. 'The club with the strict door policy. The club where you have to queue all night.'

The queue usually stretched out from the door, down the steps below and right along the glass office block. A long, thin line oozing anticipation and quite often desperation. The bouncers could seem quite whimsical some nights, but they weren't whimsical, just thorough. It was enough just to get into the place. Some nights you could queue for an hour or more. A significant part of the night was spent out there in the dark hoping that you looked the part sufficiently to get the nod from the bouncers to get into the club. It was hard for ordinary punters to know how to dress because a significant part of the evening was to be spent in the wind and the rain, and yet a coat necessitated queuing at the end of the night, and if you've pulled the last thing you want to do is more queuing. So most punters arrived without coats and stood in flimsy dresses or shirts even in the cruellest of months.

The queue always started early. It had been long that particular night. Just the way the VIPs liked it. They always said that it felt marvellous to walk right past them – the respectable citizens of this fine old town who were all queuing in the frigging rain and were soaked to the bloody skin. I still found trying to jump the queue very embarrassing. You could feel all these eyes in your back like daggers where somebody is twisting and turning the blade in between your shoulder blades.

That night, though, the door staff had got everything in hand. They had managed to get the ordinary punters right up against the wall of the building, leaving this little space to the right. The space is important. It gives the doormen a chance to see past the ordinary punters. They can then watch you as you arrive and nudge the ordinary punters even closer to the wall. There was just enough room to squeeze in in front of the paying customers. The mugs, they called them, standing freezing in the rain.

On a good night, or a bad night depending upon how you looked at these things, you would know everyone in this part of the club. Tonight, Fat Eddie was in his favourite spot, just to the right of the edge of the top bar. I bought my Rolex watch off him. Nineteen quid it cost. Of course, it wasn't real. But it looked the part in here, in this dim light. You could only tell that it was snide when you took it off. *If* you took it off, that is. It was as light as a feather. But you would never take it off, except in bed. 'Then it's too late.' That's what Fat Eddie always said. 'Far too late. You're already in there.'

Fat Eddie was always angling for this or that. Some fishy deal or other. Or else he was trying to land some gentle, wide-eyed creature who would be flapping helplessly in midair in front of him. 'I've got another one on tonight,' he would say. 'Get the landing net ready.' And he would make a little reeling gesture, or sometimes his right hand would hold the net out. It always got a laugh from the men in the know. Sometimes he would make a gesture showing the landed fish being cracked against the back of his boot. You could almost hear the thud, the gesture was that clear. The noise of death. 'The fish is well and truly fucked,' as Eddie liked to say.

Some nights Fat Eddie would have five or six snide watches on one arm. You could see the bulge in his shirt. He liked to keep them covered. He didn't need to sell them. He just did it for pin money – beer money. I had heard that he was into passing off counterfeit notes, but that was just a rumour. But a reliable one at that.

You didn't need to have money to have style. That was what they would say in the club. It was just as well. Many of them had nothing. Just a gold pass and lies and deceit about who they were. Richard was by the pillar, in his customary spot. He was big in fire insulation for factories. I mean really big, a millionaire. He was talking to Brian, who owned his own hairdresser's, or once did. I had heard that he was currently unemployed. But he could get in here for nothing and he could make a half of lager last a very long time indeed. Some other VIP would always buy him a drink. Perhaps things were a little vague around here sometimes. But they were all superstars in here. For a while. They were all living a fantasy in this desolate Northern city. They were all friends of Herol Graham, Johnny Nelson or Naz. 'I gave Naz the best advice he's ever had,' said Brian. 'Look after number one. Don't forget, look after number one.'

I was standing there waiting patiently. The last of the ordinary punters were running around desperate for their three hours away from the wife or the husband. Their three hours of freedom. Pretending to be somebody that they weren't: computer sales-man, air hostess, doctor, footballer, model, graphic designer, architect, aromatherapist, manageress at Marks and Spencer's, anything that sounded fancy and grand. Miner, steelworker, canteen girl, or, worse, ex-miner, ex-steelworker or ex-canteen girl didn't sound quite right in Style City. These ordinary punters were into deceptions that might last the whole night.

Some of the VIPs had deceptions that lasted a good deal longer. There was Frank with his Rolls-Royce parked underneath the club with just a gallon or so of petrol in the tank. If he pulled, he had to work out exactly how many miles away she lived, to see if he could get there and back without running out of gas. That was his word, gas. He said that it sounded more American, more glamorous. He knew all the districts in Sheffield and whether he could make it there or not on the gas he had in the tank. He told any attractive girl that he met that he was looking for an au pair for his children. The fact that his children were both adults who never spoke to him was never mentioned. But Frank looked the part. 'The man with the five-octane smile' is how he described himself. White flashing teeth that he liked to expose. He would bring a little phial of water with him and brush his teeth in the underground car park just before entering the nightclub. You would see these great slabs of newly polished ivory glinting in the dark of the club. VIPs who knew him called him 'the man with the five-octane breath'. He told us all that he was an entre-preneur. He had started trading cars from home – Vauxhall to Ford back to Vauxhall to Nissan to old BMW to Old Merc to old Roller. He wasn't making any money, though. He took his family on holiday to Skegness and came back in a hearse. A hearse!

Imagine how his family reacted to being picked up in a hearse. He had traded his Vauxhall Carlton for the hearse. He had tried to sell the hearse to a sandwich shop outside Barnsley. He suggested the advertising slogan 'People are dying for our beef sandwiches.' Unfortunately, they didn't go for it. He kept the Roller to give him an edge in business. 'I want people to know who they are dealing with,' he said. He had just spent the last six months collecting pigmeal bags for profit. His brother, who kept pigs, had suggested this to him. He was piling the bags in his garden, but his neighbours were all ringing the council to complain.

'It doesn't matter where you get the idea from, you know, as long as it's a little gem, a little corker.' That was what he always said. I had noticed that Frank used the same language to describe women. Little gem, little corker, and at the end of the evening, he would be out there looking for any wee bargains left. Wee bargains or cheap goods. He would take anything when he was desperate, no matter how damaged or soiled.

I was taking it nice and steady that night watching the few remaining ordinary punters make their moves and the professionals having to deal with them. I was watching Alan, a deaf bouncer, in action down on the main floor. He had a large mop of curly blond hair on a big open face and a dinner jacket that was too tight. It was buttoned up and was stretched across his ample torso. You could see that he was angry, even in the neon glow of the nightclub. The flushing of his face might not have been visible, but his facial muscles were stretched as tight as his jacket. He was standing in between two punters who had been having a slanging match. The punters had both stood their ground, but their heads had started to tilt slowly towards each other, until now only inches separated them. Alan had to move into that gap. In the seconds that it had taken him to get there, he had to make a snap decision. He had to focus on one of them. Not the bigger of the two, but the little one, the mouthy one. The little one whose face was twisting and contorting.

'Read my lips,' Alan's mouth pouted and protruded in an exaggerated fashion. No sound came out. The little guy with the cream shirt and black waistcoat and the big mouth looked quizzical. It was as if the bouncer in the tight jacket were echoing his own exaggerated social performance.

'What?' he asked.

Alan went through the motions more slowly this time. 'Read my lips.'

The man in the cream shirt thought that the bouncer was winding him up.

'Do ... you ... want ... to ... leave?' asked Alan. Each word came out with a large gap in between so that there was no overall rhythm.

Alan pointed towards the door to bring the point home. Well, not so much towards the door as at the ladies' toilet, but down past the ladies' toilet there was undoubtedly an exit. Alan watched for small, subtle indicators of understanding in this small, mouthy man, but saw none. He repeated the gesture, this time making a low, guttural sound from deep within. 'You,' he said. This time he used his index finger to take the man in the cream shirt on a more detailed journey down past the side entrance of the bar where some VIPs clustered, down past the queue for the ladies' toilet, out past the cloakroom attendant and right into the cold, misty air outside. His index finger made a short, sharp stabbing movement at the end, a stab into the smoky air of the club. This was to represent the expulsion into the cold, sharp air. The coming to one's senses.

Comprehension crept slowly and deliberately across the man's face. Starting in the eyes, moving down across his jaw and mouth and back up to the top of his head. He nodded slowly. 'I'm sorry. I didn't realise that you couldn't talk. Here, let me shake your hand. I was just having a few words, that's all. Hey, let me shake his hand as well. No problems. Sorry about that. Let me buy you a drink. Oh, sorry, it's a pity that you can't drink when you're working.'

So many words filled the balmy, smoky, perfumed air. Words about desire and social status, words to persuade and cajole, words that lied and fabricated, and Alan could hear none of them. I was sure that sometimes he was glad that he didn't have to listen to all of this.

I pushed my way past a few VIPs, now swaying gently in their alcohol-induced haze, and headed towards the toilet. The toilet attendant was looking harassed as the ordinary punters who were about to leave were trying to spray themselves with aftershave without paying the customary twenty pence. 'Come on lads, it's twenty pence a shot. I've got plenty of change. Only the best gear here. Real fanny magnet stuff,' said Paul as aftershave dispensers fired off indiscriminately into the air. 'One spray per payment, please,' shouted Paul. 'One shot each. I'm counting. Hey, sonny, you've had five squirts of Paco Rabanne. That's a quid so far. I hope you can afford that.'

He winked at me as I went into the toilet. 'You can have three squirts of whatever you like free of charge.' He pushed some Kouros my way. I didn't like the smell of this particular aftershave. It was too sweet and sickly for me, but I was too polite to refuse. I squeezed the nozzle three times as directed. 'Three's plenty,' said Paul. I went back to the wine bar and drained the last drop of flat lager from my glass. Fat Eddie was still talking away to some new muppet.

'Oh, are you coming as well?' the anonymous punter asked Eddie. He was trying to sound sincere. But this punter knew what went on all right. He knew the club wasn't really closing. Who really goes home at half past two in the morning?

'No. I'll be out in a minute,' said Eddie.

It was very late now. I saw the manager with a video under his arm and I knew what he was up to. We were going to watch an edited video from the security cameras. The story was starting just above my head. I could see the bright white light and could hear Fat Eddie moving his chair into a better position. There was no sound on the video. Pete, the owner, would almost certainly come a little later and do the voice-over. He claimed to know the words that were actually spoken on the night of the actual encounter in a dozen or so of these films, even though he was not physically present at the scene in any of them. He had told me that he would talk to his staff afterwards whilst it was fresh in their minds and remember the words verbatim. The bouncers all said that it was worse than being interviewed by the police. Pete wanted the exact words spoken before, during and after any confrontation or fight. Not just the gist – he wanted the exact words plus any ums or ahs. 'If you don't get the ums and ahs it puts your timing right out,' he always said. If he didn't get an absolutely accurate verbatim report, then the words didn't fit, and he would get very cross. 'I'd end up looking a right cunt,' he would say.

He had a script for each film, which mapped, more or less exactly, onto what was being said, give or take the odd millisecond. Nobody in the club ever disputed these words, not even the bouncers who had actually spoken them. We were all there after hours as his guest or his employee. It would have been impolite, to say the least, not to take his word for it.

The bouncers had worked out that, if they couldn't remember the words actually used, it was important to provide dialogue of approximately the right duration as the original, so that when Pete was doing the voiceover there would be no awkward silences where he had come to the end of his line but the protagonists in the original film still had something to say.

Lenny had confessed to me that whenever he was interviewed by the police about an incident in the club, he had started unconsciously doing something quite similar. He was making up whole stories, imagining conversations, constructing violent threats in his head, all of which had the exact temporal properties as the original and shared almost none of the actual meanings. The official police statistics for violent crime in the area were being badly affected by this practice.

I looked up at the video screen. A man with long permed hair was standing just outside the club. He had obviously been barred. Why else would someone be standing there at that time of night? The time and date were on the bottom left-hand corner of the screen. It was eight minutes to two. Eight minutes to get back in to the club and score. Just time for the smoochies, 'the erection section' as the DJ liked to say. The man with the perm kept putting his head around the door to talk to Alan, the deaf bouncer.

'Look at that fucking loser there,' said Fat Eddie, pointing up at the screen. What was it that J. B. Priestley had once written? First you take their faces from 'em by calling 'em the masses and then you accuse 'em of not having any faces. Fat Eddie just saw losers out there on the street and in the club, even when they were magnified on the screen in front of him. Losers with no faces, no emotions, no individuality and no biography. Losers who would all have loved to get where he was. In the middle of all this. In the know.

'Do you know him, Cliff?' he asked the police inspector in the corner. 'He looks like the sort of guy who would keep your lot pretty busy. A real no-hoper. Where's Pete? I wouldn't mind hearing this one.'

But Pete was busy at the far end of the club, so this slice of violent life was to be viewed in silence.

There was a light on at the top right-hand corner in the foyer of the club, which bathed the right-hand side of the picture in bright white light. It made Alan, with his fair hair, look serene but quite ghostly. Everything in the club was bright, everything outside was dark. This punter wanted to go from the dark to the light. Why he was being prevented was not clear. He was just barred for some minor, or perhaps major, misdemeanour. Nobody seemed to know who he was. He would have to be a nobody to be barred. That was the logic.

The punter kept putting his head round the door and getting a knock back. That's what they called it – a 'knock back'. It was a nice vague term. It wasn't like being barred, and it had no temporal dimension written into it. If you were barred, you would be barred for a set period of time. If punters were barred, they would want to know how long they were barred for. If you got a knock back, you couldn't legitimately enquire as to the duration. Plus, it had no motive. You could have a knock back on a whim or something vaguely remembered by the door personnel. You didn't really have to justify a knock back if you were a bouncer. You just had to be resolute for the duration of one evening. Just one evening. 'Come back tomorrow', the bouncer would say, 'and we'll see.'

The incident on the video was just a knock back, but it was being contested. The punter wasn't going anywhere. Metaphorically speaking, he was digging his heels in. In layman's terms, he was being a bloody nuisance. He was standing there protesting. He was breaking every rule about authority and order and who has the final say. This was worse than being a muppet in Fat Eddie's eyes.

We all sat there watching the man with the perm. Pete had now joined us.

'Fucking asshole,' said Fat Eddie. 'If I had a knock back, I would just fuck off home. Or go to another club. No offence, lads. Has that cunt got no pride?'

The man with the perm stood there arguing away outside the club, then he flicked his cigarette into the night. It looked like a tracer going through the black night air. Some girl came out and whispered in the ear of the deaf bouncer. She kissed him on the cheek. The bouncer mouthed something after her. The punter with the perm looked down the steps after the girl. He was more agitated now. He was remonstrating with the bouncer. He was making these sharp, stabbing gestures.

'He's fucking asking for it,' said Fat Eddie. 'What would you do to him, Cliff, if he was in police custody and he started pointing his finger at you like that? I bet you would knock his lights out.'

I noticed that Fat Eddie was sweating. He had also gone noticeably paler. Fat Eddie took speed, everybody knew that. The drugs made him sweat.

'Look, that's better,' said Fat Eddie, pointing at the screen. 'He's put his hands in his pockets now. Come on, Mr Psychologist, what does that mean?'

That pale, drawn face with the dark circles for eyes turned my way. The police inspector looked up from his pint of lager expectantly.

'It's hard to say,' I said. I gave a little shrug to indicate my nonchalance.

'Hard to fucking say?' said Fat Eddie. 'Hard to fucking say?' The muscles around his eyes were pinched to make a squinting sort of face. He turned his head to fix eye contact with each member of the group in turn. 'Hard to fucking say?' He tried to coax a little smile from each person in turn, a smile or a laugh, like a beggar with a cap working a theatre audience. He wasn't disappointed. 'Do they pay you for these opinions up at the university?' he said. 'Hard to fucking say? Is that what you come up with when they bring some fucking nutter in to see you? "It's hard to say." And you're meant to be the expert on this. Come on, Cliff, give us a professional opinion.' He stressed the word 'professional'. 'What does the hands in the pockets mean from a professional point of view?'

Cliff set his pint of lager down slowly on the black metallic table. It made a solid clanking sound. He cleared his throat. It made him sound serious, as if the opinion he was about to express was the product of a great deal of deliberation. I could imagine him going through the same routine in court.

'I would say,' he began. 'I would say,' he started again in a little rhetorical flourish, 'that it means that he, the man in question,

201

the suspect, the punter as we say around here, recognises the seriousness of what he's got himself involved in, and that, at this point in the proceedings, he's having second thoughts, serious second thoughts about continuing with his course of action.' He gave a cough to mark the end of his testimony.

'Excellent,' said Fat Eddie. 'Fucking tremendous. You see, Mr Psychologist, some professionals can read people like books. That was tremendous, Cliff. How did you know all that from just that one simple act?'

'Years of honest, decent police training,' said Cliff picking up his full pint mug, his pint mug that was being used against all the rules up there in the wine bar. He looked very satisfied with his own performance. 'Years of watching the evil bastards make their moves,' he said. 'And getting in there first before they've even made up their own minds about what nasty things to do. It gives you quite an edge on them. I can tell you that for nothing.'

'But what you've just said is not very scientific,' I said quickly and quite quietly and, I must confess, without much reflection.

'Not very what?' said Fat Eddie, with that squinting face of his again.

'It's not very scientific,' I said more slowly and more deliberately.

'Listen,' said Cliff, setting down his lager more forcefully this time so that a large wave of lager tipped out of the side of the pint mug all over the table. 'I didn't say it was scientific. I just said that it was based on years of experience. That's not the same thing.'

'What do you mean, not scientific?' asked Fat Eddie. 'It's tried and tested. That's good enough for me.'

'Well, Cliff could say what he likes,' I said. 'He hasn't got a theory of what's going on here.'

'Oh, I have a theory all right,' said Cliff. 'My theory is that assholes like that guy there have no bottle when it comes down to it. The drink makes them brave, but there's this little voice at the back of their mind saying, "Don't fucking push it or this big bouncer here will knock your fucking lights out. Don't push your fucking luck."'

'Excellent,' said Fat Eddie. 'That's some fucking theory, that is. Does it have a name, that theory of yours?'

'No,' said Cliff. 'It doesn't have any fancy psychological bollocks name. It's just a commonsense theory based on years of experience.'

'I wouldn't fancy being lifted by you, Cliff,' said Fat Eddie. 'You're too fucking clever. A man would have no chance against you.'

Fat Eddie and Cliff went back to their drinking. They drank in perfect synchrony with each other. The glasses were lifted from the table at exactly the same moment. They gulped within the same brief interval, and the glasses were put down again. All with perfect timing.

'But you can't predict anything with your theory, Cliff,' I said into the silence, breaking myself away from my observations. 'You're just offering an opinion. Okay, it's based on your experiences. But that's all it is. An opinion.'

'What?' said Fat Eddie. 'Are you saying that Cliff's theory based on his whole life's work is a load of bollocks? Is that what you are saying to his face?'

Cliff got up abruptly. He kicked away the nearest stool to him. It landed on its side on the metallic bit of the wine bar with a clatter that rang on and on like a tinny alarm.

'What are you fucking saying?' he said.

He moved across to me until he was standing just in front of me. I stayed seated.

'It's not fucking bollocks, and I'll tell you why,' he said. 'The cunt with the perm is going to needle a bit more and a bit more and then he's going to get fucking decked. That's my prediction. Any cunt who needles that much deserves it. Do you understand me? Do you still think that I can't predict the future with my fucking theory?'

I nodded and tried to say that I didn't think that he could predict anything with such a theory, but the words didn't come out that easily. Fat Eddie had turned his face away from me. I was sure that he was laughing.

'Cheeky fucker,' said Fat Eddie when he had managed to control himself again. 'Give him a slap, Cliff.'

'Twat,' said Cliff as he went back to pick up the stool that he'd kicked over.

The punter was still talking away on the video. The deaf bouncer, Alan, had turned his head away. I went back to watching the screen. I felt my cheeks burning. A woman in a smart suit, who was leaving the club, said something to the punter. He looked after her longingly. I found myself quite unconsciously timing this look. It was my years of training, I suppose. It was twenty-nine seconds. Nearly half a minute. That's a long time for a look of this kind. I wanted to point this out to Cliff and Fat Eddie. I wanted to display to them my precision in measurement, but I looked at their faces and guessed that they wouldn't be that interested.

On the video, you could see Lenny coming up to the foyer to check what was going on. He didn't stay long. Then Becksy came out. He had obviously been asked to have a word with the punter. You could see Lenny's upturned hand gesture in the space between him and the punter. His hand was open, helpless, imploring. But even this more primitive form of communication wasn't working.

If the punter had been an ape or a child, he might have got the message, but he wasn't. He was a muppet and he understood nothing. He didn't know the regulations of the club or the rules for surviving out there after dark. He didn't understand power and authority in this land of the vanquished. He didn't understand how these guys worked. He didn't listen or attend. He was worse than ignorant. He was wilfully not attending. I wanted to make some of these observations aloud to get back in with the rest of them who were all sitting there making comments about the action on the screen as if they understood people.

It was now after two o'clock on the film. The club was officially closing. There was a stream of people leaving – groups of men and gaggles of women going their separate ways. A small group of women were hanging about outside. One or two of them were smoking. You could see the bright glow from their cigarettes. The cigarettes seemed almost alive in the dark. They seemed to pulsate with the breathing in and the breathing out, with the rise and fall of the lungs. Then Jack arrived.

It was hard to get a sense of perspective in this shot of dark and light, but you could see that Jack was huge. A huge, dark, ominous slab in the corner of the light, behind the glass door. There was little expression on his face. His face was something more primitive altogether. No basic emotions ever seemed to register there. There was certainly no fear, but also no surprise, no happiness, no anger, no disgust. Nothing of any real consequence, just a little boredom perhaps.

'This is where the film gets interesting,' said Fat Eddie. 'There's Jack. He's the man. He's the main man. Look at the size of that big fucker. Have you really never seen this film before, Cliff? Your prediction was awfully accurate if you haven't seen it. It was spot on, actually.'

Cliff shook his head. 'No, I've never seen it.'

'But you've seen ones like it,' I said before I could stop myself. 'You know roughly what's going to be on it. You know that the guy with the perm and the bouncer aren't going to go off hand in hand.'

Cliff looked at me menacingly. He had hard, narrow eyes now. Mean eyes. Colourless eyes.

Tony, one of the new glass collectors, came up to the wine bar carrying a huge number of glasses which were slotted into each other. It looked like a fragile glass sculpture. He paused in front of the screen. The sculpture shook slightly.

'Fucking hell,' said Tony. 'He's a giant. Is it true that he used to be a professional wrestler? Jack was a bit before my time. What was his wrestling name? Giant Haystacks? Godzilla? The Incredible Hulk?'

'No, I think it was the Gentle Giant,' said Fat Eddie. 'I think that's what they used to call him. Six foot ten inches of pure unadulterated beef. But gentle.'

The punter stood there on the screen in front of us, trying to talk to the Gentle Giant. He held up an empty cigarette box. You could guess what he was saying. He just wanted to go in to get some cigarettes. He would only be a minute. Jack shook his large ponderous head and looked down at his own feet, ignoring him. The punter flicked the packet at the door. The motion caught Jack's eye. You could see his eyes opening wider. His look was almost reptilian.

'That's done it,' said Fat Eddie. 'That's him well and truly fucked.'

'Provocative,' said Cliff. 'In the police, we would describe that as very provocative.'

Here we were watching this human behaviour without the benefit of sound and coming to all sorts of conclusions about the justifications for the violence to come, because we all knew what

205

conclusion we were working towards. Or rather they were coming to this conclusion.

On the video, more girls came out in light summer dresses with bare legs. The punter got more agitated again. You could sense the excitement building in our group. We were all there now: Pete, Lenny, Becksy, Fat Eddie, Cliff, Tony, Andy and me, stuck in the middle. There were no women that night. Sandra and Michelle had cashed up and gone off for their taxis. They had avoided Fat Eddie. There was more talking on the screen, but, of course, it just came across as more silent mouthing with the body activated into gesture. Some guy left carrying his coat. Then there was a pause. This was the climax of the film. I could see it in Fat Eddie's face. The smile starting. He had seen the film many times.

Suddenly from nowhere, this left hook erupted around the door. The punter who had had the knock back couldn't have seen it coming. I couldn't see it coming and I had studied the whole episode up to that point in great detail. It was not in any way connected to the flow of the interaction. Some violence isn't. I saw nothing in the video in front of me to allow me to predict Jack's response. Nothing. There was no sound from the screen, but you could virtually hear that punch landing. I have never heard a more solid punch. Boom. The punter went down, dead to the world. The deaf bouncer, Alan, stepped back slightly. Jack had trouble getting through the door because of his size. He had to go through sideways. The punter was off camera, but you could see Jack bending over where his prostrate body must have been and waving his fist. He lifted the punter up by the shirt and punched him again. His head cracked on the paving stones. It must have sounded like a coconut being thrown onto concrete. You could almost hear the head opening up and the blood seeping out in thick gurgles.

There were two girls caught on the camera. They were still in the club looking out. You could see their faces. Their expressions were in marked contrast to everything else on the film. Emotion was written all over them. They were covering their faces with their hands in an attempt to hide just some of the emotional messages leaking from them. The man who had left carrying his coat came back and said something to Jack. Jack gave a dismissive wave and turned away. This was perhaps the real climax to the film. This stranger dragging the punter away, dragging him backwards off screen. The punter was out cold. The stranger was dragging the lifeless body the way that you might drag a bag of cement. It took the same amount of effort. The shoes of the punter with the perm scraped along the pavement. One of his shoes came off and lay in the middle of the camera shot.

I watched them all there in the club, sitting there hooting with laughter. I felt a slight sense of disgust, but I hoped that I was managing to conceal it. The word went down to the DJ to play the tape again from where the punter flicked the cigarette box. They were commenting on that punch. It was a monster hook, a big dig, the big D, a bone cruncher, a knuckle sandwich of the highest order, a goodnight kiss from the Gentle Giant. The punch KO'd the punter. It rocked the punter. It floored the man with the glass chin. The punch travelled through the man to his boots and back.

'I felt that punch,' said Fat Eddie.

'So did I,' said Cliff.

The DJ loaded a second film into the video recorder. An Asian guy was having an argument with his wife in the doorway of the club. She was screaming in his face, but there was no sound. The camera captured it all. Fat Eddie offered to do the voice-over for this one.

'You kicked my sister in the fucking cunt, you son of a bitch. Look at her! Look at her!'

The sister was walking unsteadily around gripping her crotch. She looked very small in the shot, almost dwarfish, but it might have been the camera angle. The wife kicked her husband and kneed him and head-butted him, knowing that he wouldn't retaliate in the presence of the doormen. She was trying to get him to hit her so that everyone would see what kind of man he really was. I found this film embarrassing, but the rest of the audience were creased up with laughter. There, also captured on the video, was the audience witnessing the original scene, huddled in the doorway of the club. They were clearly enjoying the spectacle of raw passion unfolding in front of them. You can see a young Naz amongst the group.

This film went on for ever. The violence was episodic. Every now and then, one or other of the protagonists would disappear down the steps away from the club, and the other would sidle up to the door and attempt to persuade the bouncers that they were not at fault. They would try to do this as calmly and as rationally as possible. Neither wanted to be the one that was barred from the club. In the middle of all that violence, screaming, blood and pain, that's what they were most concerned about.

But they were both barred in the end. They didn't just get a knock back, they were both barred.

It was funny, really, that they never talked about the real backgrounds of the individuals caught in the security cameras. They never discussed the state of their marriages, their financial problems, the effects of redundancy on them. How could they? They didn't know them. One day, they would be nameless, ordinary punters who queued up and paid to get in, the next they would have a name of sorts, the video title, and they would be barred. They never saw them again, except when they came to the door to get their knock back. These people had no real history as far as they were concerned.

I told everybody that I needed some air. The air was almost clear at that time of the morning. Presumably it would have been a lot dirtier when the steelmills were still going. The birds were singing outside the town hall long before dawn. I wasn't sure whether pigeons sang like that or not.

I looked out at the empty streets, my eyes stinging with smoke. I had been distracted somewhere along the way and had ended up in this subculture of Thatcherite values, where dog was eating dog right before my very eyes and where the only goal seemed to be to climb on the shoulder of one's neighbours in order to stand above them for just a few moments. To be a somebody was what was left. Jumping the queue so that the punters in the rain would say, 'Who's that?' Staying behind in the club after hours as the mug punters filed out. Watching videos of the punters fighting each other or trying to fight one of the bouncers and giving us all a good laugh in the process. It was just the routine of the night.

This was Big Lenny's world and I found myself being sucked into it, and I stayed there for some reason that I now find hard to understand. It was not surprising that I mentioned the forensic tape to Lenny one night. I can't remember how it came out, it just did. Perhaps I was boasting. Lenny said that he'd come up to my office to watch it. 'Or we can watch it at your house, if you want.' And he had laughed. I wasn't looking forward to it, but it was unavoidable now so I got on with it as best I could. Professionally.

SIX

I watched the video recording of the incident in the club many times after I had watched it with Lenny. I had seen the worst parts of the video recording of the murder and I knew that I could at least sit through it on my own. I knew where to stop the recording in order to miss the killing itself. I had written the time of the killing down in pencil on a scrap of paper and had underlined it. I was only interested in what happened before that point. I still had my work to do.

I thought that if I watched the death itself again it might make me emotional and cloud my judgement. My anxiety about the tape was that without the transcripts of the speech, I was in danger of making the kinds of errors that Cliff and others made when they viewed behaviour. For a while, I contemplated saying that there was nothing in the video for me to comment on. But I was a psychologist, and not just another punter trying to get by with fancy words and fragments of other people's lives. I had to see something in the tape and in the flux of behaviour. Something that Cliff and Big Lenny couldn't possibly see. Something which would tell others and myself who I really was.

I played the video over and over again in that darkened room, trying to put Lenny's words out of my mind. I watched the three men enter the bar. I timed their entrance and measured how far they sat from the other couple. Distance, time, speed, every little thing could be significant here. I didn't want to miss anything out. I watched the girl in the sexy dress give her tell-tale look. I timed it, but there was nothing that significant about it. It was a glance. Nothing more, nothing less. A glance around the room without making eye contact with anyone in particular. There was nothing to read into it, except Lenny's premature interpretation.

I wrote down: 'Room-encompassing look displayed at this point. Not significant to the structure of the subsequent interaction.'

I watched the three men give their 'sly' looks to each other. That was Lenny's word, as well. These were slippery concepts he used. Lenny lived in a world of sly looks and women with guilt written all over their faces. A world of devious and dubious meaning in behaviour, before the behaviour itself was even described. A world which was understood at a glance.

The guy in the leather jacket's face did show significant changes, though. I isolated the individual frames of the video recording of his facial movements one by one. I need still frames to work with sometimes, so that configurations can be charted. I scored the frowning upper brow, the raised upper eyelid, the wrinkled lower lid, the dilated nostrils, the open lips, the exposed lower teeth and the depressed lower lip on the face of the man in the leather jacket. I charted carefully their changes. That was a recognisable emotional configuration. I could put a name to it. It was anger.

Then I started to describe all this microscopic and fleeting action in much greater detail. The kind of detail we – psychologists – need to work with. I watched him raise his upper eyelid and scored how the centre of his upper lip was drawn straight up whilst the outer portions of the lip weren't drawn up as high, causing an angular bend. I watched him raise the infra-orbital triangle, causing the infra-orbital furrow to deepen. I scored how this deepens the nasolabial furrows and raises the upper part of this furrow. I watched him widen and raise the nostril wings, causing the lips to part.

Sometimes we think we take it all in as behaviour dances across our view, but, believe me, we miss most of what is happening out there. I could see all of this in front of me for the first time. I sat long into the night scoring those three crucial seconds of film.

The confrontation between the two was really an emotional dance of sorts. That's how I thought about it. A reaction to microscopic movements in each other, involving the muscles of the human face, one of the most sophisticated signalling systems in the world. The pars medialis, the zygomatic major, the orbic-ularois oris, the pars alaris, the depressor labii inferioris all acting and reacting. I saw anger there. I saw some surprise and, at times, a little fear. At least I did in the case of the man in the leather jacket. The perpetrator of the violence. But in the case of the victim, I saw only minimal emotion. The rest of his emotions were all dampened down by that great mask of a smile that hung there throughout and presumably by the effects of all that alcohol.

Then there were the postures of the three men who had arrived together. It was certainly a significant configuration of seated postures. Two were in exactly the same posture as each other. We call that postural echo. They had their arms folded, their legs tucked under the counter of the bar, their heads slightly turned. But the other one, the victim, was in quite a different posture to them. He was orientated exclusively towards the blonde in the sexy dress. Could this posture be construed as aggressive? Not without a detailed understanding of the subculture in which they were operating, in which a man may have certain proprietorial rights over a woman. And not without a detailed understanding of what might count as a violation of such rights. Not on the basis of the scoring of postural echo and lack of postural echo, anyway.

I looked at the final frames of the man in the leather jacket. The imminent action of this dangerous man seemed to be signalled through the immobility of his expression. The man in the grey suit smiled back at him, a wavering sideways smile. Was this where the aggression slipped in? An inappropriate reaction to a deadly threat? Perhaps he just didn't see it. Perhaps we needed the benefit of hindsight to see it. Perhaps we needed to know what actually did happen in order to allow us to interpret the seriousness of that look in the first place.

Then there was that eye contact. Two men looking at each other for a full minute. No words exchanged, mutual gaze culminating in one man trembling or shaking. This was just too ambiguous. And then the touch preceded by that small but significant gesture. The gesture where his right had stretched out, then started to make a claw and then eventually a fist. Two fingers together dragging behind the others. Then the same hand settled on the back of the girl in the leather dress and moved slowly in a smooth, gentle arc down the back of her shiny leather dress. You could see the disbelief on the man in the leather jacket's face clearly from the video. These frames were amongst the most obvious. So was that the aggressive act on the part of the man about to be killed?

That was surely the significant element in the whole incident in that after-hours drinking den. And what about the gesture that preceded it? What was that signalling? It was an iconic gesture. But what was it representing here? The whole thrust of my own research was that the gesture acts with the speech to form a single cognitive representation. But we didn't have any transcripts. And without the speech, we just had a fist shape. A fist – that could be perceived as very threatening. A fist followed by a provocative touch. These were the conclusions that I drew on the basis of what I had seen. The solicitor seemed very pleased with my report. I didn't mention this to Lenny. I knew that it would make him angry.

I got a call a few months later from another academic who had been involved in the analysis. I have a vivid memory of this particular call. 'Believe it or not, we've got some sound on the recordings now,' he said. 'There is one small thing that might be relevant in those transcripts,' he said. 'Something very small indeed. Do you remember that section of the video in which you can see this little hand gesture occurring before the victim lays his hand on the woman? Do you remember those two fingers outstretched together and then turning into a very aggressive-looking fist?'

'Of course,' I replied. 'I remember all that. That was the core part of the analysis.'

'Well, apparently,' said my colleague, 'the victim had a long-term relationship with that woman and he's saying to her at that point, according to the witnesses . . . let me read it to you, "How can you do this to me? We were so close." And this is apparently the point in time when he gestures. Do you think that the gesture could have been indicating how close they were at that point? Because that would affect the interpretation of what was going on, surely?'

He left a gap again, but I didn't say anything. He filled the silence for me. 'This doesn't significantly affect your interpretation, does it?' he asked.

I sat in my office in the dark in front of the bright screen of the monitor. I could see my own reflection. I could see my look of fear and surprise and I could see that this was certainly not fleeting or squelched. I was just relieved that nobody else could see me and my whole facial configuration at that precise instant. My research had told me all along that body language and speech work together in a complex way, but I had temporarily set my own theoretical views aside to work solely on the body language, to help out my colleague, and I suppose, if I am entirely honest with myself, to prove my own worth, to prove that I was indeed something and not just all talk like the rest of them in this faltering city.

But now I suddenly realised that a fist may at times indicate nothing more than the closing of an iconic hand movement representing togetherness. I realised at that precise point that I had been prepared to make convincing-sounding arguments on the basis of partial and fragmentary evidence. On the basis of a quick reading of the body language alone, despite all my research to the contrary. I was no better than Cliff. Or Big Lenny. Or any of the rest of them.

I sat there at one end of the telephone and I said nothing. But I knew what I had to do . . .

'Oh, and by the way,' added my colleague. 'Word of our research appears to be spreading. I have received yet another video to analyse. This was apparently a threat on some doormen by some hooded men armed with baseball bats, which turned very nasty. If you can believe that sort of thing goes on in this city of ours,' he added.

'Goodness,' I said with all the guile that I could possibly muster in the circumstances, as if I didn't know that these sort of things went on, as if I went to bed at the same time as all the other academics that I knew.

'Well,' continued my colleague. 'This act of threatening behaviour went badly wrong. Very badly wrong. According to the police, it might have been a dispute over territory or something. Four men armed with these offensive weapons went to threaten some doormen at a club, but one of the hooded men seemed to get very anxious and started lashing out before running off. There were some serious injuries incurred. This time, the police have asked us to look at the tape to see if our expert analyses can produce any psychological insights into who the attackers might be. They want a psychological profile.'

I coughed gently down the phone as if to indicate that this

was perhaps, just perhaps, beyond our current competence, a cough to signal that I was about to say something, right there and then, to indicate some reluctance or caution on my part. But the cough stood there for a moment quite alone, embarrassed by its own solitary presence, and then vanished quietly and cowardly into the silence.

'Well, basically,' continued my colleague after a pause, 'the police want anything that might be relevant to their enquiries. Do you think that we can help them out here?'

'Of course,' I said. 'We should be able to tell them something. We are the experts, after all.' I listened to my own voice saying this and I probably sounded as convincing as I could, under the circumstances. Given how I felt.

The video was delivered the following day. I sat in my room with the light off and played the tape on the large screen in front of me. The quality was quite poor on this film, but I recognised this particular club immediately. It wasn't one that I frequented, but I knew it all right. I played the tape in slow motion and stopped it when the men in hoods arrived. There was also only one close-up in the whole film. A close-up of the largest member of the gang who had been wielding the baseball bats in the moments before the violence erupted. He was mouthing something. Something short and to the point.

It was easy to recognise the first word. It has a distinctive shape. It's a bit like watching footballers on the telly. You can always make that word out quite easily. It was the word 'fucking'.

The second word was more difficult. I played it again and again until, with familiarity, I could recognise some order in the organisation of the mouth. It had a distinctive shape. My heart started to race as it slowly dawned on me what that word might possibly be.

I played it again. Then once more. I knew that word all right. I had seen it before. Indeed, I think that I had seen it before from the very same mouth that was now poking through the cloth of that dark hood. It was the word 'tasty'.

I looked at the screen and in spite of the poor picture quality I was sure that I also recognised the size, shape and mannerisms of the man who was fleeing. I was sure that I knew him as well. The man whose panic and uncontrollable emotion had evidently started the whole violent conflagration.

It was a man with a very irregular heartbeat and a very bad ticker who was rushing down some steps away from the club and away from all of this.

THE REWARD

'A sportsman is a man who, every now and then, simply has to get out and kill something. Not that he's cruel. He wouldn't hurt a fly. It's not big enough.'
STEPHEN LEACOCK, *My Remarkable Uncle* (1942)

ONE

It was a Sunday evening and my son had finally tired of watching WWF videos after five or so hours of more-or-less continual viewing, or that's how it seemed to me. But all that wrestling had had some positive effect on him; he now wanted to train all the time, to pump iron, to be like those large ballooning men on the films. He liked to practise his moves, his body slams on the settee; he had taken to lifting up the dog and threatening to slam him onto the cushions on the floor – 'rock bottom' the move would be called. The dog had taken to biting him on the arm. The leg of the settee was broken with all that force and the settee now sat at a lopsided angle.

He always asked to go training rather curtly. 'What time are we training?' he would say without even looking at me. He said it a couple of times that night until I silently packed my stuff and then nodded for him to get into the car. He doesn't talk much so I put the radio on. When I was his age, I used to *say* that what I really wanted to do was to box, but he showed no interest in that at all. It might be a class thing; I'm not sure. I used to do judo in a club down near the docks in Belfast before my teenage years and, before the judo mat was brought out, boys from the boxing club, which shared the same premises, would hang about, eyeing us up. They would be putting their gloves away. They had a confidence in their fighting abilities which we didn't have, despite our training in the martial arts, and despite our singsong Japanese words. I could always see the difference between them and us. We were all working class and came from the same wee mill houses in Belfast, but they were more desperate somehow, and thinner and harder, and I guess braver. I always sensed that. And one night, when my arm was broken in a judo match by a boy with glasses called Alan, these thin boys with white, bony chests and big shiny shorts crowded in for a look in a way that my friends didn't. Alan burst out crying, and they laughed at his big runny tears. I was afraid of boxing and those involved in a way that I couldn't articulate then. There was just something about these boys and that look of theirs and their hard emotionless expressions that frightened me, as a twelve-year-old, if I am totally honest.

I remember that Friday night in casualty waiting for my da to arrive – drunken men swearing, blood on their faces and down their shirts, that feeling in my lifeless arm. My father was as white as a sheet when he came in and saw his son 'sitting like a soldier', he always said, in a white judo suit holding his limp arm. 'My wee soldier' he called me. 'My brave wee man.' He died a year later during an operation. He was fifty-one years old; it seemed almost old then.

Today, when I see boys and men on the street like those lads from the boxing club, I have the same sort of feeling inside. Sometimes, I think that was why I wanted to be involved in boxing in some way later in life, to challenge my early irrational childish fears, to get to know those who box a little better, to understand them and to strip away their mystery. It doesn't pay for psychologists to have such persistent stereotypes, after all. I could understand why my son wanted nothing to do with the sport, though.

There was a debate on the radio about whether Mike Tyson should be banned from the ring for his recent outrageous behaviour. Some psychologist, I didn't catch her name, said that boxing was all that he had left in his life. 'Take that away, and he'll have nothing.' But I wasn't sure that was the point. Tyson had just bitten Lennox Lewis's leg during a press conference called to publicise their recently announced fight, and at Tyson's appeal before the Nevada State Athletic Commission to consider the case for him to be allowed to box in Las Vegas, his lawyer argued that it was just boxing theatre gone too far. The psychologist seemed to disagree that this incident had anything to do with theatre, as she understood the concept of theatre. The newspapers were reporting that there was a sign outside Tyson's Connecticut home that read 'Come on in, I won't bite you.'

Nobody seemed to think that this was particularly funny, except perhaps Tyson himself.

Of course, when it comes to Mike Tyson, we are all psychologists. There is something about his behaviour, both inside and outside the ring, which seems to demand a psychological explanation from every one of us. There has always been something primitive in the way that he fights. It seems to come across as barely controlled aggression, which is seen as a natural human instinct. This is not a boxer practising his trade, or engaged in the sweet science, but a boxer with apparently violent instincts for whom the context of the boxing ring seems to provide an acceptable outlet for the pent-up aggression inside. That's how most people read it, in their role as intuitive psychologist. Mike Tyson has always been an aggressive and intimidating boxer. All boxers begin the psychological battle long before they get into the ring, we've seen that already here; they play games to psych each other out. They throw challenges at each other in order to detect those little micro-expressions of fear in their opponent that tell them all they need to know, that the battle is over before it has even started. Some boxers – Muhammad Ali or perhaps even Naz himself on a good day – do this skilfully and with great subtlety so that we can sit back and admire their cunning. Great boxers often have a gift for reading the fleeting nonverbal expressions of fear that many of us miss. But there does not seem to be much subtlety in Tyson's pre-fight build-up. He sets out to intimidate his opponents, mentally and physically, to bully them. Before the fight with Tyrell Biggs, he said, 'If I don't kill him, it don't count.' Many of us can read the fear in his opponent's face before the fight even starts – consider that image of Frank Bruno facing up to Tyson before their showdown. Who couldn't read the churning emotion inside Bruno leaking out for all to see? And, of course, for some people the most intimidating aspect of Tyson's performance is for them to imagine how they would stand up to that kind of pressure themselves.

Tyson has stripped away the glitzy excitement of the Las Vegas show that has invaded boxing, the glitz that Naz and others have worked on for years. Frank Bruno once described boxing as 'just show business with blood'. With Tyson, there is less of the show business. It is back to primitive childish fear, undisguised and uncontrolled, and back to those bony white boys in the club down by the docks in Belfast. It is that determined walk of his to the ring in his black shorts and black boots. He wants to get it on and his opponents know it. His opponents sometimes seem to stop throwing punches halfway through a bout, as if they have already decided psychologically that they can't win. The effect of his punches on his opponents is devastating. My lasting image will always be of Trevor Berbick in 1986 when Tyson became the youngest ever Heavyweight Champion of the World at just twenty years of age. Berbick tried to get up, to raise himself up off the canvas after being clubbed by Tyson, but he couldn't. The image in my mind is of a zebra or a wildebeest being mauled by a lion on the great African plains.

Over the years, many have applauded Tyson's great skill, but others have been more hesitant. He was an exciting boxer but he was also a dangerous boxer and what he accomplished in the ring was a measure of his dangerousness, they said. When Tyson bit off half of Evander Holyfield's ear during that notorious fight, people pointed to this as being symptomatic of the violent and uncontrolled aggression within Tyson. Critics and intuitive psychologists alike pointed to his background – his fatherless upbringing in Brooklyn, New York, his rescue from the streets by Cus D'Amato who moulded a great fighter out of the most difficult clay. D'Amato taught Tyson about discipline and respect for his opponents. Many point to the fact that D'Amato was the father figure that Tyson never had, the one steady influence in his life. Tyson himself said, after D'Amato's death in 1985, that 'people always tell me when I'm doing good, but Cus would always tell me when I was doing wrong.' If you watch interviews of Tyson after D'Amato's death, one striking feature is how his hands, in the form of those iconic gestures that I have studied so closely, seem to articulate major parts of what he needs to say. His hands do his talking for him in more ways than one. Mike Tyson is the masculine male stereotype developed to the extreme. We expect to see no emotion from him and we don't – he ran away to cry on his own after D'Amato died. He articulated his feelings nine days after the death in his own way in an aggressive fight that he won in just seventy-seven seconds.

We know all about Mike Tyson's misfortunes outside the ring – the break-up of his marriage, his car crash, his street brawls and his conviction for rape. It has often been said, and it is a cliché, that his toughest opponent is himself. His wife, Robin Givens, attempted to have him clinically diagnosed as manic-depressive, and she is reported to have said that his mood swings were both unpredictable and violent. There seemed to be a good deal of chaos in his life at that time, and his refuge from this chaos was in the ring itself where Tyson kept expressing himself in his own way.

It has been said that part of the attraction of watching Mike Tyson in the ring is the same as watching a film like *Jaws* – his opponent is like the victim who is about to be mangled and, like Jaws, Tyson waits for his moment. Many of us, of course, have chosen to pay to watch just this.

Recently, Tyson's appearances in the ring have been less frequent. Before his fight with Brian Nelson in Copenhagen towards the end of 2001, he had not fought for a year and he had had only three rounds of boxing in the previous two years. But the big one with Lewis was being lined up whilst I was working on this book, until, that is, he bit Lewis's leg in a brawl, like a rabid dog.

The debate on Tyson on the radio broadened to discuss whether boxing itself should be banned. Paul Ingle was mentioned along the way. Old familiar arguments raised their ugly heads. 'We need a gentler society,' the high-pitched middle-class voice said, 'where young men would not or should not be allowed to do this sort of thing.'

A different middle-class voice said, 'A ban would simply drive boxing underground.'

'Where would such bans on dangerous sports stop?' an irate middle-class voice screeched.

Mountaineering was cited, and I felt myself flinching so hard that my son asked me what was wrong. It was unusual for him to take such an interest. Part of me wanted to ban everything that could destroy a family: boxing, mountaineering, fast cars, affairs, alcohol, cigarettes, nightclubs, absence of cotton wool around the human body at all times and especially after dark when dangers can catch you unawares. Of course, the experts who were asked for their views on the subject wanted to ban boxing but not these other activities. None of them mentioned compulsory cotton wool, which I thought was interesting and revealing.

'What is the point in a sport where people are deliberately trying to harm each other?' someone asked rhetorically, and I thought of Ordsall and Wincobank and American concepts of work and getting paid bugger all, and I immediately thought of an answer to this direct and searching question.

I drove faster now, with my son beside me, thinking about what boxing means, and I reflected on the nature of the boxing fan who doesn't have to step into the ring, who never has to step into the ring, but who can watch the fight and analyse all human behaviour and then talk about the fight and the courage and pain of the sport from the comfort and safety of his armchair. And from this same armchair, he can display all the intense masculinity that Mailer has discussed so poetically, through the safe process of his own talk. Boxing for the fan is not just about that sweet feeling of catharsis after the fight, when the adrenalin of the boxer and of the fan have both subsided, it is about talking knowledgeably about this side of human experience, this hidden dark side, that is only revealed in that man-to-man challenge. Boxing reminds us of another side of ourselves, a more basic side, it is a nudge and a wink to our evolutionary past and the talk about the fight might itself be like the peacock's feather, a warning to other males of our strength and prowess, and our position in the male hierarchy. I was smiling to myself as I reflected that this talk might ultimately protect us from violence. And the other fights caught on CCTV, and even the forensic tapes of the worst violence imaginable (the worst imaginable because we can imagine ourselves as the muppets in those exact same situations) might serve a very similar sort of function, a topic for talk, a topic to display our masculinity through discussion. And I thought to myself that perhaps these films are even more effective, in a way, because they are more real – and therefore truer – with no rules governing what can and cannot occur. It is human nature red in tooth and claw to be played over and over and to be discussed time and time again. Nobody ever just wanted to watch all of these different genres of violence – be they boxing or something less regulated altogether – they wanted to watch them in order to talk about them. That was one of the things that had struck me most about the subculture in which I had been living. There is all this talk surrounding violence, and all this talk is really rather poorly understood. We can talk about violence and we can construct ourselves through our descriptions of what 'goes off', of what actually occurs and why, and through our subtle and not so subtle evaluations of all the action, we can become something in the process. We ourselves can be something.

Many fans wanted to see Tyson box, not because they didn't agree that he was out of control, but because it would be a real test of Lewis's courage to step into the ring with a man like that. They wanted to see this ultimate test of courage and, of course, they wanted Lewis to win, so that they could talk in a manly way about intense fear and pain, so that others might be confronted with their constructed personae. I don't think that we will ever understand boxing and the strong feelings that people hold for 'this horrible, dirty, prostituting sport', as Brendan sometimes likes to describe it, until we understand how the talk about boxing actually functions. This talk allows an essential expression of masculinity in a world that constrains most other outlets for such an expression. And if we ban boxing, what are we going to offer those waifs and strays down the gym that nobody else wants? And what are we going to encourage those kids from Ordsall to get into instead, and those lads who get paid with bonuses of Kit-Kats at the end of a long day? And how else are we going to allow men to project themselves as men in this day and age? It's a lot to take away, that's all I thought, as I gazed at my son in the light from other cars.

Sheffield was wet that Sunday night, and the rain was pinging off the slate-grey streets just by the River Don. One lone prostitute stood under a pink-and-white umbrella with a long, shapely white handle, just down from where Caesar's massage parlour used to be. Her shoulders were hunched miserably, her arms were folded tight across her thin, white, partially exposed chest. The rain was pinging down all around her. They are trying to develop this area, to entice the yuppies of a new decade to come down here by a river with old rubber tyres half in and half out, and knotted bin bags full of rubbish bobbing in the black oily water and that lone hunched figure on the other side of the street.

I was alone in my thoughts. So what had I witnessed over those long years of studying the subculture from which Naz had emerged, with Brendan leading the young Arab lad around

225

Wincobank late at night and whispering in his ear about Muhammad Ali and what it takes to be the greatest fighter in the world? And what had happened between them that finally drove them apart? Was it just another lesson in human greed? Or was it something different altogether? Was it the fact that we all individually want to take the credit for great success, but we all want to attribute failure immediately and unequivocally to somebody else? Is this really all that I had learned – that human beings are biased in terms of how they process information about the social world and flawed when they reason about their role in the success or failure of human action? And what did really happen in the end between the two of them? Brendan's views about what had happened emerged over the course of many conversations. My understanding was that Brendan thought that Naz had some serious flaws as a man, flaws that almost certainly he himself had helped to create over those long, intensive years. He thought that Naz had wanted all of the attention for himself in the lead-up to the big fights and, therefore, that Naz resented all of Brendan's time and effort spent with the waifs and strays in the gym. But I think that all of this time and effort with society's rejects was how Brendan justified the sport of boxing – 'this horrible, dirty, prostituting sport' – to himself. Brendan also seemed to think that Naz was trying to destroy the gym and the whole enterprise, and, therefore, his life's work, by enticing many of the best fighters, like Johnny Nelson and Ryan Rhodes, away after the split. But what was Naz's view of what happened and what truth was there in Brendan's conclusions? And what about Nick Pitt's account of the episode in that limousine in Los Angeles when Naz accused Brendan of never standing up to anybody in his life, when Brendan realised that it was Naz whom he should have stood up to? How important was that one argument, that epiphany in the back of a long, luxurious car? And then, from my purely selfish point of view, what had I really been witnessing over those years? Did I really watch at first-hand a new Muhammad Ali coming into being, with all the talk and charisma and all the skill, in a northern town decimated by a government that didn't seem to care? Or was he just another boxer full of showbiz hype, showbiz with a bit more blood, on another career trajectory that climbed and climbed and then fell back to earth following a meeting one night in Las Vegas with a Mexican with both feet firmly on the ground? I still wasn't sure and that bothered me enormously.

My son and I drove around the centre of the city and down to the Hilton, based in this area as part of the whole regeneration process. There was a large black Mercedes sitting outside, the rain on the roof making it shine like glass, the engine running, the driver obviously waiting for someone. The dark windows slowly started to open as I passed. The voice came out of nowhere. 'Geoffrey, how are you?'

I looked around and saw an old familiar face peering out. 'How are you, Naz?' I popped his name into my greeting, just in case my son didn't recognise him. Naz was looking a little less lean than when I last saw him, a little rounder in the face. I could see my son smiling broadly, as I introduced him to the former world champion.

'I've known your dad since way back,' said Naz. 'How's *Big Brother*?' he asked. 'I've been watching you on that. I love that programme.'

I smiled back at him, 'Pretty good,' I said, feeling temporarily important, flattered by his comments.

'You never told us that you were the expert on that body-language stuff when you used to come down to the gym. Why did you never mention it? You can't be modest in this world, you know, or people will just ignore you.'

He shook my hand firmly and with a certain warmth. There was a lot that I wanted to ask Naz now that we had finally met up, especially as I had heard that a fight had just been arranged against the European Featherweight Champion Manuel Calvo for March. I told him that I had been trying to get hold of him for months, but had been unable to get through.

'I'll sort it out – don't worry,' he said. 'Didn't you tell my people who you were?'

'I didn't know what to tell them,' I said, smiling with almost false modesty now.

I didn't want to take any chances that night standing out there in the rain, so I threw a few questions at him anyway, when he was off guard, so to speak. I reminded him of what he had once said about how he would cope with defeat. 'So how did it feel really?'

'And you're the world's expert on lying as well, I hear,' he said, laughing. 'I'd better be careful what I say here.

'I've always believed', he continued, 'that what happens happens for a reason. There's no problem with anything, I'm as confident as ever, I'm probably even more confident now.'

But there was something about his demeanour that said otherwise. He said it so quietly, with his arms locked tightly across his chest. But I didn't want to read too much into isolated body language after what I had been through.

He told me that after his defeat, Sugar Ray Leonard had rung him to tell him that the defeat would do him good and that he himself came back as a better fighter after losing to Roberto Duran.

'I'll come back from this defeat stronger. I didn't get beat up. I'm the better fighter. I was getting the wrong advice about how to handle the fight. I was being told to go for the knock-out. I should have stayed relaxed.'

I wanted to ask Naz about 11 September because it was on my mind, and I had heard that it had been the source of a great bust-up between Naz and some of his closest friends back in Brendan's gym. Johnny Nelson had apparently asked at the time, 'Why is Naz staying silent? Why doesn't he speak out against the events of 11 September? Instead he has laid low and kept quiet. Is he with us or against us?' Naz's family had been furious at the comments. I wanted to ask whether Naz would be called to the ring again by a mullah or be fighting again with 'Islam' emblazoned prominently on his shorts in this new Americanised world of ours, but I didn't know how to slip this shot in. So I asked him instead whether he would make any changes to his 'entrances'. He evaded the question or didn't see what I was getting at.

'No, I'll still be flamboyant,' he said. 'The world likes a flamboyant fighter who deals with his opponents in a good style. You know me, Geoffrey, I like taking out my opponents in good style.'

Oscar Suarez, his trainer, came out of the hotel and got into the car. He was carrying some videotapes of fights under his arm. Naz introduced me as 'an old friend', as 'someone who used to come down to the gym a lot' and as 'the *Big Brother* psychologist'.

'Ah, a psychologist,' said Oscar.

'He doesn't need one of those, by any chance, does he?' I asked.

'Not at the moment,' said Oscar Suarez, 'thank you very much.'

Naz gave me a number to ring, and we shook hands. I asked for an autograph for my son, and he wrote it in big flamboyant style and my son released a great big uncool smile of pleasure. It was most unlike him to be that unguarded.

The electric window started to go slowly back up, as I thought of one last quip. 'Perhaps he'll need a psychologist in March, if things don't quite go his way,' I said quickly, but my suggestion was drowned out by the purring noise of the large black Mercedes moving slowly off into the wet Sheffield night. The car taking an ex-champ back to his luxurious surroundings on the far side of town, the west side of the city, the side miles from here, the side well away from Wincobank and from Ordsall and from skinny females with pink-and-white umbrellas who were out on this wet, cold night, trying to make a few quid from their bodies in hard and sometimes very dangerous times.

'Well?' I said to Sam. 'What did you think? Do you believe me now? I always told you that I saw Naz when I was out and about, and that I was a friend of his. I wasn't just messing about, you know, when I was going out.' I could see him thinking. He was looking at the rain and smiling to himself.

'I always believed that you knew him really,' he said. 'I just don't think that he's that big any more. He's not like The Rock or Stone Cold Steve Austen. He's just Naz, after all. He's just local.'

TWO

The truth is that I thought that the story would end here, at this precise point, with Naz driving off in a large Merc into the night, and my son now believing that Naz knew me all along. It might not have excused all those nights out when Sam was younger, but it created some ambiguity about what I was doing and that, I suppose, was the most I could have realistically hoped for.

The following day, I rang the number that Naz had given me and spoke to Riath, who sounded genuinely pleased to hear from me – 'Geoffrey, how are you?' But I was not optimistic about my chances of setting up a face-to-face interview. A documentary had been shown on Channel 4 a few weeks previously, which had followed Naz in the run-up to the Barrera fight. The documentary exposed the intense egotism of the Hamed camp and of Naz himself. It revealed this new world that they had created for themselves in their own image, and the contrast between this rich, soft life that they were leading and their very public dedication to Islam seemed to upset some people. The contrast between the overblown rhetoric of Naz and Barrera's more measured language also hit you between the eyes, especially given the outcome of the fight. I assumed that they would be avoiding the media. Experienced journalists were unable to get face-to-face interviews with the Prince. There were many rumours about his weight. There were one or two telephone interviews with the 'Silent Prince', as the newspapers were now calling him. Most said that the hunger had gone from Naz, and that the Prince, who had now been exposed as a pauper, was finished. I also assumed that, as in any divorce, where all of the onlookers are assigned to one side or the other, they would have thought of me as being on Brendan's side. But Riath told me to make my way down to Naz's new gym the following Monday morning.

'How will I find the new place?' I asked.

'You can't miss it,' he said, 'just look for the three big white pillars. It used to be a carpet shop and it's beside a bookie's, but it's like a palace on the outside.'

I wasn't taking any chances so I drove down London Road and Abbeydale Road the night before looking for the three white pillars, which really did stand out a mile – like a Middle Eastern palace, or perhaps an Indian restaurant – on a grey Sheffield street.

The following morning, Naz's black Merc was parked carelessly on the pavement outside. My first thought was that this was a closed private place with an intercom and tight shutters, unlike Brendan's gym, which was always open and inviting, like a church. But it's best to get rid of all preconceptions like this before an interview.

Riath and Naz looked pleased to see me. They seemed very proud of their new training location and insisted on showing me around. Riath asked me what I thought of it. There were framed photographs of Naz all over the walls, and one or two of Muhammad Ali. Old pairs of shorts, including the leopard-skin shorts with 'Prince' on the front that he wore against Steve Robinson in 1995, were framed and in a line on one wall.

'I've put my shorts up there,' Naz said. 'Just some of my shorts, mind, not even all of them. They weigh a ton, they do. When I won the world title against Steve Robinson, the shorts were so heavy. They're up there now.'

I pointed out that the year below the framed leopard-skin shorts read 30 September 1985 and not 1995.

'We never noticed that,' said Naz.

'It's funny that,' I replied.

There was a cushion cover with Naz's portrait on the front hanging on another wall. I stood there looking at the ring and then at this huge polished gallery of images of the Prince from every possible angle.

Riath nudged me. 'You can tell that his ego has landed here with all these pictures. It's his Arabness coming out; he has to have his picture on everything in sight.'

Naz intervened, but in a good-natured sort of way, 'That's bull.

That's total bull. It's just that you want to make it as comfortable as possible.'

Riath teased him a little more: 'He loves himself. He just loves himself. Look at him.'

Naz started to justify this gallery devoted to his ego: 'The fact is, what else could I put up here? I mean, I'm trying to get loads of other pictures of great fighters, and when I get them, I'll put them up but, at the end of the day, the only pictures I've got at the moment are from my own office that I had to take out of there to make the gym a little bit homely. And, at the end of the day, these are the fights that took place.'

I noticed that there was a picture in one corner of Johnny Nelson, Clifton Mitchell, Ryan Rhodes and Naz all in orange wigs. It was an image of happy days long gone; it was the craíc down in the old gym. I noticed that there were no photographs of Brendan, even caught in the background of any of the old photographs.

Riath showed me up to the gallery overlooking the ring. CNN was on in the background. I noticed that the FTSE 100 Index was being displayed. I didn't know if this was what they had been watching when I arrived. I was still looking around me, getting my bearings. I had never seen a boxing gym like this before; it was so – well – sumptuous. I was told that it had cost half a million quid. It really was a shrine to Naz, the champion of the world.

Riath obviously felt that he needed to explain the decor a little more carefully. 'In the Middle East, there are massive pictures of the President everywhere you go because it's the Arab mentality. You've got to reinforce who the leader is. It's a bit similar here. Just look around.'

Naz smiled over at me. 'You know, back in the Yemen, they took the pictures of the President down and put me up instead. In the Yemen, I've just done a telephone commercial. It's a mobile phone commercial and it's gone crazy over there. The marketing that they put into it was just amazing. And the actual pictures that they took, they're on every street in the Yemen.'

I watched Naz's body language; he was starting to stretch out with pride on the settee in front of me.

Riath added, 'The subscription levels have just gone through the roof since Naz got involved.'

I noticed that they backed each other up in conversation. They latched their turns onto each other, one ready to help the other out, the way that you might expect brothers to do in conversation, but rarely do in real life in my experience.

I sat down beside Naz on the sumptuous leather settee. The leather sighed wearily as I sank into it. I was ready to start. 'Tell me about losing to Barrera,' I said directly to Naz. 'How did that feel?'

He moved away ever so slightly. Perhaps I was sitting too close for comfort, perhaps it was the directness of my first question.

'I knew that I had lost before the last bell went,' said Naz, 'simply because I wasn't boxing to the best of my ability. But I'm making no excuses; he was better than me on the night. Full stop. He was better than me in every department necessary.'

I asked Naz if he felt good going into the ring that night.

'No, I didn't, but I don't want to make no excuses. There were loads of things going wrong. Everything that could have gone wrong went wrong that night. Me bandages, me gloves. I mean I didn't pick me gloves until ten minutes before the fight.'

I asked him to explain to a non-boxer why the gloves are so important psychologically. He looked slightly surprised by the question.

'Oh, the gloves are so important, it's untrue. You still run marathons, don't you? Well, I mean, it's like telling you to run a marathon in size eleven trainers. It's something silly like that. It's just telling you to do something that you're not comfortable with at all. I couldn't even flip over the top rope that night, I couldn't hold the ropes properly, and I couldn't get the right grip on the ropes – all because of the gloves. I wasn't getting the right grip with them at all. They were all stiff. They needed breaking in properly, and I didn't have time for that. I didn't have that much time on the pads. I was also cold. All of that didn't lose me the fight – I lost me the fight. I lost me the fight when I entered the ring and I boxed the way I did, and you can only do what your opponent allows you to do, and my opponent didn't allow me to do much that night. He'd got everything down pat, as they say in America, down pat. He'd got everything off; he knew everything that was going to happen. He had worked out all the moves; he was anticipating what was going to happen next. He was very, very good. He'd got a lot of things off pat.'

I asked Naz at what point during the fight he had realised that things weren't going his way. I tried to look supportive.

'From the very beginning,' he said. 'But I've been in loads of fights where things didn't work out from early on, and then all of a sudden things change, things can change just like that in fights. Things just change, I don't know why they do, but they just do. But I never think, "Oh, this ain't going really well." Because whatever's going to happen, it's going to happen. It happens for a reason, that's what I believe in. And I believe in God, do you know what I mean?'

I wanted to know how intense religious belief of the sort that Naz clearly possesses and sport fit together psychologically. I asked him if he thinks that everything happens for a reason because of the will of God, does that mean that he, the sportsman, can't change things.

'No, no, I don't believe that,' he said. 'There's a certain expression in our religion – in Islam – it's basically asking God for help. The only thing that can change fate is that.'

But what happens if you ask God for help through prayer, and it doesn't happen? Does this cause worry?

'No, you don't worry at all. In my religion, you just think that this is what God wanted, this is His will, and this is what's happened. And you thank Him for it, no matter what has happened – in misfortunes, in accidents, in whatever. The first thing you do is say, "All praises are due to Allah, to God." Simply because things could be worse, a lot worse. You could not be living, you know. In all misfortunes, in all mishaps, in accidents, in anything in life, the first thing that a Muslim would say is "All praises are due to Allah."'

I asked him whether he thought that the experience had made him stronger, and whether it was God's will to make him stronger through defeat in the Barrera fight.

'A hundred per cent,' he said. 'And, you know, I have got stronger, my faith has got stronger, I believe. But also I'm concentrating even more because of the losing. Losing for me has not made me change in any obvious way. People say to me, "Oh, you've changed a lot." But you can't see a change in me like that. The thing with me is that I'm a really happy guy; I'm a happy man, and I thank God for that. I'm happy-go-lucky. And I've been like that for years and years and years because I've always

234

realised the gift I've got. And I thank God for the gift I've got; I thank Him every day. For the last so many years, I've been praying five times a day and I've been going to Mecca with the family. So I have got very religious, probably in the past three or four years. But saying that, even with getting religious, you know, boxing is only one side of my life, but the core of my life, and the centre of my life is me religion. When I lost, I instantly thought that this is the will of God, and that's how I'm going to take it. I came out of the fight and I think that I was more relieved than upset. In fact, I wasn't upset at all. It was like I really never lost anything. It was like I achieved something that night. It sounds funny, but the night I lost it felt like I achieved most in my career. Because the night I lost was the night I went to town supporting Islam. I tried to promote Islam to the best of my ability. And I felt like a winner.'

Riath had been sitting quietly up to this point on a leather chair just out of my field of vision, as if he were only half listening, but suddenly he interrupted. 'The thing is it's very sensitive especially now because all of a sudden religion, well, Islam in particular, has become the number-one focus. Islam is being blamed for a lot of things that are happening in the world, but there are fanatics in every religion. But all of a sudden we are getting questions about our religion. And we get people coming up to us saying, "Are you going to calm down your religious presence in the arena? Are you going to have any consideration for what happened on 11 September?"'

Naz shifted position uncomfortably on his seat. 'You always get this. You get four guys who rob a bank, or do something bad, and they are Christians, and you get four guys that have done something but they are Muslims. Immediately, they'll say, "And four Muslims have done such and such, and we don't know who they could be working for." Now if they were Christians, they wouldn't mention their religion.'

I asked whether in America they would be putting a lot of pressure on them to tone down their overt religious display.

Riath answered first. 'Not so much in America but over here. They've asked for some consideration for what's gone on. They don't want us to come out with any kind of religious overtones of any kind whatsoever in our upcoming fights.'

Naz joined in. 'But, as I've said, it all depends on how I feel on the night, or coming up to the fight. If I want to promote Islam, I will. If I don't, I won't, and that's how I've left it. I'm not saying to them, "Oh, I totally understand", although I do totally understand. Our hearts are full of sadness for them all. Which hearts wouldn't be? Only a person with no feelings at all could have no sadness in their heart for the people who died on 11 September, those innocent people whose lives were taken.'

I enquired whether Naz was worried about the way that the Yemen was being drawn into America's hit list at the moment.

Again, Riath got in first. 'Yemen is kind of changing to be honest with you. The President of Yemen has gone over to Washington, and everything's all pally-pally now. So that's kind of resolved now. I think Yemen has just been caught in the crossfire because of some of the recent terrorist activity in Yemen, which is completely against what the government of the Yemen believe and the people of the Yemen believe. And you get these terrorist elements everywhere, which you know all about, my friend, coming from Ireland as you do. A lot of them think, "Oh yeah, Yemen." They think there's a lot of terrorists out there because they are harboured sort of thing, and it's a kind of breeding ground for terrorism, but it's not true. Wherever you go, in the world, in the most obscure places in the world, there are terrorists everywhere.'

Naz interrupted and leant forward slightly. 'Changing the subject completely and going back to boxing, which I do want to focus on anyway. After the loss, before I came back to England, I went on a nice vacation with me wife and me kids. We went to the Bahamas and stayed in a beautiful hotel. We just had a fantastic time, and we just chilled out. Coming out of the ring that night, losing on points, yeah, there was something about it, as I said to you, I thought that I achieved more that night than I had in my whole career. I mean, I competed at the absolute best of all, at the top of my division. And nobody can ever say, "Well, I mean that guy won everything, and he got out of boxing when he did, but at the end of the day he never boxed the best in his division." Well, you can say that about a lot of fighters, like Chris Eubank, Nigel Benn, all of them. Obviously, I give Nigel Benn a lot of credit for boxing McClelland, but the circumstances that McClelland was under before that fight – losing something like sixteen pounds in twenty-four hours – was just absurd. I don't even know how somebody could do that and stand up, never mind box. So it just shows what can happen to a fighter when they drain themselves and drain their brain that much.'

I reminded Naz that in the past I had written about this terrible thing that boxers have to go through to make the weight. I asked him directly how tough it was for him now.

'It's tough. It's very tough. It's tough training for three months solid. And I'm talking about being right on course and bringing your body to the peak of its fitness and dropping the weight and feeling strong at the weight. It's not just about dropping the weight. I mean, you've got to go in there with something, you've got to go in with the right ammunition, knowing that you are strong enough in every department to beat your opponent.'

I asked whether it was getting tougher as he was getting older and also whether he was going to continue fighting at featherweight.

'I'm staying at featherweight. I don't know what it is but, when I'm getting into the fights, I feel really, really much stronger. I mean with Barrera in the last fight, in every single round even up to the last, there was something about the feeling of the fight and me feeling stronger and me looking in the guy's eyes and me knowing that the guy was afraid for twelve rounds. I felt that he was afraid for twelve rounds and that he was very wary in case he got caught. Then again, he had a lot of things covered, and I admire him for that. He's a great champion, and I give it up. I mean fighters like Kevin Kelley when I knock him out in his hometown and he just makes complete excuses – they're not champions, you know. A champion's a champion when he can say that he's been beat by a champion. And then he'll come back to beat that champion. I said Barrera was better than me on the night and on that night only. You know, it was written for him to win and, at the end of the day, the credit is due to the guy, because he won the fight clearly. He won the fight hands down. But then I look back and, in the space of one year, the best in boxing had got stopped and knocked out. Look at Lennox Lewis; he got knocked out directly after my fight – that totally over-shadowed my loss. You got Felix Trinidad, one of the best pound-for-pound fighters in the whole world, who beat Oscar De La Hoya, and then he got knocked out by Bernard Hopkins. He got pounded and knocked out. You got Oscar De La Hoya; he got beat by Sugar Shane Mosley. This is all in the space of a year. And then you got Sugar Shane Mosley who, just the other week, gets an absolute pasting and loses on points. I mean, after beating Oscar De La Hoya, Sugar Shane Mosley was rated as maybe the best pound-for-pound fighter in the whole world. But he got dropped. And when I look at my loss compared with all of these big massive unification bouts in boxing, I think my loss was a little points margin thing, whereas these guys are getting absolutely hammered. Now, as I said to you, the first thing I said inside the ring with me father and me family was "Thank God. Praise is due to Allah. Praise is due to God." Simply because the guy never hurt me, the guy never stopped me, the guy never put me down, the guy never knocked me out. I was thinking, you know, I've got two beautiful kids, I've made an absolute fortune; I have a lot to be thankful for.'

I asked Naz how much he got for the fight.

Naz was very cagey about the money, though. 'What did the papers say?' he asked.

'Millions, many millions,' I replied.

'I think that it is still rolling in today,' Naz said, as if he couldn't be sure of the final figure anyway.

'You got a lot of money?' I asked again, trying to pin him down to a set of figures.

He was getting a little impatient with me. 'The only reason for not telling you,' he said, 'being honest with you, is that ... I'll tell you why, when people read this, I don't want people to read about a guy talking about the fortune he has, what he makes, what cars he has, what he drives, what he's got, the luxuries in life, where he lives, all that sort of thing. I'm just saying that I don't want to be a guy that turns round and says here, "Geoffrey, I've made this, I've got this."'

I changed tack somewhat. 'Can I just go back a bit, Naz, because I was reading bits of interviews that I've done with you before, on the way up in your career. Now, you've had a unique background, you would agree to that?'

'And thank God,' he said. And then there was a slight pause. 'Are you meaning family?' he asked.

'I mean everything,' I said. I was watching his face carefully for evidence of little micro-expressions that might reveal his true emotion. They were there all right; he knew where the interview was going. 'I was reading again the stories that I wrote about you being in the gym since you were seven and so on. Do you think that being absolutely focused on boxing from that early age was essential to your success?'

'I think it played a big part,' he said, 'because there was always this dream and there was always a goal at the end of that with me training every single day. There were days when the sun would shine, and I would smell the breeze and the air and I'd think, "I just don't feel like going to the gym today." But in the back of my head I'd be motivated by this thing and, even as a kid, I'd be motivated by this thing in my head telling me that I was going to be the best in the world. I wanted to be the best fighter, one of the best fighters that ever lived. And I wanted to be on that world stage of boxing.'

This was obviously the moment to ask him about Brendan. He knew that the question was coming. I could see it in those little micro-expressions that flitted across his face more regularly now. 'I was shocked when you and Brendan split up because the last time I spoke to you the two of you were together. Can you just explain to me what happened between the two of you?'

'I don't honestly know if I want to go into that,' he said. 'I mean, I'll go into it a little bit, but I don't want this interview to be overshadowed by this thing about Brendan. I'm sick of publicising this man. I'm absolutely sick of publicising him. But a lot of people are looking for me to slag this man off, I'm not in line to do that. If anything, I'm in line to give this man credit. Credit in that he had time to spend on me, and time he did spend on me. And the thing that I recall most that came out of this man's mouth when I was growing up was "You can tell people from all over the country that this kid right here is going to be my meal ticket for the next ten years."' He glanced over momentarily at Riath, perhaps for support, perhaps for encouragement, and continued without a pause. 'And, boy, I was. And he was building something up to become this special thing. And I give it him, you know. He used to take me for walks every Sunday, and he used these brainwashing techniques – he was very, very good. But I'm going to be honest with you. I learned a lot from the gym, and I learned a lot from Brendan, and it was a fantastic step in my life, and it was a fantastic journey that I took, and I'll never regret it, never. It was an experience. But I

239

know a hundred per cent that it's eating him away like a cancer – the bitterness that's inside him, and I don't want him to do that. I mean, there's many a time when I've said to myself, you know, "Maybe we should make up," because the last thing I want is enemies. Not even enemies, I don't want people having bad feelings about me. I don't want that. I've got on with my life. I've been successful leaving the gym, unlike a lot of people when they left the gym. You know, I moved out with me brothers. We made a decision that we were going to move out to the big wide world of boxing and take it by storm and we did. We're one of the biggest promotional companies there is now.'

Riath interjected, 'As well as promoting Naz, we also do twenty-six Sky promotions a year for other boxers.'

But Naz took over the floor again on the theme of Brendan. 'There's simply nothing in my heart against the man or against his family, against what he's done, but all I want to bring up to you is good.'

But Riath wanted to make his point. 'In actual fact, hate is against our religion. Another thing is, Geoffrey, that you've got a certain idea of him; you've got a certain image of him.'

Naz: 'You've known him for years?'

'I've known him for a long time,' I said.

Riath: 'But the thing is you don't know the dynamics of how their relationship was – day in, day out. You didn't live with it. As a psychologist, you know yourself you can only know the true individual if you've had that kind of closeness, or proximity on a kind of continuous level. It came to a point where the relationship was just unhealthy.'

Naz: 'It was unbearable at one point. It literally became unbearable. We could not work with each other in the end.'

Riath: 'He was writing a book at the same time as working with Naz and being paid for training the Prince, which was more than offensive. I mean, it was kind of a betrayal.* I mean, imagine you're working for me and then, at the same time, you're writing a book. Or, I'm working for you and, at the same time, I'm writing a book about you and your life and then it's going to be published on the week that we separate. Imagine what kind of betrayal that

---

* It is important to note that while Brendan co-operated with Nick Pitt he received no financial gain from the book, and was not writing one himself.

is. He was making money from us while he was compiling this book.'

Naz interrupted. 'It's not just about money, Riath; you're dealing with somebody for over eighteen years of your life. You've nearly spent the whole of your life with somebody. At one point, he even wanted me to move into his own house. You know where I lived – I lived literally two minutes away from him. He wanted me to move into his house and live with his family. He wanted to try and take that much control of my life. This was as a kid.'

Riath spoke again. 'I think Brendan thought that Naz's family was too much in his life. But that repulsed us.'

'Not just that,' said Naz. 'He wanted to brainwash me that good that he wanted me to live with him. But as I said, it got to a point where there were quite a few fights, where there was an atmosphere there between us. I always wanted to move out of the gym and do something else with him in terms of setting up a training camp before fights. I wanted him to put the whole attention on me, with me being the main man, as in I had the most important fights coming up. And I thought that whoever had the most important fights coming up in the gym, all attention should be on them. But to get thousands and thousands of kids – that's what it felt like – thousands coming in and professionals and amateurs and the whole shebang training together. What bugged me was going into that gym and doing every little thing the same every single day and not being trained and them getting absurd amounts of money for doing it.'

Riath intervened. 'The thing is, Geoffrey, this is being said not with any kind of malice. But Brendan would take this with malice. He would take every single thing what we've said with malice. Especially because it's coming from us, because the way he sees it is that we've cut his lifeline, that's how he sees it. To be honest with you, there was so much respect in the relationship from me to him all the way up and an acknowledgement of the contribution he has made to Naz. And my dad acknowledged that and my dad went to his house on several occasions to show him good will.'

Naz spoke again. 'I think the book was one of the things that really, really bugged us and bugged me dad because the book led to another book and it led to things in the paper and it led to

241

everything else. My dad says to him, "Whatever happens between you and my son, don't write or talk about my son." And he gave my dad his word on that.'

I wanted to be very clear here. 'So talking about your personal life, is that what Brendan said he wouldn't do?'

'He talked about everything he could,' said Naz. 'Things about me driving, things about love, which I don't even want to go into. I don't want to talk about it; it's just promoting the Nick Pitt book even more. Do you know what I mean? The point I'm getting to now is betrayal, and the point is he gave his word. And I made this man financially secure – him and his family. But that was a big step that I took in life – leaving his gym. Because when you've been in the environment for like eighteen years, growing up with certain people, going down to a certain gym, living in a particular spot, it was like how can you leave that kind of place and delve into something else? It was like hard.'

'It was the fear of the unknown', said Riath, latching on to Naz's response.

'As Riath just said, it was the fear of the unknown,' continued Naz. 'Really and truly, I should have split up way before we did split up because things weren't working out, you know. I think there was a big, big problem before the Kevin Kelley fight, where Frank Warren had to get us both together, because we was going to split up before the Kevin Kelley fight.'

I mentioned that I had read the Nick Pitt book and reminded them of Pitt's conclusion that the argument on the way from Los Angeles International Airport to the Sheraton Hotel was the critical moment in their breaking up. I asked how accurate this was.

Naz said that he could recall this particular incident but emphasised that it had nothing whatsoever to do with the break-up. 'No. It was nothing to do with that; in fact, it was just a little argument in that car. We had little niggles throughout life with each other. We had little niggles and we had arguments.'

Riath was, however, keener to apportion any responsibility or any blame for these little arguments. 'Brendan would have niggles with Naz. Brendan would have niggles with John, his own son. Brendan would have niggles with me.'

'The one thing throughout my time with Brendan and his

family,' said Naz, 'the one thing was I never saw love between them. Never. And when I say love, I mean love.'

'Not the way we express our love in our family,' added Riath.

'Yeah, the way we express our love,' said Naz. 'And the way that you should treat your own brothers and your own sisters and your parents. Let me ask you one thing, have you ever seen them hugging?'

'No,' I said.

Naz: 'Never?'

'Not really,' I said again. (When I played this part of the tape to Brendan later he commented that, 'In Ireland they shake hands, that's what they do; over here the English will put their arms around you and stab you in the back. They put their arms around you and it's all false.' This to me sounded like a fair comment by Brendan.)

Naz continued, 'In the time you've known them, you've never seen them hugging. Have you ever seen them with any kind of affection for each other in terms of any kind of body language? Because you know psychology. You know body language – you work on body language. You don't see it with them because there isn't any. Now, I didn't grow up this way. You've seen that I've got a tight-knit family, but they were different. They were always trying to compete with each other as to who was going to make what, as to who had got what fight. And I'm not saying it's got nothing to do with me, but that's what I've seen, and you could see that they despised each other. I'm talking from father to son, from brother to brother.'

Riath intervened again. 'I wouldn't say despise. Despise is too strong a word here.'

Naz responded. 'Well, there was jealousy between them, I should say, and envy between them, because it was like which one was going to work in the corner. There was quite a bit of rivalry, you know. And you'd look at the family as a whole and you'd think, you know, "How can this be a family?"'

And at that point, I noticed Naz's hand gestures – the hands apart, the palms facing downwards, the hands moving up and down, each hand depicting members of Brendan's family vying for position. Naz's fighting hands revealed how he felt about the family that had welcomed him as a son for eighteen years or so.

Riath added, 'But that's the truth, and I can honestly say to you, everything we've said is the absolute truth. It's in our hearts, we're not trying to manipulate anything. We're not trying to slag anybody off.'

'I'm not interested in perpetrating a slagging match at all,' I said. 'I'm really not interested in that. What I'm interested in is explaining what actually happened in your opinion, so that people can understand your side of the story.'

Naz looked pleased. 'Well, I hope this will be the start of many more interviews because, to be honest with you, this is what I tell all journalists. When you have an interview with somebody, you see how that one goes and you see how they write it, and you read it, and, if you think that they've made a complete fair assessment of it all, you think, "He's definitely getting another interview."'

Riath added, 'But you did a brilliant interview the first time around. I mean, we're not saying brilliant in order for you to blow smoke up your own ass kind of thing. It's just that it's fair.'

Naz interrupted him, laughing. 'I don't like that saying, though. I really don't like that saying.'

I told them that I didn't know what this saying meant.

Riath explained, 'Basically, you know, kind of bigging yourself up. We're not bigging ourselves up, and you're not bigging yourself up. Do you know what bigging yourself up means?'

'He means blowing your own trumpet,' Naz added. 'But coming back to boxing, the split with Brendan gave me a chance to try another trainer.'

'So what was Manny Steward like?' I asked.

'I think the best thing that he did was just make me laugh,' Naz said. 'The one thing that I admired about Manny is that throughout everything the guy could have a laugh. And that was one of the best things, but to come back in the early rounds of the fight and say to you, "You need a knock-out to win," I think that's absurd. That kind of advice for a fighter in the corner is just crazy. But, as I say, it gave me a chance to work with Oscar Suarez, who I get on well with now, and you get to see different things in boxing – different things and different techniques – and you put your mind on something else because when you are in a certain environment and a certain place and when you've grown up in a certain way, in an environment of boxing you only see one method of boxing – that's the only thing in your head. But when you move out and check different things and you look at different aspects and see how things work, and how things can be, it gives you a lot more to work on and to think about and to improve. Whereas before, you just think, "Stick to this, I know this, I know what I'm doing." It's all about moving into the unknown again.'

I looked around at the plush surroundings and felt that I had to ask him something quite directly. 'You're very comfortably off now, more than comfortably off. You don't need boxing any more. You've got all this beautiful stuff; this gym is amazing. So how difficult is it to step from this into the ring again?'

'I'm going to give you the true answer here,' said Naz. 'The feeling inside of me is that I haven't made it.'

I thought that I had misheard him here. 'You haven't made it?' I asked.

'No,' said Naz. 'Even though I know I've got it, inside of me I feel as ordinary and as equal as everybody living. That's me. I'm a humble man. This is because of the upbringing from me parents and me religion, the way it makes you. It gives you a certain way of thinking, once you're religious. And you've got to know that you are equal to everybody else. Equal. You're no bigger or no smaller. You have to see yourself as equal. And, as I said, I'll come back to the feeling I've got in my heart no matter what I've accumulated or what I've achieved. Inside of me it feels the exact same way I did as a kid. That is, you start with nothing and you end up finishing with nothing anyway, because when you're gone you're gone. You can't take nothing with you. But I know that I've accumulated things and I've done really, really well and I've achieved things that people can only dream of really. I know I've done well and I'm proud to say that I've done well and I thank God firstly for letting me do so well, but I don't get that feeling that it's hard to go back in the ring – it doesn't feel like that. This is what I do. It's a part of me, it's just a part of me; it's second nature. You know to come down and train is second nature. You know, at one time I had so many lay-offs, which was crazy. The lay-offs that I used to have in between fights was mad, but at the end of the day that was how I wanted to play it at that particular time in my life. And I've never felt that "Oh, I've got all this materialistic stuff" because I've done so well with all this materialistic stuff in front of me that it would stop me or make me have a feeling of complacency or give me that feeling of "Who needs boxing?" Boxing has been great for me, but I honestly believe I've been great for boxing.'

I wanted to push him on this one. 'But what I was going to say, Naz, is part of this feeling that you've not completely made it is because when you were young you had this goal of emulating or being Muhammad Ali.'

Naz responded immediately. He sounded slightly irritated. 'No, not Muhammad Ali, I never had that goal. The goal that I had as a kid was to be known and to be seen as one of the best fighters who ever lived. Because there were many great fighters and there are many great fighters today. To be on a world stage with them and to be talked about on the same level for me is fantastic. To retire and to be remembered as one of them great fighters is incredible, and I believe it will happen.'

'So,' I asked, 'Muhammad Ali has no special significance for you?'

Naz: 'The only significance that he had in my life was how cool he was in the ring, his class, his class in and out of the ring. The way he presented himself, you know. I wouldn't even call him an idol. I don't really believe in the word "idol". Probably at one time as a kid I'd say he was a boxing idol but I don't like using the word "idol". He inspired me just like he inspired millions of other people around the world, and not just boxers. When I looked at Muhammad Ali and I seen the class, the moves, you know, something that you will never ever see a heavyweight do, you'd see Muhammad Ali do. His sayings, his funniness, his charisma, his flair. He attracted people to boxing, the people he attracted to boxing was the people nobody could attract to boxing. The superstars who rolled up to watch him against Joe Frazier in '71 in Madison Square Garden were incredible. So I suppose he's a guy who you look at and say, "Oh, imagine if I could do a little something like that." I didn't want to be him because I always wanted to be myself; I always knew I was different from a lot of fighters. I always knew that I wanted to drop it, in a totally different way to other fighters. If I could change anything, I'd like to change everything compared with somebody else. If it suited me I'd do the same as them. But that's why there's so many things that I change. I've even started running. In fact, I love running now.'

I reminded him that he used to hate running.

Naz: 'But I can't box without running now before a fight. No, I can't box without running. At one time, I could stay two or three hours in a ring, and the ring fitness was untrue. I'd be first one into the ring and I'd be last one out, and I'd spar with people from flyweight to heavyweight, and I'd beat all of them up to the body and I enjoyed doing it. But the thing was I had that ring fitness then as a kid. I was never out of the gym. But from the age of seven to the year of '96, I never ran in my life. I never ran for a fight in my life. And when I started running, I felt that this was a whole new different thing for me, and I realised I can run. I never ran really before much at all. And then I realised when it came to running, I loved the feeling in me lungs. Just me lungs opening so well. And getting so much wind that you can take off like. I run in the mornings. I like to catch the Morning Prayer in the mosque so I used to run before that. We used to get down to the gym at half past four or five o'clock. We used to just drive right up to the moors, right up top. And we'd run up there at about half four, quarter to five, five o'clock. You know, that coldness and that air is beautiful.'

I said that he had changed a bit. I remembered the time when he only liked to train at night.

'I loved training at night at one time,' he said. 'But I've got kids and everything and I want to see my kids and my wife. It's nice to do your training early and get it out of the way and work hard and then spend some time with your family, if you can. That's one of the biggest reasons that I had a gym done like this so I can be so comfortable in the gym. I study fights up here. I got my computer, I've got actually a whole living room, I've got a kitchen. I've got the gym downstairs and some kind of other gym below.'

We both glanced around the gym more or less simultaneously. 'So does anybody else train here apart from yourself?' I asked.

'Just me and my family,' he replied.

It was a very big change from the old gym. I asked whether he had kept in contact with any of the lads from the gym.

'I have been in touch with Ryan Rhodes,' he said. 'I've even spoken to Johnny Nelson now and again. There was a little bit of a fall-out at one time but we seem to speak now. But that was one thing that I couldn't get to grips with. When I left the gym,

I honestly thought that the kids that I grew up with would show me some kind of support. We literally lived with each other, we went everywhere together and we travelled the country and some parts of the world together. And then you leave a gym, after spending your life down there, it felt like the whole of my life because I can't remember anything before it, do you know what I mean? And you find it hard to have a complete break from everything, the whole surroundings and everything.'

Riath and Naz were unhappy that Ryan Rhodes and Johnny Nelson didn't move across from Brendan too.

'They didn't want to take that step,' said Naz. 'I'm not really dwelling on that aspect of it. But we did end up meeting with Ryan after a few years, and I met Johnny once or twice after leaving but not for the last year or two. It was hard because I grew up with this guy. This guy was my friend. It was hard at first to believe that these kids could just totally blank me.'

'Like you didn't exist,' said Riath.

Naz: 'Yeah. But I get on with some of them now, and we keep in touch now. I speak to Ryan now.'

I asked how Ryan's career was going at the moment.

'His career?' Naz said.

'Down the toilet,' Riath interjected.

'I wouldn't say down the toilet,' said Naz. 'That's a bit harsh. When the kid was starting out, it was unbelievable what the kid could achieve, and all of a sudden, they see him get beat. I mean he's probably only boxed once or twice in the year.'

Riath took up the theme. 'I remember, even with Johnny, and it's not that we're having digs, you've got to understand that, it's not really about having digs, it's about facts and about relationships and the longevity of relationships with people. And I remember Johnny had such a weak confidence level behind him. I mean his reputation spoke for itself. And even Brendan said after that fight at the City Hall against Carlos de Leon that Johnny killed boxing for the next ten years after that in Sheffield.'

'Did you hear Brendan say that?' Naz asked me.

'No, I've never heard Brendan saying that,' I said.

Riath: 'Well, everybody in the gym heard it, and Johnny's confidence was absolutely rock-bottom but then, when Naz was making it big time, he spent so much time with Johnny – it was just unbelievable. Naz was putting his confidence back; every time that Naz fought, he would talk to Frank Warren and say, "Make sure that Johnny is on." And all the time and energy what we put into him, into the kid, and everything else. But when it came to the crunch, and Naz did leave Brendan's gym, Johnny wasn't interested.'

Naz leaned back on the swish leather settee. 'No, I suppose he became the big fish in the pond then when I left.'

Riath: 'You spent virtually every day of your life from eight years old with them. You interacted with them. You were with them virtually every single day. You sacrificed spending time with your own family, at one point, because you were there most of the time. Because that's how Brendan wanted it. He wanted the gym atmosphere to be so cliquish and interactive all the time with him and the boys. So boxing would completely overshadow everything else in Naz's life. And then it comes to a point when the relationship was so unhealthy between us and Brendan, and Naz and Brendan, but they weren't like men. They didn't think that whatever Naz wants to do, he could do, he can go to another gym, but I'm not going to stop speaking to him because of Brendan.'

Naz took up the story. 'But looking back on it, I only wish now that I'd left before I did leave. Because me leaving, in fact, saved me career because from the age of ten or eleven or twelve I'd stopped learning in that gym. I stopped learning. So I had to create everything for myself, from the age of twelve upwards. Now I just thought that with nobody willing to teach anybody anything in that gym you just had to progress with your own experiences and your own everyday training and realise what was right for you. In those days, I realised that if you could fight, you were going to get through.'

I asked Naz for his evaluation of Herol Graham, the role model in the gym when Naz was young.

'I like him,' Naz said. 'We get on with him.'

Riath added, 'He's the one who was constantly calling and wanting to come round after Naz left to see if there's anything he could do and that kind of thing.'

'Herol went through a hell of a lot,' said Naz. 'And I could relate to a lot of things that Herol went through because I was getting it all in my ear in walks with Brendan. I've seen Herol's career go up and down for many years. I just think that Herol was one of the unluckiest fighters that ever lived. But I think you bring it on yourself. Things that you do in life.'

'You reap what you sow,' added Riath.

'Yeah, definitely,' said Naz. 'Things can catch up on you. I don't blame it on anything or put it on one specific thing why he never won the world title. But at one point I really believed that he was a world-beater but Herol brought his style with him and brought his ability with him. Herol was like national champion for years before he came to Sheffield, from Nottingham as an amateur. He was a superb fighter. And he was a made fighter before Brendan got him. That's not taking anything away from Brendan. Did he improve when he got to the gym? Yeah, I think that he probably improved. But there was one thing that was taught in that gym and that was "Look, do what he's doing, or try and do what he's doing." Whichever guy was doing well it was like look at him and with your own particular way of fighting or whatever, try and focus and get round it in your own way, in that way.'

I asked Naz whether in training these days he used any of the routines that he had learnt in the Wincobank gym.

'Yeah. There's a lot of things that I like doing and, even with my trainer now, he can relate to some of the stuff and he can see why I like doing certain things, but one thing that is great about him is that he says, "Whatever makes you comfortable I'm happy with."'

I decided to throw in a strange question, which I knew, being a psychologist, that I could get away with. The spectre of Brendan seemed to be in everything Naz talked about. So how did Naz's unconscious deal with Brendan? 'Do you ever dream about Brendan?' I asked him quite suddenly.

Naz looked taken aback. 'Never. I've never had one dream about him, but I've got no bad feelings about him. I don't want anything to happen to him. I don't dream this or that. It was a stage in my life that took place for a long time, but it's a part of my life that's gone. And I'm glad it's gone.'

'You know when you've been in an unhealthy relationship,' Riath added.

'It was an unhealthy relationship,' said Naz.

'You know when it ends,' Riath said. 'And then, all of a sudden, you think how long had that been going on – three years, three and a half years, whatever it is – you look backwards just with a sigh of relief that it ended.'

'That's what I mean,' said Naz. 'I'm just so glad I left when I left because that could only have destroyed my career.'

'So what was the final straw? What really happened?' I asked.

It was Riath who answered. 'It was the book that was finally the *crème de la crème* or *la pièce de résistance*.'

There was a certain irony in this. Nick Pitt was trying to identify precisely what had caused the split between them, but Riath was saying that it was the book itself.

Riath: 'After the book, there was one fight left.'

'The book was the nail in the coffin,' said Naz. 'The McCullough fight was left.'

They were both laughing now.

'What's so funny about that?' I asked.

'I'm looking at Riath,' said Naz, 'because Riath had so much problems before that fight. Listen to this, and this is what you gotta realise. Brendan had one thing in front of him that meant everything to him. And that was Frank Warren. He did not want to upset him in any way possible, so the morning of the fight he comes into me room crying. You never see your trainer crying, or the man that you've known for like eighteen years crying, sobbing and crying. And it was all "Oh, Frank Warren is going to leave" and it was all Frank Warren this and Frank Warren that and "there's that many problems between us and all of that, and with your brother Riath" because Riath was just getting to the stage of really controlling things and was asking that many questions. Do you remember?'

'Yeah. I can't forget that,' said Riath.

(Brendan later said that he remembered the incident well but he focused on Naz rather than on his own emotions in his account: 'When it happened with Frank Warren, I went down to the room and Naz was there and I said, "Frank Warren, he's gone." So Naz came over and put his arms around me, and said, "You don't realise the money Frank Warren is making." He said, "Stick with us. He's making millions out of me." I said, "Naz, he's the promoter, he's done the deal."')

'And that was a particular point when I knew it was hard for Riath,' said Naz. 'It was very hard. It was probably harder for him than for me. At the end of the day, I just felt like Brendan tried

251

every little thing to make one man – Frank Warren – happy. Whatever you do, you don't come in any circumstances whatsoever to your own fighter, the morning of the fight or a day before the fight, whatever it was, crying, literally crying, that the promoter may fly back, and then who's going to promote the fight?'

'What was the problem, then, with Frank Warren?' I asked.

Riath was now laughing very loudly indeed. 'I was the problem.'

'To them he was but really and truly all he was doing was looking after me,' added Naz.

'I'll tell you why,' said Riath. 'One of the reasons was that the contract was basically coming to an end, and I was trying to work something out.'

'So what I realised,' said Naz, 'was that Brendan at that particular time was trying to use some sort of emotional tactics on me to tell Riath to back off. And I actually did. I said, "Riath, whatever you do, smooth it over because ..."'

'You didn't say it horribly,' interrupted Riath.

'No,' said Naz. 'I just said, "Riath, just please smooth it over because I don't want him coming to my hotel room like the morning of the fight crying. I don't want that, Riath. I don't want to see grown men cry." Not just a grown man; he'd played such a big part in my life, at one time, and to see him at this particular point breaking down because of the love of Frank Warren.'

'Because of how Frank Warren was feeling about us, well, about me in particular,' said Riath.

'I mean, I couldn't believe it,' said Naz. 'I had to get hold of him and give him a hug and say, "Bren, don't worry about it. It'll be all right."' Naz finally added, 'Nobody has got that story, by the way. Nobody's got that information before. We were on Concorde when I made the decision to finally split from Brendan.'

'From New York to London,' added Riath. 'And we said there's no way on earth that we can work with these people again.'

Naz summed it up. 'Yeah. We made a decision then. We made a decision together as brothers and as family that it wasn't right for us. We felt it wasn't right for us – things was going that bad, they couldn't have been worse.

'What about this, Geoffrey,' continued Naz. 'Could you imagine fighting the biggest fight of your life, never fought in the States – it's your first time in Madison Square Garden – and deep down in your heart you feel that the corner men aren't fully behind you? There was that many problems before the Kevin Kelley fight. Actually, at one point, Brendan refused to train me before the fight. John, his son, had to step in. But imagine being in the biggest fight of your life. You've gone down twice, three times, in fact. Like once in the first round, maybe the second or whatever, and you feel you can't look back at your corner.'

'For advice,' said Riath.

Naz said, 'I had this feeling: "Do they care about me? Or what should they tell me?" Or whatever. And you've got to pull it out of the bag yourself.'

This surprised me more than anything so far. 'You really felt that Brendan didn't want you to win that one?'

'I felt it and not only in that fight,' said Naz. 'In the McCullough fight I really, really felt that he wanted me to lose. Did you see the big argument in the corner in the middle of the fight? I wanted space to breathe and to relax when I got back to the corner, and he was right in me face. Like trying to give me advice or whatever, but I was saying "step back, step back" and I had to get up and step back – we was fighting in the corner. I was fighting in the fight and actually fighting in the corner with him. I was getting no peace.'

(When I played this part of the tape to Brendan he laughed. He said that he did everything he could to assist Naz, even, 'Dancing and making an arse of myself to take the pressure off [before the fight], because Naz was under a lot of pressure.')

Naz continued, 'To be in a fight thinking and knowing that your trainer wants you to lose is a terrible feeling, terrible.'

It all struck me as quite extraordinary that Naz should feel this way, especially because Brendan had told me that he was behind Naz all the way in this fight. This really was the psychology of the boxer exposed. The fear and the loneliness all leading to this. I asked if Brendan ever articulated any of this. 'Did he ever say anything? Or was it just something you felt?' I asked.

Naz answered, 'No, it was something that I really, really felt. I mean, who would argue in the corner in a big world title fight with their own fighter that they've known, in their eyes have raised, have brought them up in their eyes? And arguing with them in the corner in the middle of the fight.'

'Did you feel it through his body language?' I asked.

'Through his body language?' said Naz. 'Through the tone of voice. It was everything because as you know I'm very, very good me at reading body language. I'm very good at reading people – their mannerisms, the way people act, what they do. You know their mannerisms, what they do, the whole facial expressions.'

Riath: 'The last three fights of the relationship with Brendan was absolute hell.'

And Naz added, 'But it wasn't just them it was way, way, way, and I mean way before then. The only people who could tell you are the people that were there. The people who were there were the guys who lived in the gym. Like your own so-called friends that you thought you had who saw everything and heard every argument that you had and why it went on and what started it and how it finished. And it went on in the gym, it literally went on in the gym.'

'That's why it was so unhealthy,' said Riath. 'It was such a bad, bad relationship. It was like a bad marriage. And sometimes you only stay together because of the kids, and I think in some ways they only stayed together because of the kids that were in the gym. They were the kids in a weird kind of way.'

Naz continued, 'Well, not just that. Don't forget it was the sense of insecurity of basically another trainer. Going out into a whole new world, it was a whole new life. It was like seeing a whole new you. Because everything that you've seen, through your growing up, will completely change. It's like saying to you, Geoffrey, from now on you are never going to see a pen and a pad. But coming back on a boxing point, I've never been happier, I've never been happier. And, even after losing the fight, I've still never been as happy.'

'Just one last question about Brendan,' I said. 'Do you remember one of the first articles I wrote about you and Brendan making the weight together? Do you miss going through that with him?'

There was no real hesitation. 'No, being honest with you now,' Naz said, 'the thing I miss, and I don't even know if I really miss it now, was the actual gym and the environment. And the laugh we had together as a whole gym. And even taking it with us when we went out to different boxing shows and that. We had a certain craíc about us that nobody could beat. It was the fun and it was the laughter, and we made it work, we made it work for us, in what we were doing. I suppose that's one of the biggest things that I really, really miss. But even if I could have it now, I wouldn't want it, because I've slipped out to a whole different new way of what I like now. I suppose one of the big things that I learnt directly after leaving, and even when I was there, was that the only real friends that I wanted anyway were my own family. And they're the only people I could really, really ever trust.

'I don't think', he continued, after a moment's reflection, 'that what happens in other sports is like boxing. What happens in boxing is not like what happens in other sports. I think boxing is on its own. It's unique with its own unique problems. I remember Brendan saying when we were growing up that boxing is a dirty, horrible, prostituting game. I remember him saying that when I was really, really young. And it's true.'

But through boxing this little lad from Wincobank had seen the world, and his other stories reflected this. It wasn't boasting, it was just some of the things he had seen and some of the people he had met.

'I really, really liked spending time with Muhammad Ali,' he said. 'He lived at the top of boxing. Things that happened with him were so special but not just that, it was the fun that we had. He's funny.'

'Even now,' added Riath.

'He's very, very funny,' said Naz. 'His family too, his wife and the people around him. And they are really, really nice people.'

'You've met everybody,' added Riath.

'Michael Jackson was all right,' said Naz. 'We had a good laugh, and he invited me and my wife to go over to his house one New Year's Eve. It was after the Kevin Kelley fight. We went as well and had a good laugh. We stayed in his premises and everything.'

'In Never Never Land,' said Riath. 'Is that what they call it?'

'It's supposed to be Never Never Land,' said Naz. 'People could not believe that this man would go down a back street, to a boxing gym in New York, in the dark, to watch me training. And we got it on tape. I really couldn't believe it.'

'I was really shocked,' added Riath, 'when I saw him and Elizabeth Taylor together. I'd already met Michael a few times, but I love Elizabeth Taylor. So I wasn't really starstruck with Michael any more, but I was with Elizabeth Taylor.'

'She was telling me stories about Sugar Ray Robinson,' said Naz. 'She was just so nice. She was telling me that he shouldn't have fought this one and that one. What was she saying to me? "Sock it to him baby" or something like that.'

'Yeah, it was "Give it to him" or something like that,' said Riath.

'Or "Take him out" or something,' said Naz.

'And then Naz had this massive diamond ring on,' said Riath, 'because Naz loves his diamonds. And she was looking at it in the light, and she took his hand. "That's beautiful," she said. She was really admiring it. It was like a big testicle. I talked to her for ages about *Cleopatra*; I love that film. I thought in my eyes that was the best film that she ever made.'

'I've met a lot of people out of boxing,' said Naz. 'Will Smith, Puff Daddy, Wesley Snipes; there's quite a few people. It's amazing to think of yourself boxing as a kid and growing up in the gym from the age of seven. And all of a sudden if somebody had said to you, "Listen, you know when you get to such and such stage in your life there's going to be so many superstars who are going to really admire what you do and like what you do and actually respect you for what you do." There've been that many superstars or whatever, and all I remember about myself is being just that kid from Wincobank.'

Sooner or later I felt somebody was bound to mention the Channel 4 documentary, so I brought it up.

'Some people loved that film and some people hated it,' said Riath. 'I just think there was more to that film that people didn't see.'

'There was a lot more to it,' said Naz. 'I think there were certain points that were highlighted, like the hairdressing thing, and we wish we'd never had it in.'

'It was a bit unfortunate, to be absolutely honest,' I said.

'There was one side of me', said Naz, 'that thought I want it out. But there was one side of me that wanted it in. And, at the end of the day, if something important comes up you want your hair the way it is supposed to be. And I was being me. I mean the music they put around it made it look unreal. It was the camerawork and that music, that's what was terrible. The actual thing itself wasn't like a put-on; it was like me wanting my hair done in a certain way. And that's the thing I really want to tell people; at the end of the day, I'm not a false person. I'm a real person that will be real in a certain way. That's one thing I liked about that documentary, that at the end of the day, people want to see me how I really was, in a way. But then again, it all depends on what mood I'm in. I don't really care about the hairstyle, but maybe at that certain point I wanted it done in a certain way, I didn't have any barber there and I wanted it in a certain way.'

'And if you'd won the fight, of course,' I added, 'it all would have seemed different.'

'Everybody says that,' said Riath. 'One thing that really pissed me off, though, was, when it came out, the guys who sort of hate us in the boxing fraternity, they went to town on it. You know when you've participated in something you think, "Oh, people are going to take it for what it is." It was actually "pick of the week" in all major magazines, you know in *Time Out* and all other magazines, and *The Times* wrote about it, and other papers wrote about it, and nothing was nowhere near as cutting as the guys who are boxing journalists. They went to town; they wanted to vent their feelings towards us. Whenever he's done something wrong, they want to jump on him, and that was their opportunity. The thing with Naz is he crossed over from being just a fighter; there's not many people who know many fighters in England. If you went out on the streets and asked about the likes of Nigel Benn, people wouldn't know who he is. Naz crossed over because he was getting like ten or eleven million viewers on ITV. He was the highest-rated fighter on ITV. He moved on to Sky and he was getting the highest pay-per-view figures on Sky. There's no disputing he's made colossal amounts of money. He moved on and then he kind of crossed over to the celebrity bit. The celebrity bit was really interested in him and wanted him as a product for interviews and things. He was doing all kinds of things. At the same time, there was a battle between the boxing fraternity, who probably thought he's young, he's got money and maybe our extraction of origin isn't what they wanted it to be – that's my personal opinion; I think race issues come into play. And to be honest with you, ninety-five per cent of sports journalists are white. They all kind of come from the same background and have ideas about what traditional boxing should be.

And so what you see when they write is a kind of anger or venom against him. And some of the younger ones, who are kind of in their forties or late thirties, when they do end up writing about him, some of them tend to have the same view as the older ones because they get ostracised if their views are different.'

It was an interesting world view that was expressed here, almost paranoid in its tone and content.

But inevitably the topic turned full circle back to the Barrera fight. Naz perhaps felt that he hadn't had sufficient opportunity to express how he felt, so he tried again.

'I one hundred per cent feel that I am better than him. And I one hundred per cent feel that I will be back to beat him definitely, God willing. But I suppose that's what makes champions, real champions. I reigned for six years as a world champion, and it was a great feeling, and then you lose, and you know it's your first real loss. When people said to me afterwards, "How do you feel?" and "Did it break you?" and silly things like that and they even mentioned retirement. And I'm like "How can a guy who feels like he's boxed all his life, who has reigned for six years, who has not been beat on paper in twelve years," like the last time I got beat before this one was in '89 as an amateur, and people thought I was robbed then. It's a big amount of time without getting beat.'

I watched his hands again, articulating this length of time through the silent and subconscious language of the body. In his mind, it was a huge amount of time, the hands apart as far as they could go. A lifetime of winning in that gap.

'So when the laws of averages comes up,' he said, 'and it happens, it's no big deal. There's been better fighters before my time that have been beat, and there will be better fighters after my time that's going to get beat, because my parents explained that to me, before I got beat. "This is sport, this is what sport is all about, people win and people lose in sport. Even though you've done so, so well, and it's a gift from God. But at the end of the day, it's a sport, people win and people lose." And that's exactly what happened.'

I asked him if he got depressed at all after the fight.

'No, throughout all of it there's not really been one bad feeling whatsoever. Because, at the end of the day, I feel it's preordained and that is it.'

'And we went to the Bahamas as well,' said Riath. 'So we were all there – my mum and dad – and honestly we had such a laugh.'

'It was like I'd won the fight,' said Naz.

'That's how much we really didn't give a fuck,' said Riath, 'pardon the language, we really didn't, because life is too short. All these people who think he's going to crumble and wither away and evaporate once something major happens like that are mistaken. Our lives so far have been good because, thank God, there have been no tragedies. There's no life disasters, there's no major trials in our life that have brought us to our knees, there's been no deaths or miseries or this or that or illnesses. God has blessed us in that way to keep us away from those kinds of trials in life. And when this comes up in the scheme of things in life, it's so irrelevant and pathetic, do you know what I mean?'

Naz was now displaying some intense emotion. 'One day, this journalist thought that he was really clever amongst all the press and he says, "Naz, is this fight the most important thing in your life?" And I looked at him, and the press was looking at me, and what must have come over my face must have been unbelievable, because the feeling that I got in my body was to say to this man literally, "How stupid can you be to ask me that kind of question?" Even though it was the biggest fight of my career, and a lot of people may have said, "Well, Naz, he has a good point," but to say that to a religious man.'

'And a family man,' added Riath.

'Yeah, a family man,' said Naz, 'with two kids. I mean, I looked at him and said, "How could this be the most important thing in my life?" I said, "The core of my life, the centre of my life, is Islam; boxing is far from being the most important thing in my life. I've got a family, I've got kids, I've got me parents and my brothers and sisters and most of all I've got the worshipping of God. The most important thing in my life is the belief and the faith I've got in God."'

He looked relieved to have got this out.

I asked him finally what he might do when he retires from boxing.

He sounded very relaxed. 'A lot of people are suggesting different things, maybe presenting, maybe doing a bit of acting. And I'm cool with it because I'm not concentrating on retiring yet. I think I've got quite a bit of time inside of me to box. I love it. I like boxing.'

'In two years he'll probably think about it,' added Riath. 'It could be a year, it could be six months, it could be two years, it could be three years. When he feels he's ready to retire then he'll retire.'

And then Riath said something very interesting.

'I always believe that fighters never know when to quit; I think they need to be told when to quit. That's my belief. I think fighters right from when they start out think that they can go on for ever, and that they can carry on and on and on. But I think people close to them have to say, "The time has come now where you don't need to do it." That's not what I'm saying to him, though, don't get me wrong.'

'In a lot of people's eyes,' added Naz, 'it's like "Naz, you've earned this kind of money, you've got this kind of name, why do you want to box?" And I'm straight back with my answer – I really and truly want to become one of them greats, one of them fighters that people talk about when they've retired in a good way. And I want people to say that I've done something for boxing because I believe I have done something for boxing. I believe that what I put into boxing there wasn't much of it at that time. You know for a guy to come on dancing and doing everything and doing that somersault. But I don't just want to be known for "Oh, this guy is a great entertainer." I'm a fighter first and foremost. At the end of the day, for people to see those knock-outs in the lighter division – in the featherweight division or even in the super bantamweight division, and even in the flyweight division when I first started as a professional – it was like you don't see people getting stopped and getting knocked out that way, the way I was putting them away.'

Could he ever imagine training some younger boxers like his former mentor Brendan? I asked.

'I couldn't do that,' he answered snappily. 'I couldn't. I've always said that when I finish boxing, I finish boxing and I'm out of the game totally. I don't want to be one of those guys who stick around to do this, to do that, to make themselves busy.'

The words reminded me directly of Brendan himself. 'Making himself busy' is how he always put it, exactly how he put it.

Naz continued, 'When you're out of the game, you should just relax and do what else you have to do. And, don't worry, there will be something for me to do.'

It had been a long interview, a whole morning. Naz slumped back on the expensive leather settee and sipped his fruit drink, watching me carefully, trying, I imagine, to work me out, trying to interpret my response to their version of the road to greatness, the version I had not really heard before, bumps and all. A version where all of the intensive psychological coaching by Brendan had become, in Naz's descriptions, a form of brainwashing, a version where our understanding of a complex relationship all depends upon fragments of body language at critical moments, which may possibly give the game away, if you believe in these sorts of things.

Finally, Riath and Naz showed me around the remaining parts of the gym, with its white marble jacuzzi and its white marble steam room and its weights room, all the very height of luxury. The best money can buy; that's what they say, isn't it? It was the best money could buy. This was what greatness had got them – all that luxury. That and an empty gym devoted to one man in his future pursuit of greatness in a damp, grey city. It was worlds away from Brendan's gym in Wincobank, where all the troubles and anxieties of the world came through the door on a daily basis carried by insecure and frail seven-year-olds who sometimes knew a little too much for their own good. Here the troubles were less diverse, but I suspected no less intense. And, as I left, Naz and Riath were climbing into the ring for their midday prayers, to prostrate themselves before Allah, to seek help and guidance in the trials and tribulations that were to come, both inside and outside the ring. And, ultimately, through such trials and tribulations, to find an answer to the question of what kind of a man and what kind of a champion Prince Naseem Hamed really is.

THREE

I went back to see Mick Mills one last time because I realised that boxing is more to do with Mick and his life than the private gyms and white marble steam rooms of former world champions. I discovered that Mick had left the club where he had worked for years following some dispute and was now working in another club across the street. Gary had walked out along with him. I like loyalty in friends. The new club was very different to what Mick was used to. There was a large team of doormen with earpieces in the huge darkened doorway, which was full of young people, high as kites on a Saturday night. I asked one of the doormen where Mick was.

'No idea, mate,' he said.

I found Mick at the top of the large staircase stopping swaying glassy-eyed teenagers from walking back down the staircase with glasses or bottles in their hands. He looked so small in here. There was a neat little arrangement of bottles around Mick's feet, almost hemming him in. I watched him from a distance for a few moments. Some large shaven-headed man with a lime-green shirt out over his trousers handed over his bottle with a look that said that he wasn't happy about this, and then he tried to walk down the stairs. But he slipped on the way down and skidded on his backside down nine or ten steps. It was like a toboggan in action. He got up as he reached the first landing as if nothing had happened and continued walking unsteadily.

Some large Asian guy approached Mick. I stood watching the two of them. I could tell by Mick's facial expression and by his gestures what he was talking about. It was his glory days in the ring. The Asian guy looked too young to remember any of Mick's fights, but Mick was taking him back to one of his fights, perhaps the one at Bramall Lane in front of thousands, the one where Mick had his jaw broken. It was the fight that had ended his career. I could see the cupped hand pointing towards the face, showing how the jaw hung from his face in this most dangerous of sports. The hand hung there slightly to one side of the face and trembled faintly, perhaps signifying the pain of the whole thing, perhaps something else. It was an odd conversation in the middle of a sea of people who passed them, many brushing against the walls for support in their drunken state. Saturday night in this huge, cavernous, dark club was what most of them aspired to. These would be their glory days. I went close and could hear the conversation now.

'What about Naz, then?' said the Asian guy. 'What do you make of him?'

'Well, he did it,' said Mick, smiling slightly, 'he took on the world and he beat them and you have to give him credit for what he did.'

But I noticed that it was all in the past tense.

Then he added, without any hint of jealousy, 'And that's not bad for a little guy from Sheffield.'

And then Mick stepped back slightly, and his hands took up a boxing stance, his facial expression changed and became more serious, more manly in every regard. The stance was part Mick 'the Bomb' Mills, part Muhammad Ali, part Marvin Hagler, part Sugar Ray Leonard, part Oscar De La Hoya, part Antonio Barrera and even part Naseem Hamed. But it was oddly genuine, and those hands, for the few moments that they remained there, said a great deal to the waves of ordinary people who made their way unsteadily past.